Such Things Happen

The Life of a Typographer

JOHN LEWIS

Such Things Happen

The Life of a Typographer

JOHN LEWIS

1994
Unicorn Press

First published 1994
by Unicorn Press
College Farm
Forward Green
Stowmarket
Suffolk IP14 5EH

ISBN: 0-906290-06-6

Produced by Hugh Tempest-Radford *Book Producers*
Typeset by Galleon Photosetting
Printed in Great Britain by St Edmundsbury Press

DEDICATION
To Griselda with gratitude

Contents

Prologue   vii

Part 1   Life Class

1   Childhood   1
2   Charterhouse   14
3   Bart's   25
4   Goldsmiths'   29
5   Freelance Illustrator   40
6   Camouflage   54
7   War in Canada   69
8   Secret Devices   81
    In Limbo   93

Part II   The Printer's Devil

1   Life in a Printing House   102
2   Manningtree   122
3   Painters and Musicians   131
4   Divided Loyalties   140
5   The Royal College of Art   148
6   Trans-Atlantic Ephemera   160
7   Meadow Cottage   168
8   The Book Factory   170
9   Art Schools   174
10 An Irish Story   179
11 Boats and Books   185
12 Casting-off   189
Appendices   203
Index   207

*Plates between pages 36 and 37, 84 and 85, 132 and 133, 180
and 181*

Prologue

IF YOU ARE Welsh it is difficult not to be descended from parsons, schoolmasters or coal-miners. My mother's father Ben Morris, who died when she was nineteen, had been rector of the Parish of Cadoxton, Barry, in Glamorgan for twenty-eight years. It was indeed a churchy family. His father, the Rev. Ebenezer Morris, was Rural Dean of Kidwelly (he is reputed to have drunk ten pints of beer every day of his life and weighed over twenty stones). His cousin Charles Green was the first Archbishop of Wales and three of his brothers were parsons. My Uncle Sam was Chaplain on HMS *Victoria* and, in 1893, with most of the ship's company, went to the bottom of the Mediterranean when his ship was rammed by HMS *Camperdown* in an ill-conceived battle manoeuvre.

The Mediterranean fleet, under the command of Admiral Tryon, was steaming in two parallel columns. At the point where they were to come about and retrace their steps, the Admiral thought it might be more interesting if they turned inwards rather than outwards. In spite of the protestations of the Captain of the *Victoria*, Admiral Tryon insisted on his orders being carried out. *Camperdown* and *Victoria*, being in the van of each column, swung inwards. The inevitable happened; *Camperdown* rammed *Victoria* amidships. Admiral Tryon remained in the corner of the bridge and said not one word as he, my Uncle Sam and 800 officers and men went swiftly to the bottom of the sea.

At Cambridge Ben Morris was Captain of Boats at Trinity and he was also a fine swimmer. Some years later, he became great friends with Tom Joseph-Watkin who had been at Caius and whose absorbing interest was heraldry. He was born Tom Joseph but, with his brothers, had re-adopted the family name of Watkin. He joined the College of Heralds in 1894, being appointed Portcullis Pursuivant and then Chester Herald. He was a great genealogist and traced the family history, through the female line, back to AD 948 to Owain ap Howell Dda, King of South Wales. Owain's wife was Angharrad, daughter and heir of Llewelyn ap Mervyn, Prince of Powis. This greatly reinforced my mother's Mrs Micawberesque belief in the gentility of her family.

It was Tom Joseph-Watkin's sister Kathryn that my grandfather eventually married. She was seventeen years old and brought with her a dowry of £10,000. Her father, Thomas Joseph, owned the Dunraven Colliery which, not long after his daughter's marriage, he sold for a handsome sum. Under the new owners, it became less prosperous. Maybe the seams were worked out. There was talk of closure.

One day a deputation of miners visited Thomas Joseph and said quite bluntly to him: 'You were a good boss, Mr Joseph. The pit's in trouble. Buy it back man, and we'll work for you for starvation wages.' Much flattered, he did so and lost every penny he had.

Katie Joseph was as pretty as a picture and sang like a nightingale. Ben was exactly twenty years older than her. They were deeply in love and lived in a handsome house near Barry called Twynedd, where practically every year she produced another baby. My mother, her third child, was born in 1883 and christened Margaretta Maria. When my grandmother was twenty-nine, after the birth of her last baby, she contracted puerperal fever and went out of her mind. Pretty little Katie and her capital of £10,000 were taken in care by the Master of Lunacy. She lived a mindless, care-free and apparently happy existence until she was seventy-eight, by which time her capital had dwindled to a few hundred pounds. I was twenty-six at the time she died and until my mother told me of her death, I had never known she was alive. My mother had told me, when I was quite young, that she had died after the birth of her last child.

'You know,' she later explained, 'we didn't talk about lunacy in those days. It was thought to be a disgraceful thing to have in the family.'

My grandfather was completely broken up by his young wife's mental breakdown. He lived for nine years struggling to bring up a young family with the help of his servants. When he died of pneumonia in 1902, he left nine children: six girls almost grown up, and three little boys. He also left a load of debts. The two eldest girls, Louisa and Mary Nest already had jobs, one as a nurse and the other as an organist and music teacher. My mother, who was considered delicate, was given a temporary home by her father's sister, her Aunt Julia, who, for her second husband, had married General Sir George Greaves, at one time second-in-command to Lord Roberts in India. He was kind to this orphaned girl. My mother was indeed fortunate, for the Greaves family lived in a spacious Regency house called Netherwood at Saundersfoot in Pembrokeshire. After living in a rectory among a large and noisy family, with no mother and a grieving father, she found Netherwood quiet and civilized.

I can remember my mother saying that her Uncle George should have succeeded Lord Roberts as Commander-in-Chief in India, but as the result of what *The Times* called 'a piece of political jobbery', due to a change of Ministry, the post was given to a protégé of the new government.

'Uncle George wasn't in the least embittered about this blow to his army career,' my mother said, 'after all, he had a very pleasant life at Saundersfoot.'

As he had 4000 acres of rough shooting, a number of horses, seven dogs and three small racing yachts (one designed by Dixon Kemp with which he won numerous cups), that was probably an understatement.

He was, according to his contemporaries, a fine soldier who did much to modernize the army. He also had a very wide circle of friends which included the Kiplings.

While my mother was enjoying this brief interlude of gracious living, terrible things were happening to her three little brothers. My grandfather's eldest parson brother, the Rev. Rees Morris, took it upon himself to dispose of them. The eldest boy, Tom, he sent to sea in a training ship, SS *Deanmount*. A pathetic letter to his eldest sister survives. In it the little boy wrote:

> Uncle Rees must be a brute to give you all this trouble, and I like to tell him so . . . I want to buy a pear [*sic*] of boots, a suit of go-ashore clothes and some underclothes and socks. I was sent to sea with a very poor outfit, nearly all the clothes (rags rather) I have got left are what I have got from the other boys. To tell you the real truth, as you are my loving sister, I don't care for the sea at all, I believe Uncle Rees only sent me to sea to get rid of me. He hated me when I was staying with him, because I used to be such a rogue . . . I will never forgive him for telling me that I killed father, that it was through me that he died. He is a proper hipocrit [*sic*], there is no other name for him. We do not get any money for working . . . I have only got a shilling with me . . .
>
> I remain, dear Louie, your loving brother
> T. W. E. Morris.

The two other little boys were shipped off to farms in Ontario as indentured labour, which amounted to virtual slavery.

My mother felt that she could not live indefinitely depending on the kindness of her aunt and uncle, so she took a job as a music teacher (she was a tolerable pianist) at a school in her father's old parish in Barry. Soon after that she met my father. His first name was Claude, a name with 'greenery-yallery' connotations. My father was the antithesis of that Oscar Wildean world. He was a bustling, bristling, exuberant extrovert, rather like the wire-haired terriers he later bred.

When they met, they were both acting in an amateur production of *She Stoops to Conquer*. My father played Tony Lumpkin and my mother Kate Hardcastle. Soon after that they became engaged. She was penniless. It was four years before they could marry. They were an incongruous couple.

My father was born in 1882 at Cross Oak House at Talybont-on-Usk in Breconshire. He was Christened Claude Pritchard. He was one of seven children. When he was two years old, the family moved to Llangattock-vibon-Avel in Monmouthshire, where his father, William David Lewis, had become the village schoolmaster. Llangattock was a feudal village. The schoolmaster, the parson and the doctor provided a social middle ground between the peasants and Lord Llangattock's family. One of the Llangattock boys was Charlie Rolls. He was a few years older than my father, but they used to play cricket together when they were children. He later became famous as a racing motorist, as an aviator and as the co-founder of the Rolls-Royce Company. According to my father, everybody in the village loved Charlie Rolls and they were all brokenhearted when, in 1910, he was killed in a flying accident.

When he was sixteen my father, who was reputed to be the brains of the family, was put into a branch office of a private bank, the Metropolitan and Birmingham Bank, at the little mining town of Mountain Ash, a few miles down the Cynon valley from Aberdare. This was not at all what he wanted. His one ambition then was to become a doctor and to follow in the footsteps of his father's brother, his Uncle Christopher, who was a successful heart specialist in Birmingham.

There was some tenuous family connection with this small bank which, very soon after my father had become a clerk in its employment, was swallowed up by what is now the Midland Bank. In the early 1900s my father was posted to the Barry branch. There he joined the Territorials and was commissioned into the 12th Battalion of the Welch Regiment. The army was to become his university.

In 1910 my parents married and took over the lease of a little house in Rhoose, overlooking the Bristol Channel. It was there that I was born.

Part I

Life Class

All students please turn round and look the other way.

1. Childhood

I WAS HAULED squalling into the world a fortnight before Christmas, just in time for lunch, in a semi-detached villa called Fontenay at Rhoose, a straggling little village some twelve miles west of Cardiff. The year was 1912. Apparently I was a sickly child and more than once my parents despaired of my life, particularly after a young nursemaid, who was meant to be looking after me, left me out in my pram in a snowstorm. I was kept alive by a saline drip. As a result of this treatment, throughout my childhood, I could not stomach ham or salt beef.

Just before war was declared, my father was ordered to join the training battalion of the Welch Regiment at a camp called the Buttrells at Barry. They left Rhoose, and my mother, Judy, our wire-haired terrier, and I moved into rooms near the camp. These rooms were owned by a Mrs Burton. Her daughter Dorothy became my nursemaid. My first memories are of Dorothy playing with me and taking me for walks. She could only have been about fourteen or fifteen. To me she seemed quite grown up and I loved her dearly.

The Burtons' terraced house was set on a hill with a little lawn which sloped steeply down to a brick wall, the top of which was level with the grass. There was a drop of eight or nine feet to the pavement below. One day I had been left in my playpen on the lawn whilst Dorothy went indoors to fetch something. Somehow or other I scrambled out and the next thing I was rolling down towards the drop onto the pavement; but for Judy my life would probably have ended there and then. The little dog rushed at me and grabbed my frock in her mouth, her fearful growlings and my yells brought the household tumbling out on to the lawn. From that moment onwards, Judy barely left my side, presumably regarding me as a large and incompetent puppy. It was not until I was eight years old and went away to school that we were parted.

Judy had been intended to be the mother of the Fontenay kennels from which my father had hoped to make a fortune. In her first litter she produced a world champion which was sold to a United States dealer for £450, quite a sum in those days. Then the war came and after that she never produced another puppy worth anything. This meant nothing to a little boy. She was the dearest and most understanding companion any child could have wished for. Fond though I was of my mother, it was to Judy I told all my troubles.

At the end of 1914 my father departed for the Western Front, serving with the 1st and 2nd Battalions of the Welch Regiment. My mother and

1

I moved to Abergavenny to be near my father's sister and mother. My memories of what my father went through are a jumble of names: Ypres, the Somme, Passchendaele, Hill 60, the Marne, Le Cateau, St Quentin, St Omer, Paris and Cologne. By the end of 1915 he was a Company Commander. He seemed to spend most of the war deep in the mud of the trenches. The hours spent waiting in dug-outs were made tolerable by a liberal supply of whisky and the game of bridge at which he became very skilled. Those awful years seemed for him to be full of happy memories. The friendships he made then were for life. His unhappiest memory was of being in charge of a firing squad for the execution of a young fresh-faced boy who came from a remote farm in one of the Welsh valleys. He had been court-martialled and sentenced to death for desertion and cowardice in the face of the enemy.

My father's leaves were rare. I can remember one when we stayed at Jules Hotel in Jermyn Street. This man in khaki with a loud voice seemed to me a quite unwarranted intrusion into our tranquil life. He must have thought me a spoilt brat. I could not understand why my mother was so upset when we went to see him off at Victoria Station. He had one longer leave, after being frost-bitten, and I remember staying at Brighton and being carried round the Aquarium, perched on the shoulder of a gigantic Sikh, dressed in hospital blue.

My conscious memories really date from the time we moved to Abergavenny. My mother had taken a semi-detached house in a quiet road of similar stone-built, slate-roofed Victorian houses. It was on the northern edge of the town, at the foot of the Sugar Loaf mountain which, in winter time with a capping of snow, looks like Fuji Yama. My father's sister, my Aunt Sah, began to play a big part in my existence. She had been christened Sarah Ann Hughes, and because of her initials everyone, except my grandmother, called her Sah. To my granny she was Sally. She was a female counterpart to my father, volatile, hot-tempered and very generous. She had been married rather late in life to Harold Pegler, the manager of a local printing firm. He was a kindly, if insignificant, little man, with a bald head, a loud sonorous voice and gold *pince-nez*. He was also a church-warden. Uncle Harold, on medical grounds, had been rejected by the army, but once a week he used to don khaki and go off to parade with the 1914–18 equivalent of the Home Guard. My aunt was in charge of the local Red Cross hospital which she ran with great flair. Finally, she quarrelled with her committee and flounced out in a blazing temper.

My father's mother looked like a little Welsh peasant woman. She dressed entirely in black, except for a little trimming of white lace at neck and wrists. When out of doors she always wore a bonnet with two black satin ribbons trailing down the back and black buttoned boots. She had dressed in this manner ever since my grandfather had died in 1911 and she continued so to dress until she died in 1938, at the age of 94. Apart from my dog Judy, I was on better terms with my granny than

2

with anyone else. Once a week we used to walk up to the cemetery to visit 'the grave', to change the flowers and, usually, to have a row with the custodian because he had not kept the rectangle of gravel clear of weeds. The grave was rather like a double-bed and was indeed, in course of time, also to accommodate my grandmother. The fact that my inoffensive Uncle Harold, whom my grandmother detested, had been tucked in there long before she died, did not please her at all. Finally my Aunt Sah completed the quartet; but that was many years away from those wartime visits.

I have nothing but happy memories of those early days in Abergavenny, I suppose mainly because of the kindnesses my childless Aunt Sah showered on me and the tales my granny used to tell me of life in the Welsh valleys and of a ghostly coach-and-four that used to drive through Llangorse Lake at Talybont-on-Usk.

Each year my mother and I used to go to the Mumbles. The Mumbles is a little Victorian seaside resort across the bay from Swansea, at the beginning of the Gower peninsula. We always stayed in the same rooms let by two maiden ladies. For breakfast we had laver bread (a kind of seaweed) made up into cakes with oatmeal and fried with bacon.

During one of our visits to the Mumbles my mother went to an auction sale and bought, amongst many other things, an old model sailing yacht. It was almost as big as I was, a full thirty inches long and with a battered schooner rig. An old sailor re-rigged her for us.

'She didn't ought never to have been rigged as a schooner, Ma'am; plank-on-edge cutter, pilot cutter, that's what she is.' And that is what she became and a lasting joy she was to me.

All day long I used to play about in the rock pools of Limeslade Bay, sailing my boat accompanied by Judy, whilst my mother read or bathed. One of the great joys of the Mumbles was the Mumbles Railway. This was really a tramway that ran round Swansea Bay. It was drawn by a superannuated Great Western tank locomotive. The first class was a very old passenger coach, the second class consisted of three ancient trams and the third class of a couple of open trucks with hard back-to-back benches.

The next station to the Mumbles was West Cross where two of my mother's aunts lived. They were Aunt Jane and Aunt Jessie. They had a large Victorian house with a cedar-shaded lawn. When days were fine and warm, Aunt Jane used to work in the garden, sitting in a basketwork chair that looked like the kind of chairs club porters used to sit in. Aunt Jane was a very severe lady who disliked small children and was referred to by my mother as a 'blue-stocking'. My furtive attempts to look beneath her long black skirts to see whether her stockings really were blue were completely unsuccessful. Her reputation for her 'blue-stockingness' was, I imagine, because of her close personal friendship with Howell Gwynne, the editor of *The Morning Post*. I think she must have written articles for the paper because I can remember her working on galley proofs. (I had no idea then what those long strips of paper were.) She referred to me as Noel, which was one of my names, but I was always called Dodo by my mother.

Aunt Jessie, who always dressed in lavender grey, was as gentle as her elder sister was obdurate. They had a box of painted tin-plate soldiers. Whenever we went there, these were brought out, presumably to keep me quiet. The day we left the Mumbles for the last time, Aunt Jessie came over to say goodbye and presented me with the box of soldiers.

For the Christmas of 1917, my father sent me, from the BEF in France, a copy of *The Water Babies* illustrated by W. Heath Robinson. I could not read but I could look at the pictures. My mother read the book to me and I loved every word of it – and even more I loved the illustrations. No sooner had she finished than I made her start all over again. Kingsley's description of Tom's flight from Harthover Place over the precipitous Harthover Fell and down into Vendale imprinted itself on my mind and was the beginning of my love for that fine northern country. The drawings by Heath Robinson, with his child-like vision, were drawings I could understand and indeed I read into them as much or as little as I wanted. Half a century later I still loved them.

The last time I saw the old Mumbles Railway was on a wet November day. I was standing by the window in our sitting room, blowing on the window panes and trying to whistle. At the very moment when I first achieved a shrill squeak, the train pulled out for Swansea in a cloud of steam and my mother burst into the room and clutched me to her. She was crying and laughing at the same time.

'Listen, Mummy, I can whistle!' I said, trying to disengage myself from her grasp.

'Can you, Dodo darling? Well, today you can whistle as much as you like.'

'Why?'

'Because the war is over. They've signed an Armistice.'

'What's that mean?' I asked.

'It means your Daddy will be back soon.'

'I don't want him back!' I said rather truculently, thinking he would probably tell me not to whistle. I doubt if my mother even heard that ungracious remark, for she must have suddenly realized that after four long years, she could at last stop trembling at the sight of a telegraph boy. All would be perfect from now on, so she thought.

In the early summer of 1919 my father returned most reluctantly to civilian life and to his job as a cashier in the bank at Barry. He and his former Battalion Commander built a couple of bungalows at Rhoose. They were no more than converted army huts, sited in an open field overlooking the Bristol Channel, with the Exmoor hills on the distant skyline. A couple of fields away, between the bungalows and the sea, was the loop line of the Great Western Railway. Twice a day the Swansea–Newcastle express thundered past, often drawn by a famous and gigantic locomotive called *The Great Bear*. It was a sight to inspire any little boy with hopes of becoming an engine driver.

Rhoose was on the edge of the Vale of Glamorgan, which was an unspoilt stretch of country. There were no tarmac roads there then and when our doctor came to visit us in the summer in a pre-war Humber motor car (he was the only one of our friends who had a car), he would leave such dust clouds behind him that they turned the hedgerows white.

Sometimes my father took me for walks along the cliffs. On one of those walks we stumbled across a corncrake's nest and I collected my first bird's egg. There was plenty of shipping to look at, going up and down the Bristol Channel. There were occasional sailing ships, little coastal schooners and tall nitrate barques from Chile and there was a never-ending stream of heavily laden colliers from Cardiff docks.

'Now listen to this Dodo, Cardiff is the biggest coal port in the world,' my father would say. 'Those ships take Welsh anthracite to every port in Europe and across the Atlantic, even to South America . . . there are twelve miles of docks.' He said this with some pride.

I was duly impressed, yet I was always frightened of this quick-tempered man; so much so that I used to make up any answer that I thought would please him to the questions that he fired at me. Of course, he always found out that I was not telling the truth. This resulted in fearful lectures on the importance of being truthful. Tearfully I promised never to tell another lie and five minutes later, out came another whopper! We returned home in ominous silence, until he could vent his fury on my poor mother for bringing me up so badly. His rages were like thunderstorms in their elemental force. My mother was soon reduced to tears and I started howling to keep her company. He must often have wished he was back in the trenches. Whether his fierce temper turned me into a coward, or whether it was just the way I was made, I was certainly a craven little boy. I really began to hate him. My poor mother was more forbearing. Dr Griffiths, our family doctor, had told her that after four years on the Western Front, my father's nerves were shot to pieces. She just had to be patient with him. It was an uncomfortable household for an only child. There were endless rows and I usually seemed to be the cause. I found some comfort later about this untruthfulness, when I read that Kipling had said that when he was a child he had developed the same habit of telling lies. 'This, I presume, is the foundation of literary effort,' was his comforting conclusion.

In the winter of 1919 we spent a couple of months at Paignton in South Devon. My father had been sent as acting manager to the local branch of his bank. I remember playing alone on the sands on a cold November day. I noticed something unusual in the breakers. A big wave suddenly swept it up beyond the tide line. I ran over to see what it was. Before I had reached it, I realized it was a body. From the blue jersey and serge trousers I guessed it was a sailor. It was all rather alarming but before I could do anything about it a crowd of people gathered and some busybody hurried me away.

I was full of my discovery when I got home. I told my mother I had found a drowned sailor.

'He looked all soggy,' I said 'and he had some seaweed in his mouth.' When my father came in, my mother told him of my adventure.

'Pack of lies!' my father snorted. 'Probably just a baulk of timber.' I was then soundly berated for getting some tar on my new white jersey. A few minutes later, the maid brought in the evening paper. Although the drowned sailor was headline news, I cannot remember my parents apologising for their disbelief. I supposed it was all part of the unfairness of grown ups.

At the end of 1920 the bank offered my father the chance of opening a new branch at Farnham in Surrey. They had made a wiser choice than they probably realized. His heart was not in banking – soldiering was what he liked. Farnham was only a few miles from Aldershot and Camberley, the very heart of the army in England.

In the spring of 1921, he opened his bank in Farnham and within a few years it looked as if he had most of the British army banking with him. He had a profound contempt for his head office, referring to them as 'a bunch of counter jumpers'. God knows what they thought of him, but they left him in tolerable peace as he made handsome profits for them. At one stage, they offered him a job at head office. His distaste for bureaucratic authority resulted in a disastrous interview and he returned to Farnham to go his own way.

My first impressions of Farnham were not very favourable. We arrived by train on a winter's night of driving rain. The Bush Hotel, where we were to stay, was a gloomy great building, with faded red plush curtains and an odour of port and Stilton. My mother took me to church on the first Sunday we were there. I thought the singing was beyond word feeble, and the parson, Canon Crum, preached a sermon in a thin and reedy voice about subjects far beyond my comprehension. I missed the Welsh fervour. There may have been intellect there, but there was certainly no *hwyll*.

A young brewer was also staying at the Bush Hotel. He was married to a pretty girl with a lovely voice. One morning he heard my mother referring to me as 'Dodo'.

'Is that the child's name?' he asked.

'Good Gracious no, it's only a nickname. He is called Noel,' my Mother answered.

'That boy is no Noel!' the brewer said. 'Hasn't he any other names?'

'Well,' said my mother, somewhat abashed, 'he was christened John Noel Claude.'

'I can't imagine you would want two Claudes in the family. What is wrong with "John"? I think "John" is a fine name.'

6

My mother meekly acquiesced and from that day I shed my childish nickname and never had to answer to Noel again, except from my old Aunt Jane, who could not stomach any kind of change. From that day onwards I became 'John'.

The first few months we were in Farnham, I attended a dame's school run by a kindly disciplinarian called Grace Buckle. She was the daughter of a long since deceased admiral. Among the dozen or so children there was a very pretty golden-haired child called Diana. I was fascinated by her and remained so until she eventually married a respectable stockbroker, the first of her three marriages. Her mother, twice married and twice widowed, was as dark as her daughter was fair and as pretty. She was also staying at the Bush Hotel and my father was clearly very taken with her.

In the hotel's garden, shaded by fine cedars, there was an aviary of exotic birds, mainly Chinese pheasants. Not long after we arrived there, someone presented the hotel manager with a baby red squirrel, which had fallen out of its nest. This little animal was given to me and I was allowed to keep it in one of the cages which were big enough to walk about in. The squirrel was the dearest and tamest little creature, and I lavished more love on it than it probably wanted. By the summer, the baking hot summer of 1921, when we had moved into a house on the outskirts of the town, the little squirrel was needing his freedom. We released him just near Blacklake, J. M. Barrie's house at Tilford, where he had originally been found. I opened the door of the basket in which he had travelled: he climbed up on to my shoulder, took his bearings and then leapt into the branches of a nearby spruce tree. He stopped, turned and looked at me, as if he was memorizing what I looked like, then he was away, jumping from branch to branch.

We returned to that spot several times and saw various red squirrels leaping through the tree tops, but there was no means of telling whether any of them was my squirrel.

The time was approaching when I was to go away to school. The school had already been chosen. It was called Bigshot and my cousin Frank had been there; when he was there it was called Bigshotte Rayles. It had been built as a shooting lodge by the Dowager Marchioness of Downshire. It was an unlikely looking building, half timbered and once thatched. But by the time that I had arrived there the thatch had gone, because of a fire in the surrounding pine woods which had threatened the school. It was roofed with corrugated iron painted pink. Frank had been utterly wretched when he was there and had been beaten unmercifully by a sadistic headmaster. This had no influence on my parents' choice. In fact that awful headmaster had departed and in 1921 the school was owned and run by George Gordon Brierley, who proved to be a good and kind friend to me.

The intellectual prowess of my cousin Frank was constantly before me. From Bigshot he had won two scholarships to Marlborough, where he had become head boy. He had gone on to Cambridge with more scholarships. There he took a Double First. In those days I was rather frightened of him. My first conscious memory of him was when we were both staying with my Aunt Sah in Abergavenny. The house was full and we had to share a bed. I was five and he was thirteen or fourteen.

'If you pee in the bed, I'll beat you!' he said ferociously.

At the end of the hottest summer of this century, my mother and father took me over to Bigshot and left me to the mercies of sixty other little boys. I probably ought to have been homesick and frightened. In fact, I was blissfully happy there, though I missed Judy. It was the most humane of schools and Brierley soon made it clear to my father that whatever talents I might have, I was certainly not scholarship material. My father did not take to this observation at all kindly. If his parson brother Tom could have a son who won scholarships and became a Senior Wrangler, why the devil could not his son? However, Brierley was quite undeterred and told my irate father that he knew a lot more than him about the capabilities of small boys.

My reports used to have such comments from the headmaster as 'A struggle between a naturally volatile temperament and the need to work and concentrate steadily,' or 'Full or energy but unfortunately only a small percentage is applied to his work,' though there was one that said 'Dawning signs of Grace!' My father never saw the joke.

Brierley came to stay for a night or so during one Christmas holidays and gave me a rugger ball as a Christmas present. He impressed on me that on no account was I to tell the other boys. Then he kissed me warmly, much to my mother's surprise. He was a great one for kissing, particularly after he had beaten one on one's bare bottom. I was always getting beaten and always being kissed. I did not see anything unusual about it and, like many of the boys there, I adored him. He may have been inspired to give me a rugger ball as a result of my using a wastepaper basket in place of a ball. My attempt at converting a goal over a row of desks, resulted in the basket soaring up in the air and upending one of the hanging oil lamps with which the classroom was lit. A sheet of flame cascaded down onto the floor and only the prompt arrival of Mr Phipps, one of the masters, with a fire extinguisher prevented a devastating fire. I was not even chastised for that.

On Sunday evenings Brierley used to read to us. In that particular year, he chose *The Wind in the Willows*. He read well and we hugged ourselves with delight at the doings of Mole, Ratty and particularly of Mr Toad. Also, that remark by Ratty about there being 'Nothing – absolutely nothing so much worth doing as simply messing about in boats' lodged in a corner of my mind.

For one term we had an elderly temporary master, who looked like Sickert's portrait of George Moore. He had a drooping moustache and a watery eye. He was tall and thin, with a pronounced Adam's apple and a resonant voice. After exams were over, he introduced us to

Dickens. His reading of 'the death of Nancy' from *Oliver Twist* sent agreeable shivers of horror running down our spines and Sidney Carton's last words from the scaffold reduced us all to tears.

The staff at Bigshot in my time, apart from the headmaster, consisted of Brierley's younger brother Mick, who took the sixth form; Mr Kingdom, a lovable man who was the games master; and Mr Phipps, who had been a cinema pianist and was a movie buff. Mr Phipps had a hand-cranked 35 mm projector and a print of one film, a two-reeler called *The Brotherhood of Man*, which, judging by the clothes the characters wore, must have been made while Queen Victoria was still alive. On every wet afternoon, he used to run this through, slowing down or speeding up the action as he felt inclined. He soon, with Brierley's backing, progressed to more sophisticated equipment and every Saturday night we screamed our heads off at the antics of Harold Lloyd, or loudly cheered Douglas Fairbanks, supported by Mr Phipps' tremendous work at the piano.

The younger Brierley was a mousy little man who looked like the conventional idea of a curate. There was more to him than that. He had a very good brain, and was a brilliant actor and master of drag. At the end of every Christmas term, we used to have a play written by the headmaster, which always included some eccentric female character which his brother would play. The pinnacle of his performance was when he played a female male impersonator, impersonating a bishop. It was a wonderful impersonation of a bishop, but he gave the impression that the bishop was really a woman!

These plays always gave the headmaster a great chance to dress up all his favourite little boys as little girls. The plays were written on two levels, because both parents and boys seemed to enjoy them equally, though I noticed the grown-ups used to laugh at bits we did not think were funny.

There was one thing about Bigshot that I did not like and that was the choice of pictures. They were mostly sepia Medici prints after the Florentine painters. A Madonna and Child by Raphael which hung behind the desk from which Brierley took prayers has put me off Italian Renaissance painting for life!

I never had the slightest qualms about going back to school at the end of the holidays. As an only child, I always seemed to be in the middle of a tug-of-war between my father and mother. Sometimes the tensions were too great for comfort. On one occasion I lost a brand new cricket ball my father had given me. I lied like a trooper about how I had lost it until, at the end of the affair, I could not remember what *had* happened. Anyway, I was sent to bed in disgrace.

We were then living in a house called Thornfield which had a lawn big enough for a cricket pitch. Our gardener-cum-kennel-boy Harry used to bowl to me by the hour. I loved the game and in my third summer at Bigshot, I scraped into the first eleven. My pride was short-lived, because in a practice game, fielding at silly point, I stopped a full-blooded swipe from a big boy. I came to, lying on my bed in the dormitory with a lump as big as a duck's egg over my right eye. I heard the tea bell ring, so I struggled to my feet and dizzily made my way downstairs. As I reached the dining room door the matron came rushing after me.

'Good gracious, child, you shouldn't be down here!' she screamed. She was probably right, because at that moment I was suddenly very sick.

The doctor arrived and pronounced severe concussion. The next day my parents came over in the large blue Austin 20 they used to hire. The chauffeur was a little dark man called Blake and I liked him. His right index finger was missing and he had very hairy nostrils. My father had bought me a large and expensive Paisley-patterned green silk handkerchief which was tied round my head and over my right eye. I felt very piratical and rather proud of myself.

As the limousine drove down the long gravel drive, I noticed there was something missing.

'Where's Judy?' I asked, but knew the answer before my mother spoke. She leaned forward and took my hand.

'She died last week, she died in her sleep.'

This was my first contact with death. I did not say anything. I looked out of the car window, through my one open eye and felt cold inside. Dear, kind Judy, long suffering and always understanding. I have never owned another dog.

I spent about five weeks at home, the first week in a darkened room. I rather enjoyed it, as soon as my head stopped thumping. I have a lump over my right eye to this day.

It was not until after the bang on my head that it was discovered that I was very short sighted. I was taken to a Harley Street oculist and in due course fitted out with old-fashioned gold-rimmed spectacles. My father was so horrified when he saw them, he ordered me to stop wearing them until I had had some horn-rimmed ones made. These he reluctantly accepted.

The day I returned to Bigshot, my mother was taken ill with tetanus. She was lucky to have for her doctor a very handsome young man, who was standing in for our GP. The locum had had much experience of this awful disease in Salonika during the war. By the time the car came to take me back to school, she was delirious. I wondered if I would ever see her again.

Delicate though she was, and thanks to her doctor, my mother recovered, but before she was out of her convalescence, my father went down with appendicitis. He was operated on at home, in an upstairs bedroom on a kitchen table, by Dr Hussey our old GP and made a quick recovery.

Even so, this was no house for a noisy little boy to return to. Clients of my father called Kerr came to the rescue and invited me to stay with them for the holidays. They were a Scottish family and lived in a lovely Voysey house called Lowicks, set in fifty acres of pinewoods near Tilford in Surrey. It was the first time that I had stayed in a house where money did not seem to matter. The family consisted of three sons and two daughters. The eldest son, Jack, had lost a leg in the war. To a little boy's eyes he had an aura of brilliant elegance about him. He also had a $3\frac{1}{2}$-litre Bentley. The second son, Tim, was an artist whose posters were to be seen on the Southern Railway hoardings. The youngest boy, Pat, who was fourteen, had just gone to Harrow. Marjorie, the elder of the two girls, had been to France as a VAD ambulance driver. She ran the house when she was not looking after her Kerry Blue terriers which she bred at Lowicks, or running the *Four and Twenty Blackbirds*, a teashop at Rocquebrune in the south of France. The youngest Kerr sister was called Jean. She was then sixteen, plump and pretty and I think regarded me as a tiresome child.

There were various other people staying in the house, including two quite lovely American girls who came from Georgia. I thought they were all wonderful people, even Mr Kerr who was a dour Aberdonian, and Mrs Kerr who looked like a little Kashmiri woman and was as volatile as a butterfly.

I was absorbed into this household and their sybaritic way of life. The hall was full of golf clubs and tennis rackets and the stables were full of motorcars. Apart from Jack's Bentley, there was a Bean, another Bentley and an Angus-Sanderson. This was a vehicle belonging to a heroic age, Paddington green in colour, with gleaming brass and beautifully lined; it must have weighed a couple of tons. One day, when we were driving down to the sea, the Angus-Sanderson's radiator boiled and we all had to get out and walk up the long hill over Bepton Down. When the radiator had cooled down, Marjorie once again coaxed it into motion.

The breakfasts at Lowicks were something to remember. There was a great choice of cereals such as shredded wheat, creamed barley, puffed wheat, grape nuts, cornflakes and so on. (At home we only had one, called Force, that tasted like soggy sawdust.) After that came kippers and haddock, bacon and eggs and sausages, cups of coffee and toast, honey and marmalade. Everyone seemed to be talking and laughing all the time and the morning sun floodlit their happy faces.

It would have needed a more perspicacious eye than that of a ten-year-old boy to foresee the shadows that were closing in on that household. The first of a series of tragedies happened a year or so later, when Jack was killed in a shooting accident; going over a stile with a shot-gun under his arm, he slipped and his artificial leg gave way under him. The gun went off wounding him mortally.

My last childhood memories of Lowicks were of Jack's funeral at Tilford Church. It was a cold, wet morning. As his coffin was lowered

11

into the grave, a piper played a lament. It was unbearably mournful. It seemed as though the gods had no place for care-free beautiful people.

When I returned home, I sensed things were a bit awry. The trouble – not for the first time with my father – was money. He had been living far above his income; once or twice small legacies to my mother had seen him through various crises. This time his overdraft, with the expenses of their illnesses on top of everything else, had become too much. Finally, the bank recognized that his troubles were at least in part due to his entertaining their customers and they came to his rescue on condition he sold Thornfield. On the morning that he heard that he was at last in the clear, he made me go down on my knees and thank God with him for this help. I was acutely embarrassed and was struck by the illogicality of this behaviour, for he was anything but a believer.

Before Thornfield had been sold, my father's friend Charles Craig told my parents that they were leaving their house in Castle Street. My mother was already in love with this house and persuaded my father to take over the lease. It was a pretty old house that had been refronted in Georgian times. Castle Street is a handsome street of houses with eighteenth-century façades that runs up to the castle which had been the Palace of the Bishops of Winchester for the previous eight hundred years.

Charles Craig's German wife Clara was a woman of extravagant tastes, so my parents benefited greatly from the quality of the curtains and carpets that they took over. The house was owned by a spinster lady who lived next door. Within a couple of years an old aunt of my mother's died and on the strength of the legacy she had been left, they were able to buy No. 9 Castle Street.

I soon grew to love the house and particularly my lattice-windowed bedroom that overlooked the formal walled garden, with its neat rose-beds and little box hedges. The house had rambling, low-ceilinged attics with crazily sloping floors which I used as playrooms and ultimately as a studio.

My particular friend was Michael Gordon, who lived with an aged and very Victorian great-aunt in a huge gloomy, eighteenth-century house in West Street. His elder brother Colin, who was a tremendous athlete, was at Charterhouse where Michael was destined to follow. Because my cousin Frank had been at Marlborough, that was the school chosen for me. However, when the time came for me to go there the Bursar at Marlborough had made some kind of mess-up over my entry papers and told my father I would have to wait until the following year. My father was far too impatient to put up with this. Finally, through various bits of string pulling, I was offered a place at Charterhouse at the beginning of the summer term in 1926. My father and Brierley had some acrimonious correspondence about this, Brierley saying that he thought I would be much happier at Marlborough, where many

Bigshot boys went. My father was an impetuous and headstrong man and took up the Charterhouse offer, which had the proviso that I had to satisfy the examiners.

Towards the end of the Spring term, I presented myself at Charterhouse in company with two other boys. We were examined by a dear old man who I later discovered was called 'Cissy' Rice. I came to know him well because he was the form master of Shell, the bottom form, in which I was placed with one of the other entrants. The third boy was in floods of tears all the time, so we assumed he had failed. In fact he was placed several forms higher than either of us. On the day of our examination, the sun shone and the almond trees outside the Shell classroom were covered in pink blossom.

Charterhouse Founder's Court, by John Thirsk.

2. Charterhouse

AT FIRST SIGHT Charterhouse seemed to be a pretty place with its grey, lichen-covered sandstone Gothic Revival buildings and its aubretia-covered garden walls. It looked much less raw than Marlborough's red brick, which I had seen when I had been taken there in the previous term. I had not seen Lockites then, the house in which I had been placed. In company with two other houses it was set on the sunless side of Charterhouse Hill; facing north, it was a dark and gloomy prison-like building.

So, through my father's impetuosity, I found myself at a soccer school when as a Welshman, of course, the only game that mattered was rugger; and it cost my father a lot more money than Marlborough would have done. Anyhow I felt that Michael Gordon would soon be following me there, so I would have at least one friend. I did not know then of the embargo at Charterhouse on having friends who were not in your own house.

In the Easter holidays, before going off to school, I went to stay with Margaret Dalton, a second cousin of my mother's who had married an old Carthusian. Neale Dalton had been at Weekites, the house further down the hill from Lockites. He had left school in 1915 to become a soldier and had been badly shot up on the Western Front. His one claim to fame, so he said, was that he was the last boy at Charterhouse officially to drink beer for breakfast. In the few days that I stayed with the Daltons, Neale coached me assiduously in Charterhouse folklore and Charterhouse language. He told me never to refer to other boys as 'chaps', they were 'fellows'. Matrons were called 'hags' and masters 'beaks', prep was 'banco', baths were 'toshes' and beatings were referred to as 'cocking-up'. The cooked dish, such as fried sausages or beans on toast, which was served for the evening meal, had the odd name of 'home-bill', because originally the boys had to pay the house butler for it. The paying habit, so I was told, still continued if one wanted (or could afford) to have the butler cook extra eggs.

There were customs to be observed, such as on my three-buttoned jacket (we dressed like embryonic barristers in black jackets and lined trousers), for the first year all three buttons had to be fastened; in one's second year one button, and in one's third year, two buttons could be undone. After one's third year one could carry an umbrella, a habit that seemed to stay with Carthusians for the rest of their lives. There were house colours and nick-names to be learned, such as 'The Berry' for an irascible little master called Pilsberry, 'Daddy' Page for the founder of Pageites, a lantern-jawed old man who was then in his nineties, but still haunted the grounds; 'Lucy' Lovell for the Duckites house tutor and 'Jazzing Judas' for the Rev. L. J. Allen, one of two clergymen on the staff. All this knowledge was in preparation for one's 'New Bugs' exam, which took place at the end of the first two weeks of one's first term. During those two weeks, new boys were excused fagging and were under the guidance of an older boy, known as one's 'father'.

The Summer term (or in Carthusian language, the Cricket Quarter) was a good term in which to arrive, though the boys who had come earlier in the year could lord it over us. Among these was one who was considered, quite erroneously, to be weak minded. He was an amiable creature called Stafford Palin, who later became a close friend. His father was an elderly, once successful, portrait painter. Palin had been to a London day school and he found boarding school life something of a problem.

Stafford Palin's father, W. Mainwaring Palin, was a portrait painter of some repute. The Palins lived in Fulham but also had a house in Walberswick. Here old Mr Palin painted rather attractive little landscapes. Stafford took after his father and drew quite well. He also played the flute like a professional. In many ways he was a flawed genius. He invented what must have been the first automatic gearbox for motor cars. When he failed to renew the patent, one of the motor car companies pinched the idea.

There was one other new boy in Lockites. He was a bright and attractive child and his attractions were soon appreciated by the older boys. At the age of thirteen, I apparently had no sex appeal, which was perhaps just as well. Apart from fagging, I found life tolerably easy and by some miracle I avoided being beaten. The 'cocking-up' was of a very different kind to Brierley's affectionate tannings. The Lockites head monitor, a sadistic little brute, took fearful pleasure in breaking ash 'plants' across the backsides of the little boys, nearly always on the most ludicrous pretexts. My first quarter came to an uneventful end. I think I almost enjoyed it.

In the middle of the Cricket Quarter we had an exeat. This was a long weekend holiday. It usually coincided with the Aldershot Tattoo, which my father took us to with monotonous regularity. The Tattoo was a forerunner of *son et lumière*. The floodlit Laffan's Plain provided a fine setting for 'The Relief of Lucknow', 'The Charge of the Light Brigade', or 'Queen Elizabeth addressing her troops at Purfleet'. The heart-stopping moment always came with the distant sound of pipes, as the Seaforth Highlanders or the Black Watch emerged from distant woods to the rescue of one beleaguered garrison or another. It made me feel very patriotic.

In my first summer holidays my father took me to the Oval to see

15

England playing Australia in the final Test Match. My great hero then was the Surrey and England batsman, Jack Hobbs. When I was younger I had regularly included him in my prayers, putting him one place in front of my mother. It was a Tuesday morning in August and the third day of the match. England had trailed Australia by 22 runs on the first innings. Hobbs and Sutcliffe, the opening batsmen, had scored 48 runs on the previous evening. During the night it had poured with rain, but by the time we reached our seats, the sun was shining and the wicket was actually steaming. There was no covering of the pitches in those days. The result was a pitch of some malevolence and a paradise for any bowler. As Hobbs and Sutcliffe walked out to resume the innings, no one would have given them much chance of surviving long.

Hobbs, however, played the innings of a lifetime. Sutcliffe, with Yorkshire grit and caution, hung on to his wicket and managed to collect 17 runs while Hobbs reached his century with such a display of skill as I have never seen before or since. It was not for nothing that he was called 'The Master'. Lunch was taken with Hobbs on 99. I felt sick with anxiety in case he should not reach his century. A quarter of an hour after the lunch break he took an easy single. The cheers that went up from the Oval must have been heard in Westminster. Soon after, while still on 100, a beautiful ball from the fast bowler Gregory clipped his off bail and sent it spinning down to third man. It did not matter. He had made his century and drawn the teeth of the Australians. As a result of that, we won the match and the Ashes. I can see every moment of it still.

In the following year I was taken to a charity cricket match which was being played at the Staff College at Camberley. It was an England XI against an army team. The adjutant was a friend of my father's. During the lunch break, he asked me if I would like to meet any of the team. What a thing to ask a cricket-mad little boy! He first introduced me to the Middlesex batsman Patsy Hendren, an endearing man with a face like a bog Irishman and a sense of humour to match. Then I said 'How do you do?' to the Sussex fast bowler Maurice Tate, a great, burly, sun-burned man with a lovely laugh. He was smoking a huge pipe. Lastly, wonder of wonders, I was presented to Jack Hobbs. He talked to me for a full ten minutes and asked me about my ambitions and how I played. I had to admit that my love of the game was greater than my skill at it.

'That's enough, isn't it?' he said with a shy smile. I told him I had been lucky enough to see his innings at the Oval, in the previous year. All he said about it was: 'Well, it *was* a sticky wicket!' He was everything a little boy's hero should be. I walked on air for months after that.

During my first quarter at Charterhouse, Mrs Wilson, my house-master's wife, introduced my mother to the 'Bates System of Perfect Vision without Spectacles'. My father was delighted at the prospect and I was taken up to London to see a Miss Kate Beswick, one of the Bates's practitioners. The first thing she did was to break my expensive horn-rimmed glasses. The next, to set me to work on a series of eye exercises. She also put me on a high vitamin diet, with a lot of orange juice.

The system worked, up to a point. My eyesight improved, but never to full normal vision. For the rest of the time I was at school, I never wore spectacles.

My second quarter at Charterhouse was not so agreeable, in spite of the arrival of ten new boys who were all junior to me and so had to answer fag calls before I did. Even so, I was still pretty small fry and younger than all of them. There was one boy with whom I seemed to have quite a lot in common. His name was Ralph Cusack and he came from near Dublin. He was almost pigeon chested and had a witty, lopsided face. He was musical and he could draw and paint and was a most imaginative boy. However, he had an appalling temper.

We seemed to have similar views on many things. Together we joined the 'Studio' – this was the art school run by a lovable old man, C. W. R. Johnson, known as 'Purple' Johnson. He was so named because of his one recipe for watercolour painting. This was summed up in his often repeated phrase: 'Remember boy, no matter wherever you are painting, there will always be a certain amount of purple in it.'

This resulted in generations of Carthusians producing awful little watercolours loaded with cobalt violet.

'Studio' was a refuge and a joy, even more to Ralph than to myself, for I liked playing games, particularly cricket which was anathema to him. 'Purple' Johnson's interest seemed to be more in the illustrators of his time than in the painters. He introduced me to the work of Phil May and Charles Dana Gibson. The latter had a baleful influence on

'Purple' Johnson and the young Osbert Lancaster. Drawing by Sir Osbert Lancaster, OC, from his book *An Eye to the Future*.

my pen drawings for some years. I was fascinated with the complicated pen technique with which Gibson drew his girls. When I tried my hand at drawing in this manner quite imaginary naked girls, I was gently rebuked with: 'Now, boy! That's not Studio work!'

One of the best things about Studio was that one could meet and talk to boys from other houses. There was a very talkative boy from Pageites who was mad on the theatre. His name was Philip Hope-Wallace. His great hero was Claud Lovat Fraser, an old Carthusian who had achieved fame through his designs for Nigel Playfair's production of *The Beggar's Opera*, at the Lyric Hammersmith. There was another boy, a quiet solid boy from Saunderites called Richard Guyatt, who was to come back into my life a quarter of a century later at the Royal College of Art, and a little red-headed boy called Peter Baden-Powell, who lived near Farnham.

There was a marked difference between Charterhouse and Bigshot, where most of the boys had been sons of soldiers or sailors, bank managers or solicitors, parsons or doctors. At Charterhouse, they mostly seemed to be the children of landed gentry or wealthy stock-brokers and City merchants, a world where a boy was judged by the make and size of his father's car and whether he had been to St Moritz for winter sports. For the first time in my life, I became conscious of this attitude and when I was asked by a very rich boy what my father's job was, I said he was a banker, which I thought sounded better than a bank manager. Ralph Cusack's parents were clearly much better off than mine. For one thing, they were separated, and you needed money for that. His mother lived in a villa in Menton and his father spent most of his time on the Irish racecourses. My stock went up considerably when, at the end of the summer holidays, I arrived at Lockites in a Rolls-Royce. This belonged to the Baden-Powells.

When Peter told his father I wanted to go in for art, the Chief Scout and hero of Mafeking said to me: 'I would gladly have given up every-thing I have ever done, if only I could have spent my life painting or drawing.'

Lord Baden-Powell was a shortish man with a large bald head, heavily freckled, and he had a white moustache. He talked to children as if they were grown up. He must have been at least thirty years older than Olave, his dark-haired wife. She was a formidable lady and after I had left Charterhouse she organized me into escorting her elder daughter Heather to numerous dances during the London Season. They varied from very grand affairs in large ballrooms to crowded little 'hops' in poky Mayfair houses. Sometimes we went to three or four dances in one night. However, that was some years ahead.

Stafford Palin was another boy who frequented Studio. He had a disastrous beginning to his career. He was birched by the headmaster for allowing himself to be seduced by another boy, who was expelled for his precocity. These birchings were medieval in their savagery. They were carried out by the headmaster, in the presence of the school doctor, with the culprit strapped down by the school sergeant. Not until his naked backside had been flayed to the appearance of raw steak was the wretched child released. Sir Frank Fletcher, the headmaster, a Cromwellian figure and the severest of Puritans, would then retire to his study to prepare the sermon for the following Sunday. As often as not, the beaten culprit would have to retire to the sanatorium.

The matter of corporal punishment is no longer a debatable subject. To have allowed often viciously sadistic boys of eighteen or so to break ash 'plants' across the backsides of their juniors was quite monstrous. I remember once sitting in Long Room (the combined dining and common room in Lockites) and listening to Ralph being beaten in Hall, the monitor's dining room which led out of Long Room. Every blow made me feel sick. When he emerged, his face was white and twisted with pain, his eyes dry and glittering with impotent rage. The following Sunday he was singing the treble solo in a Christmas anthem in chapel, something about 'Good will to all men'.

As we were walking back to Lockites after the service, Ralph said: 'All the time I was singing that anthem, I was thinking about what I would like to do to that bugger who beat me last week.'

'What would you like to do?' I asked.

'Kill him,' was his stern reply.

Twice a week the local tradesmen's representatives attended the 'young gentlemen's' needs. Mr Rowe from Pitchers, the tailors and outfitters, Mr Hambling the bootmaker, and Mr Wimple from Holdens, the rival bootmakers. They lined up in one of the changing rooms awaiting their orders or bringing garments and boots to be fitted.

The little boys addressed them nervously as Mr Rowe or Mr Wimple, but within a year they learned to adopt a hectoring tone and were saying: 'Look here, Wimple, those boots are not good enough!' or, 'How many times do I have to tell you, Rowe, that I like bones in my collars.'

These patient and worthy men remained polite, even obsequious in the face of intolerable insolence. Mr Rowe was a very little man, a tailor by profession, and because of his smallness, he was subjected to merciless teasing and even to manhandling; but I never saw him lose his temper.

'The young gentlemen will have their fun,' he said pathetically to one of his fellow tradesmen as he packed up his wares.

The most pitiable creatures were the buttery boys, who waited on us at table. They were usually called Leslie. There was one poor lad with fearful acne, whose life must have been made intolerable by the sixty or so boarders; he was at the beck and call of anybody and in mortal fear of the irascible, bottle-nosed, boozy old butler, who had a marked likeness to the American actor, W. C. Fields.

As I had been placed in Shell (lower than that one could not be), it meant that if I followed the normal practice of one promotion a year, it would take me five years to reach the Under Vth. As School Certificate was taken in the Upper Vth, I could see that was not much good, so by dint of doing some work, I usually managed to get promoted after one term; though I stuck for a whole year in Middle IV, in part due to the fact that I had pneumonia during the summer term.

The happiest time in my academic career was during my second cricket quarter, when I came under the spell of J. R. Darling, who was later to become headmaster of Geelong Grammar School in Australia. Darling at that time looked like P. G. Wodehouse's Bertie Wooster. He had a languid air and conducted his classes lying back in an armchair, with his feet on the table in front of him. His special subject was English literature and he filled my young head with a love for it. He also taught me a little about writing. One of our set books was *Pilgrim's Progress* and he gave us the task of illustrating Pilgrim's journey in any way we thought fit. I drew a set of pictures showing Pilgrim on his troublesome journey, borrowing heavily from a Victorian illustrated edition. To my astonishment, I won a prize, a copy of *The Velvet Glove* by Seton Merriman.

The best time in Studio was the oration quarter, when most of the boys who could draw spent their time decorating little wooden boxes for Christmas presents. I tried lino-cutting, and for a Christmas card cut a simple design of a fat monk. Why I drew a monk, I cannot think. I must have had a liking for them, for my first attempt at oil painting was a study of a tonsured monk, based on a photograph of one of the sculptures in Chartres cathedral.

On the walls of Studio were drawings by Carthusians of earlier years. There were reproductions of illustrations by Thackeray and John Leech; there were caricatures of masters by Max Beerbohm, book decorations and stage designs by Lovat Fraser and some very funny line drawings signed 'Lancaster, O., Pageites'.

The winter evenings, drawing and painting in Studio, were in comforting contrast to the cheerlessness of Long Room. There were, however, rare glimpses of domestic life.

One morning after prayers, the housemaster stopped me and said, 'Raumph!' (He always started any sentence with this strange grunt.) 'Raumph! Mrs Wilson would like you and Cusack to come to tea on Saturday. Four o'clock on private side.'

I passed this invitation on and we wondered with some nervousness what we were in for. On Saturday at one minute to four we were washed, our hair brushed and as tidy as we could make ourselves, though Ralph had not been very successful at removing the food stains that covered his tie and jacket. We passed through the communicating door to the private side of the house. It seemed like walking out of a barracks into civilization. Patience Wilson was a fluffy-haired, pretty little woman, years younger than her fierce, wall-eyed old husband, though on this occasion he unbent to the point of actually making some jokes about the curry stains on Ralph's tie. However, his temper had a low flash point, as we saw when one of us remarked how we appreciated the hot cups of coffee that we could now have before going into early morning school.

Mrs Wilson absent-mindedly said, as she poured milk into the silver sugar basin, 'Coffees of what—?'

'CUPS of coffee, you fool,' roared her husband 'and look at what you are doing!'

'Oh, Fred!' was all she said, in a meek voice.

When the remains of the delicious tea was cleared away, Fiery Fred, as he was called in Lockites (the rest of the school called him 'The Hun'), made some excuse and left us. We pulled our chairs up to the fire. The curtains were drawn, but the lights were left unlit. In the company of this gentle creature, in the flickering firelight, we expanded and talked and talked.

She told us how she had met her husband. 'Alice and I were staying in a hotel on the west coast of Ireland. This funny old schoolmaster was there too. I thought he was rather taken with Alice, then quite suddenly he asked me to marry him. I was so surprised I said, "Yes."' She paused for a moment, and then rather quietly she said, 'I don't think I was very sensible.'

We did not know what to say. She brought her confidences to a close by saying, 'You won't tell anyone about this, will you?'

We continued to sit by the fire and talk. For a short while we felt we were back in civilization.

Fiery Fred was a good housemaster: fierce, but basically kind, and we all loved Patience Wilson and her attractive younger sister Alice, who used to come and stay with them quite often. Alice treated us as human beings, and equal ones at that.

In my third year, F. R. L. Wilson retired from his housemastership at the end of his allotted span of, I think, fourteen years and was succeeded by Reggie Poole, a bachelor who lived with his ageing mother. He was an amusing man but not a good housemaster. The humanizing influence of Patience Wilson was hardly matched by old Mrs Poole, who was as deaf as an adder and interested only in her equally deaf tabby cat.

I spent every spare moment drawing or painting, both at Charterhouse and at home. It was during the Christmas holidays of 1928 that my father persuaded one of his clients to come up to the house to see my work. Her name was Mrs Radcliffe-Wilson. She was married to an artist. I showed her my immature efforts. She was kind and she said she thought her husband, Hugh, would like to see them.

A few mornings later Mr Radcliffe-Wilson arrived at the door of our house. He had driven up in a beautiful little car with a fabric body. It was one of the first of that famous marque, the Riley 9. He was a stocky, plump-faced, twinkling-eyed man with a trim moustache and swept-back hair. He looked at my drawings and began to criticize them, telling me how, for reproduction, I ought to simplify them. He had brought with him a set of drawings he had just completed for a child's reader. I looked at them with awe. This was the real thing, and the first glimmerings of what I really wanted to do came into my mind.

As Mr Radcliffe-Wilson got up to go, he said quite casually, 'Come over next week and have tea with us.' So started a very long friendship and an influence that changed the pattern of my life. From then onwards, during every holiday, I would take a bus out to Crondall, where the Radcliffe-Wilsons lived in an old tile-hung cottage, to show them the drawings and posters for concerts and cinema shows that I had done during the term. Their house was full of old Persian rugs, eighteenth-century furniture and a lot of early Staffordshire pottery. They had one child, a red-headed little slip of a thing called Anne. She was then about nine or ten years old. Hugh Radcliffe-Wilson's studio was a brick-built structure across the garden. Inside it was piled high with magazines and books and no one was ever allowed to dust them. It was quite an obstacle race even to reach his drawing desk. I thought how wonderful not only to be an artist but to be able to work at home and to have a studio in one's garden.

*   *   *

Setting for the Charterhouse Masque, my first drawing in *The Greyfriar*.

My years at Charterhouse were, on the whole, happy and relatively trouble-free. I was an idle boy, never working harder than I had to, either at lessons or games. On Sundays, sometimes alone, but usually with Ralph or another of my friends, I bicycled over to Farnham to have lunch and tea with my parents. The house was a cosy retreat after the prison-like surroundings of Lockites and my mother and father were welcoming people. There were other times when, instead of going home, I visited my mother's friend, Miss Edgar. She lived with her brother in a rambling great Victorian house called Ravenswood, set on the side of a steep hill and surrounded by giant Douglas firs and huge monkey puzzle trees. The front of the house overlooked the Wey Valley at Elstead which was only about five miles from the school. Miss Edgar, like my Aunt Jessie, still dressed in an Edwardian style, with high-waisted skirts reaching down to the ground, always in lavender grey and white. She was plump, with white hair piled up on top of her head and she had a pretty pink and white complexion. She always greeted me with a kiss. Her cheek felt like the soft underside of a muffin.

Those Sunday outings were always limited by time, for we had to be back for Chapel at 5.30 pm. Though I was by no means a religious child, I enjoyed Chapel. There was one thrilling Sunday evening when the Rev. H. Studdert-Kennedy, known by the troops in the First World War as 'Woodbine Willie', gave us a most moving sermon on the plight of the out-of-work on Tyneside. He asked us to spare any old clothes we had. We stripped our wardrobes for him. On another Sunday evening, Canon Crum – the same Canon Crum who had been Rector of Farnham when we first lived there, preached a bewitching sermon on sounds.

He paralysed us with these words, saying in a thin and reedy voice: 'I was wandering through the primeval rain forests of the Amazon, where all was silent; when coming to a clearing I suddenly heard . . .' he paused, giving us time to wonder what poetic sound he had heard, then he continued, 'when I heard . . . the sound of a gramophone.' This unexpected commonplace remark was met first with a titter, then someone laughed and suddenly great guffaws of laughter filled the chapel. This ascetic man beamed down at us from the pulpit, implying by his smile that there was room for laughter in his religion.

My last year at Charterhouse was very enjoyable. I never became a monitor or even head of Long Room. I had no responsibilities and I coasted along in an easy indolent way. My drawings had been appearing for some time in the pages and on the covers of the school magazine, *The Greyfriar*; I designed posters for concerts and film shows, including one for *Q Ships* and another for *The Schneider Trophy* film.

During my last quarter, I spent most of my time drawing or talking about art with Ralph. On hot Summer afternoons, we would take a rug out onto Green and watch the First XI playing cricket against some other school or the I Zingari or some such club. We would eat ice creams or read a book.

'This is sheer bliss,' I said on one particularly lovely day.

'I bet you'd rather be playing out there instead of lying here,' Ralph said. 'I know I would.'

'I thought you hated cricket.'

'I do,' he answered 'but somehow to be a "Blood" would make one feel one had done something.' He rubbed his nose and then smiled at me 'You know I am talking rubbish, don't you? I'd far rather paint a decent picture than play cricket for England. Anyhow, I don't suppose they'd have me because I'm Irish.'

The last day of the cricket quarter arrived and, as was our habit, we all left the House before 7 am. I was back home in Castle Street by breakfast time. Before we had finished the bacon and eggs, I was having a monumental row with my father.

Drawings by Claud Lovat Fraser, OC. *Curwen Press.*

3. Bart's

'I DON'T WANT to do medicine,' I said, as I took a nervous sip of my coffee.

'What!' my father exploded.

'I don't want to do medicine. I want to take up art.' Ever since I was ten or eleven years old when I had said I wanted to be a doctor, my father had seen a chance of fulfilling a lifelong ambition, even by proxy, of being a doctor.

'After all we have done for you, all the sacrifices your little mother has made for you, you throw this in my face. It was a great mistake ever sending you to Charterhouse. Art indeed!'

Finally exasperated beyond bearing, he said, 'Either you do something useful and become a doctor, or you go into the army.'

As my idea of army life was heavily coloured by occasions when I had been dragged off to Bordon or Camberley to watch the Welch Regiment's or the Black Watch's Regimental Sports (on one occasion I had diarrhoea behind a marquee), I felt the army was not for me.

Still overawed by my fierce parent, it never occurred to me that I could go off on my own and get a job; so I gave in and plumped for medicine. I had taken the School Certificate with five credits, enough to get into a Cambridge college but the credits were not in the right subjects for entrance to a London teaching hospital, so I had to do some cramming for the London Matric. I carefully avoided chemistry and physics, two sides of the First MB triangle.

When the time came for the exam, my father took me up to London and we stayed at the Vanderbilt Hotel in South Kensington. He lavished every care on me and fed me to bursting point, presumably on the same principle as Mr Squeers had followed when he stuffed young Wackford. It must have done the trick, for I sailed through all the papers. My father was so delighted that he offered me the choice of going to Cambridge (he seemed to have no doubt that he could get me into St John's College, where my cousin Frank had been) or to St Bartholomew's Hospital. After too little thought, I decided that if I had to do this medical thing, I had better get on with it and go straight to Bart's. It was the wrong choice, but so was medicine. I had not reckoned on First MB chemistry and physics.

The only reason, when as a child, I had said I wanted to be a doctor was that the Medical Officer of Health for West Surrey was a young Scot and a friend of the family, who had a big American car, a de

Soto coupé, in which he spent most of his days driving around the countryside. I thought that looked more promising than working in a bank. A year later I had decided I was going to follow the immortal Jack Hobbs and become a professional cricketer. That unlikely ambition was followed by ideas for various and often improbable careers, until half way through my time at Charterhouse, I *knew* I was going to be some kind of artist.

In September 1930 I went to live in rooms in Fentiman Road, opposite Vauxhall Gardens, which by then had rather lost their Regency glamour. They consisted of two hard tennis courts and some bedraggled plane trees. I went to Fentiman Road because my cousin Frank lived there. Having ended his Cambridge career as a Senior Wrangler, he then decided he wanted to become a slum parson. The rooms were kept by a splendid old biddy, whose remedy for any ailment (or crisis) was rum. As I was plagued with bronchial colds, she gave me rum in my tea, rum in hot milk, rum by itself and so on, all for 25/- a week board and lodging.

In the following January, in company with my cousin, I moved to St Paul's House, a clergy house in Deptford High Street. The rector was a smiling, bald-headed young man called Douglas Robb. I lived there for the next four years. There were two other curates apart from my cousin. One was an ascetic young man and the other a lively and robust rugger-playing fellow, who once lent me a crimson silk-lined opera cloak and opera hat to go to some gala dance at one of the Livery Company Halls in the City. They were relics of his more worldly times at Oxford. As well as the curates, there was a deaconess and an elderly Grey Lady, who came from a very grand family. It was a happy household without any excess of piety or holier-than-thou attitude. The fact that I hardly ever went to church, except for a short while when I had become infatuated with the local vicar's daughter at Farnham, was never held against me. St Paul's, the church at Deptford, was a beauty, built in 1730 by Thomas Archer, a pupil of Vanbrugh's.

The only thing I did not like about Deptford was the soap factory. Fortunately it was a very small factory and it only boiled up the fat for the soap on Thursdays. Even so, it produced a smell out of all proportion to its size, a smell so heavy you could lean on it.

Deptford was a fairly rough neighbourhood. On one evening I walked right into the middle of a street fight. A huge cockney stevedore, pushing me out of the way, said, 'Sorry, Guv, this ain't your battle.'

Before I had even begun at Bart's, I had my first real experience of the medical world. A surgeon friend of Frank's invited me to Westminster Hospital, to see him perform an operation. I was gowned, gloved, capped and led into the theatre.

'Just stand behind me,' he said, 'and you should be able to see all that is going on.'

The first operation was the insertion of a radium bomb into the uterus of a poor old lady who had cancer. She looked as old as my grandmother. She was lying on her back with her knees up in the air, supported by slings, as if she was a chicken waiting to be degutted. I could see much more than I wanted to, so I focused all my attention on the heavy white woollen stockings in which she had been attired for the occasion. Long before the operation was finished, I had decided I would opt for being a physician. Surgery was not for me. I also wondered if medicine was.

Once established at Bart's, the first-year students used to be allowed, in fact encouraged, to watch operations. These took place in very modern theatres in a multi-storey building. One watched from behind plate glass in a little gallery almost over the operating table. The most notable memory I have was of seeing a famous Harley Street surgeon make, by mistake, a great slit in the patient's aorta. A fountain of blood shot up in the air. Apparently unperturbed, he called for a needle and gut and sewed up the artery.

Every Saturday morning we used to gather in the old operating theatre, an oval room with tiers of benches, there to watch the weekly Caesareans. This was thought to be highly entertaining. It was a scene that might have been drawn by Thomas Rowlandson. After the morning work was done, we trooped off to the White Hart, a pub in Giltspur Street, which was practically part of the hospital.

At the end of my first term at Barts, I was taken winter sporting, to a little resort in the Bernese Oberland called Les Diablerets, by my father's friend Guy Breton, a retired Captain RN. I was to be an escort for his two daughters. Guy Breton's ideas of clothing suitable for skiing were clearly based on an earlier pioneering age. The proper dress, he assured me, was riding breeches, puttees and heavy army boots (with an adjustment to the heel to keep the ski fastening in place) and a windcheater.

The snow was early that year and I spent a blissful two weeks. Not only did I learn to ski, but also found myself part of the crew of a two-man bobsleigh. This happened because an unfortunate young man had broken his leg the day before the local championships. Our bob was the favourite for the race and we were the first to start. The course was an unbroken sheet of ice. We shot down the first two kilometres in what must have been record time because I could not find the brake handles. When I did get hold of them, I managed to slow us up to such good effect that our time was ruined and we only came in second.

It was the skiing that really excited me most and not just shooting down the *piste*, but skiing across country through deep, untouched powder snow. That is still one of the most enthralling things I have ever done.

I made two more visits to the Bernese Oberland in the 1930s, to Gstaad and Saanenmoser, in company with the Diana of my kindergarten days. In those uncrowded times, the ski slopes seemed like fairyland. Otherwise most of my holidays were spent in Abergavenny, pursuing two pretty cousins, walking in the Black Mountains or the Brecon Beacons and maintaining a link with the land of my fathers.

Recollections of my time at Bart's are hazy. My first set-back there was, that in the ill-lit lecture theatres, I could not see the blackboards. Ever since I had discarded my glasses during my first term at Charterhouse, thanks to working away at my eye exercises, I had managed perfectly well. The classrooms at school were better lit and I usually grabbed a desk near the front of the room. The eye-man at Bart's pooh-poohed the Bates theory and fitted me out with spectacles to match my degree of myopia. (Incidentally they were less powerful than the ones I had needed five years before.)

Now I could see, but it was of little avail, for apart from biology, in which I was interested, I could make nothing of the First MB syllabus. In physics, I spent most of my time weighing something called a copper calorimeter, without knowing why. In chemistry, particularly organic chemistry, I got nowhere. The fact that sucrose could be broken down into fructose and glucose may have meant something to the future doctors of England, to me it meant nothing. One of my friends, Teddy Smyth,[1] used to say it did not matter not understanding it. All I had to do was to memorize it. And that was the rub. At school, my inability to memorize more than about four lines of verse at a time, earned me, from a discerning form master, a lasting exemption from such learning. It was no use explaining this to the London University examiners. At separate times, I passed each part of the London University First MB, but never all of them together. Finally after some weeks of cramming, I took the easier Conjoint exam. The crammer bet my father the full cost of the fees that I would pass. I failed every part.

4. Goldsmiths'

IT WAS A murky October afternoon. The city was lost in fog. Dr Shaw, a gentle grey-bearded man who was the Dean of the Medical School at Bart's, received us in his study. After a few polite words my father came to the point.

'My son wants to give up medicine and take up art.' I never thought at the time how much it must have cost him to say those few words. His ambitions, mistakenly transferred to me, of a great career as a famous surgeon, were to be replaced by something as nebulous and futile as art.

The Dean's reactions were somewhat different. He beamed at me and said, 'That's the first sensible thing I have heard about him since he came here. I have seen his zoology drawings; if he wants a career as a medical illustrator, we can give him a job here, right away.'

That was the last thing I wanted. If I was not going to be a doctor, I was certainly not going to spend my life among hospital sights and smells, doing detailed drawings of rotting tissues and obscene tumours. I made my excuses, the Dean shook us warmly by the hands and we found ourselves outside the hospital, walking towards the Old Bailey.

'I hope you never find yourself in there,' my father said, rather unnecessarily, I thought, presumably coupling a career in art with a life of petty crime. He gave a short laugh, then said, 'Radcliffe-Wilson said Goldsmiths' was the place, didn't he?' I said that he had. 'In that case, let's go and get it fixed up. It's at New Cross, near Deptford, isn't it?' I said it was. 'That's convenient for you, anyway.' He turned and hailed a taxi that was cruising alongside the kerb. We got in and I gave the driver instructions.

'It'll cost you a bit, Guv'nor; it's quite a way to New Cross. Reckon we'd best go over London Bridge and down the Old Kent Road.' As we crept through the rush-hour traffic, I felt nervous and anxious, full of doubts as to whether Goldsmiths' would take me in. My father, on the other hand, seemed quite elated. He was a man of action and here he was doing something to launch his only son on yet another career.

The fog was thicker south of the river and by the time we had reached the Marquis of Granby, the turning point for the Lewisham High Road, visibility was down to a few yards. I directed the driver to the entrance gates of Goldsmiths' College.

'Do you want me to wait for you, Guv?' the cab driver asked.

'Yes,' said my father. 'I shall want to go to Waterloo.'

'Then you can look forward to a nice slow drive back,' the cabby replied.

I led my father through the long corridor, crowded with students from the Teachers' Training College, and up the iron-barred concrete staircase to the School of Art. A couple of minutes later we were seated in the Principal's office. Clive Gardiner, the Principal, was then in his thirties. He had a soft speaking voice and a shy manner. My father explained the purpose of our visit.

'I think I know this young man, he has been coming to evening classes during this last year.' My father looked surprised but did not say anything. Gardiner turned to me.

'I have an idea you said you were interested in illustration?' I nodded my head. 'Well,' he continued, 'before you can become an illustrator you will have to learn to draw and to paint. And that will begin, but will not end, in the Life Class.' He turned to my father with a diffident smile. 'He has got a long road ahead of him. More than anyone here, life itself will be his teacher. I know, I am still learning. The sooner he starts the better.'

There was no question about whether I was good enough. It was simply agreed there and then that I should enrol on the following Monday. I had only missed the first couple of weeks of term.

*   *   *

My first days at Goldsmiths were euphoric, except for the time spent in the Antique Room, painstakingly drawing the Dancing Faun or the Discobolus. An amorphous mass of students resolved themselves into individuals. Among the new students were two or three very pretty girls; one in particular was a startlingly pretty blonde girl called Valerie White, to whom I soon became very attached. In contrast to her was a young bespectacled girl called Betty Swanwick, who had a very personal, rather naive style of drawing. Among the boys, the first one I spoke to was Cedric Rogers. He had a mop of straight fair hair that flopped over his forehead and a pronounced limp, as a result of his hip being damaged when he was born. As he worked he sang everlastingly a mournful song called 'Lullaby of the Leaves'. There was a fair, curly-headed, rather girlish boy who had run away from Repton, called Denton Welch; and a little dwarf called Ian Hennessy-Smith whose personality more than compensated for his lack of size. He drew so beautifully we all felt he would outpace Henri de Toulouse-Lautrec. In fact, he remained a permanent student and was to be seen in the corridors of Goldsmiths' for decades after all his contemporaries had moved out into the world. He was a lovable little man.

Goldsmiths' only had about sixty full-time students, so the divisions between the first, second and third year students were blurred. Among the older students there was an inseparable couple, Helen Roeder and Carel Weight. The latter, even in those days, was thought of as a painter of more than average promise. He had a look of Coco the Clown, a look that quite belied his very shrewd brain. Carel, in fact, was a bit older than most of the other students, except for an endearing and Rackhamish little gnome of a man called Paul Drury, who hovered round the etching room. Carel had first had ideas of being an opera singer and only belatedly turned to art.

He had studied singing with an enormously fat lady who used to make him lie down on the carpet when she would pile volumes of the *Encyclopedia Britannica* on his chest and make him sing scales.

'Sometimes she would sit on my stomach,' he said, 'so I began to dislike singing.'[1]

Carel Weight's paintings, from the time he was at Goldsmiths', always contained some hidden drama. The first picture that he showed at the Royal Academy Summer Exhibition was titled 'An episode in the childhood of a genius'. It showed a baby hanging from the top of a pub sign, with a crowd of worried onlookers below.

Paul Drury was the son of a famous sculptor called Alfred Drury. Paul was a very talented etcher. In spite of his gnomish appearance, he was a witty and friendly man, who was particularly kind to younger students.

We were a very happy bunch of students and we all seemed to be brimming over with confidence. This was, I think, a peculiarity of the time, even though it was just after the slump. Because of its great tradition of illustration and print-making, students at Goldsmiths' set out with the idea that they were going to earn their living by the skill of their hands. If they felt they could not make it, they would then opt for the 'College' and a career in teaching. Few of us ever bothered to take the NDD or the Intermediate examinations. Our sole objective was to develop our skills. Looking back, it makes me shudder to think on what a slender foundation I hoped to build a career.

To begin with, during each week, we spent one day in the Antique Room, two days in the Life Class, a day in the engraving department and a day doing illustration. Our tutors for life drawing were James Bateman RA (always known as 'Cow' Bateman because of the success at the Royal Academy of his painting called 'Cows in a Rickyard') and a fat, jolly, bearded man called John Mansbridge, who had a strong resemblance to the Frans Hals painting of 'The Laughing Cavalier'. We had E. M. Dinkle for the Antique, Stanley Anderson RA for etching and engraving and Rowland Hilder and Edward Bawden for illustration.

Clive Gardiner looked at such drawings as I had brought with me on the day I enrolled and, after working out my timetable, said, 'Most of your time will be spent drawing and painting. About illustration, Edward Bawden is a very clever fellow, but he is much more of a designer than you will ever be, so I think you had better go and work with Rowland Hilder. Let's hope that he can do something with you.' So the die was cast. Edward Bawden, even in those days, was an austere figure, close shaven and with a bony forehead and something of the Jesuit novice about him. In fact he had been to a Quaker school. Bawden was a highly idiosyncratic, witty, Edward Learish illustrator, but with a very strong understanding of the design of the printed page. I was no born draughtsman like Hilder, and if I had known that most of my working life was not going to be spent illustrating, but in designing books, magazines and other bits of print, it might have been more sensible if I had worked with Bawden. Even so, I owe more than I can say to Rowland Hilder. He helped me in so many ways and not only in the art school curriculum. After I had left Goldsmiths', he took me into his house and gave me somewhere to work, and he introduced me to boats and sailing. This thing about 'messing about in boats' clearly did not further my career as an illustrator, but it brought a new dimension into my life. All this was to come later. My interests when I first went to Goldsmiths', apart from my work, were confined to girls.

Billie (as for some sentimental reason I renamed Valerie) was young and plump with puppy fat. To begin with our relationship never went further than lingering goodnight kisses as I deposited her on the doorstep of her aunt's house in Blackheath.

Things might have gone further on the night of the Goldsmiths' dance. I was spending the night at Billie's aunt's house. We arrived in long after the old aunt was fast asleep. We crept up to Billie's bedroom, she shut the door firmly, switched off the light and flung herself down on the bed. She was there for the taking, but for some reason or other I held back.

For the next year there was a certain coolness between us. Anyhow I was occupied elsewhere, going to dances with various Farnham girls and having desperate struggles on the back seats of small cars. Making love under such circumstances does indicate how strong the urge must have been.

The following summer – I think it was Midsummer's Day – a party of Goldsmiths' students arranged a picnic in Ashdown Forest. I was struck with how lovely Billie looked. She had suddenly grown up. That night we stayed together in a farmhouse. The next morning I very earnestly promised to marry her if she found she was pregnant.

She laughed ruefully and said, 'You dear silly child!' The fact that she was three years younger than I was seemed to be irrelevant. From that moment onwards I became her slave. She had a very strong personality. Henri Henrion, with whom, after we had parted company, she lived for several years, said that her will was so strong that she was the only girl he had ever known who, by will power alone, had turned her rather sturdy legs into limbs suitable for a Miss World contest.

At Goldsmiths' she developed into a talented and capable graphic designer. Her real ambition, scarcely expressed at that time, was to go on the stage. In due course she achieved her desire and became an actress of authority and great sensibility.

My three years at Goldsmiths' passed all too quickly. Early in my second year, I produced my first illustrated piece of print, an appeal booklet for the restoration of St Paul's church, Deptford. At the same time, through some chance introduction, I sold for five guineas to a brewing firm, a drawing of a negro barman frenetically shaking a cocktail. My father thought I was made and was all for me starting on a freelance career right away. I managed to persuade him that I still had something to learn.

In the summer of 1934, a group of Goldsmiths' students rented a house in the fishing village of Brixham in Devon. During this holiday I painted a number of ginger and blue water colours of Brixham and neighbouring harbours; I used this unappealing colour scheme because one of my tutors had told me to limit my palette to burnt sienna and cobalt blue. On my return home, a friend of my mother's, in her kindness, bought most of them. Billie was there, of course, and caused something of a sensation by swimming some way across Tor Bay.

We had hired a fishing boat for the afternoon. When we arrived at the quay at Brixham, which was crowded with holidaymakers, someone shouted, 'Where has she swum from?'

'Portland Bill!' I cheerfully answered. Movie cameras whirred, Kodaks clicked and a young reporter was standing on the steps ready to interview the beautiful blonde swimmer.

The effect was somewhat spoiled when the boatman said: 'That will be five shillings,' and Billie, who was the only one who had brought any money, had to grope in the boat for her purse.

'What! Five shillings for rowing from Portland Bill?' gasped the reporter.

'Who said anything about Portland Bill,' answered the boatman. 'We've only been out to the Old Harry Rocks.'

Denton Welch was with us on that holiday. He was effervescent and amusing. In our innocence it never dawned on us that he was homosexual. He was a fawn-like creature, apparently quite remote from the stresses of sex and love. Within six months he was to have the terrible accident that ultimately was the cause of his death.

Denton had quite an influence on our lives. He had a room on Croom's Hill overlooking Greenwich Park. In practically no time he had filled it with pretty things that he had bought in junk shops; Persian runners, old furniture, pieces of Oriental and English pottery. Denton had an unfailing eye for quality. Once, rummaging about in a second-hand clothes shop in Lewisham, he spotted an old tea caddy stuck away in a corner. It was so grimy that it was impossible to see what it was. He bought it for a few shillings and took it back to his room. After he had cleaned it, four exquisite Rajasthani miniatures were revealed.

'How did you know what it was?' I asked him.

'I didn't,' he replied, 'but somehow I felt it was something.'

This intuitive sense he owed largely to his mother, a Boston lady, and to being brought up in Shanghai.

'When I was in China,' he told us, one evening at Brixham, 'my mother used to collect Chinese porcelain. She let me handle the stuff. She had a jolly good eye for spotting fakes – and my goodness, can't the Chinese fake!'

There was something about Denton that singled him out from the rest of us. In many ways he seemed more like a pretty girl than a boy. He had a lovely complexion, a high domed forehead and curly brown hair. He normally wore spectacles, but not if he was being photographed. There was a hard core that belied this gentle exterior and also a certain feminine shrewdness in the way he talked about people. We soon learned that he had hated Repton. His father was a wealthy merchant in the Far East. His mother, to whom he had been devoted, died when he was eleven. His landlady at Croom's Hill was a Miss Sinclair, who came to be known as Evie. She mothered him – as, indeed, did practically every middle-aged lady who came in contact with him, including Edith Sitwell. He enjoyed shocking them by uttering schoolboy improprieties. At Goldsmiths' he never seemed to finish any work. Many years later I asked Bawden what he had thought of Denton as a student. 'Most unsatisfactory,' was his reply.

*   *   *

My pattern of life in those days was to spend the week at St Paul's House, where I now shared rooms with Michael Gordon. He certainly helped to offset the weight of four parsons. Michael was a cheerful, sporting, extrovert person and the best companion anyone could have wished for. I introduced him to my Goldsmiths' friends, and in no time he had fallen hopelessly in love with Billie. Even this did not spoil our friendship.

Early in 1932 I had persuaded Douglas Robb to get rid of his old Morris Cowley and to buy a Riley 9, a motor I had admired since first seeing Hugh Radcliffe-Wilson's car. Douglas Robb, the most generous of men, used to lend me this desirable little motor whenever I wanted. My stock at Goldsmiths' was high; any student with a car was worth cultivating!

I saw a lot of my cousin Frank. He was a plump, lethargic, unfailingly good-tempered man, with an unselfconscious flow of bad language that punctuated his talk and might have been more suitable for a barrack room than a clergy house. We used to share a bathroom which made a splendid confessional. One night whilst he was wallowing in the hot water, I was shaving and telling him of my love affairs.

He endured this for a while and then said, 'That's a lot of bunkum! Do you know what your besetting sin is?'

'No.'

'Sloth!' he replied. That brought me down to earth with a bump and from then on I began to work harder, much harder.

At weekends, with almost unfailing regularity, I used to go down to Farnham in the summer for endless tennis parties with the daughters of the retired soldiers who lived there and then on to Aldershot with the same warm-hearted girls to dance at the Officers' Club. Only too often have I sat in the car park until a quarter to one. I might so easily have suffered the fate of Miss Joan Hunter-Dunn's young man. In the winter I used to play golf with my father on Hankley Common. It was a game for which I had little aptitude.

At Goldsmiths' we had two rather special models in the Life Class. One was a striking-looking Eurasian girl, called Maxine; the other a well-rounded, middle-aged French woman called Madame Paul. She always brought some toys with her; quite often they were sugar mice. She would contort her ample figure into the most graceful poses. On one occasion she decided to climb to the top of a ladder so that we could paint her as if she was floating in the clouds.

As she started to climb, she said rather coyly, 'All students please turn round and look the other way until I have taken up the pose.' We obeyed politely.

Hard though I struggled with Madame Paul's Rubensian curves or Maxine's lithe body, I never did a decent life drawing until one day I got a commission from the Society for the Propagation of the Gospel to do a poster of a Borneo fisherman. That week we had a male model, a rather stocky Italian. I posed him as my fisherman. John Mansbridge came into the room just as I was finishing my drawing.

'Good Lord!' he said. 'What's come over you? That's not a bad drawing.'

John Mansbridge was a good teacher. He was the son of Albert Mansbridge, socialist and educational reformer. In the Life Room he used to talk to us by the hour about life in Paris, conjuring up visions of *La vie Bohème.* In comparison to Montmartre, New Cross seemed rather drab. He also talked to us about painting and painters, of Picasso and Braque, of Giotto and Giorgione and many others. In those days the history of art was not taught as an academic subject. One learnt it from one's tutors in relation to what one was doing. Every crumb of information was gobbled up.

In addition to the sixty full-time students at Goldsmiths', many times that number attended evening classes. We were also expected to go to them at least three nights a week. Apart from the extra life classes, the most interesting evening class was Commercial Art, taken by Freddy Manner, a thin, bird-like man. Manner introduced us to the work of the great French poster artist Cassandre and to the American E. McKnight Kauffer's work for the London Underground. The first time Manner showed me some of Kauffer's posters I was so excited that next morning I rushed up to St James's Park, the London Underground Headquarters, and bought several of them for half a crown each. I proudly pinned them on the wall of my room at St Paul's House.

There was no talk of graphic design then. Either you painted pictures to satisfy yourself, or to exhibit at the Royal Academy, or you did Commercial Art to satisfy your clients. Commercial Art basically meant either illustration or posters, show cards and press advertisements. Layout and typography was something we had heard nothing about, until at the end of my second year, a former Goldsmiths' student called Milner Gray started a new class about packaging and layout. I remember attending one or two classes and drawing an advertisement for the Chase National Bank of New York. Below the drawing Milner told me to rule in very carefully a number of double lines to represent type. I did not feel that this was my thing at all and I soon went back to drawing and illustrating.

Milner Gray was for over fifty years one of the most successful graphic designers of his time. He started the Bassett-Gray Studio in the 1920s. This became the Industrial Design Partnership in 1935 when he was joined by Misha Black. He was also one of the prime movers in the founding of the Society of Industrial Artists. He had an eternally youthful appearance and even when he was over ninety years old, he still had the same baby face. While I was still at Goldsmiths', Billie and I stayed with Milner and his wife Gnade more than once. He was a helpful friend and wrote an introduction to my first book.[2]

My potential skills as an illustrator were obviously limited, but Rowland Hilder did what he could with them. My appetite for romance, on the other hand, was unbounded and this he satisfied to the full with his romantic drawings of ships and sea. He also communicated something of his feeling about boats and yachting, of which at the time I was quite unaware. Then one day he introduced me to 'the punt' and that is where my sailing career began.

On a dull February afternoon Rowland drove me down to Greenwich; the tide was out and the few yachts still on their moorings were high and dry, canted over on their bilges with masts pointing in all directions.

'There she is,' Rowland said, pointing to a little boat alongside the hard which, unlike all the others, was sitting bolt upright. Her white planking was bespattered with mud, but unlike most boats in winter time she looked in no way neglected.

'This boat (I don't call it a yacht) is a work boat. I don't use it for racing – perish the thought! I use it as a means of transport to get me to places on the river where I can draw.'

'How far do you go?'

'Oh, down to Sea Reach, to the entrance of the Medway, then through the Swale to Whitstable or to Faversham Creek and the Shipwright's Arms. That's a place you should see. Miles of saltings and little creeks and hardly a soul about. But I only go there when I have a week or two spare. At weekends I go up past Limehouse, perhaps as far

Aunt Jane was a 'bluestocking'.

My great-grandfather, the Rural Dean of Kidwelly.

My grandmother.

My grandfather (standing) and the Chester Herald
Tom Joseph-Watkin.

The sinking of HMS *Victoria* and the end of Uncle Sam. *National Maritime Museum.*

My mother as Kate Hardcastle.

My father as Tony Lumpkin.

2

The Mumbles Railway.

'And played leapfrog with
the Town Clerk'.
Illustration by W. Heath
Robinson to *The Water
Babies*.

'I was brakeman on a two-man bobsleigh'.

St Paul's Church, Deptford.

Ian Hennessy-Smith and the Trojan Toys Exhibition at Goldsmiths'.

Denton Welch at Pitt's Folly, 1942. *Photograph by Gerald Leet.*

'The Shipwright's Arms'. Watercolour by Rowland Hilder.

'The Punt'. Drawing by Rowland Hilder.

6

Ralph and Kira at Cap Martin.

The Riley 9.

Boulton and Paul Defiant.

'The Review'. 2nd AA Division Mess decorations.

SS *Queen Elizabeth* on the Clyde.

The assembling of a convoy.

as the Pool, usually on Sundays. It's quiet then, practically no move-ment of commercial traffic. Even the barges and lighters are tied up.'

'Where do you do most of your drawings?'

'Limehouse Reach.'

'That doesn't sound very salubrious.'

'I'm not looking for salubrity. Limehouse Reach is still, in parts, just as it was when Whistler was doing his etchings of London River.'

A flurry of snow brought our conversation to a close and we ran back to the car for shelter. As we were driving back to Goldsmiths', my mind was lost in a long past world of sailing ships and scented harbours, of rusty steamers (nice stuff to paint, rust – just a dab of burnt sienna) and I was thinking of that little flat-bottomed boat.

It was that afternoon that formed my attitude to boats and sailing. In fact another five years had passed before I bought my first boat – that very same punt.

The artists whose work Rowland then favoured and to whom he exposed us were E. J. Sullivan, Brangwyn, Muirhead Bone and Samuel Palmer; also the illustrators of the 1860s, Pinwell, Boyd Houghton and, of course, with his watery bent, Whistler. To offset this romantic attitude, Clive Gardiner who sometimes took us in life drawing and painting, would expound the current theories of 'significant form' and talk about Cézanne, the only artist that mattered to him.

Clive Gardiner was a remarkable and most likeable man. His father was the literary editor of *The London Daily News* and an essayist of note who wrote under the pseudonym of 'Alpha of the Plough'. Clive as a young man had been a close friend of Paul and John Nash, having lived very near them at Great Missenden in Buckinghamshire. He quietly achieved much at Goldsmiths'. He painted well and he wrote well. Every Christmas he used to write a fantasy for their Toy Theatre, which became a great feature of Goldsmiths' life. Betty Swanwick was a protégée of his and, in fact, rather more than that. She played a large part in the Toy Theatre productions. Clive made Goldsmiths' a very happy place.

Betty Swanwick, though a most private person, in time achieved some fame, becoming a Royal Academician in 1979. Whilst she was still at Goldsmiths' she designed posters for Shell-Mex and the London Passenger Transport Board. Her work had an almost childish naivety but nevertheless the designs were most arresting.

*　　　*　　　*

Each year I used to drive my parents down to Abergavenny for what was always referred to as 'Granny's last Christmas'. Once again, on Christmas Eve in 1934, we set off from Farnham in a hired self-drive car for Wales. It was snowing by the time we reached the Cotswolds and if I had not been able to hang onto the tail of a car whose driver seemed to know the road much better than I did, we would have arrived much later than we did. As it was, we were late for dinner. My Aunt Sah was a fine cook, and like most good cooks, she did not like her meals being spoilt. She had seated us at the dining-room table almost as soon as we were through the front door.

We were busy tucking into a saddle of Welsh mutton before my father noticed my Uncle Harold was not with us.

'Where's Harold?' he asked.

'Oh, he's not too well,' my aunt answered casually. 'Touch of 'flu, I think.'

'Upstairs?'

'No. As a matter of fact, he is down at the Cottage Hospital. I thought we would be more comfortable over Christmas without sickness in the house.'

'How long has he been there?'

'Only since this evening. I could not get an ambulance, so I ordered a furniture van. We put him in an armchair in the back and wrapped him up well.'

Having dealt with Uncle Harold, we then got down to the serious business of eating. Feeling benign at the end of the meal, my father suggested, as my aunt had no telephone in the house, that he and I drive down to the hospital to see 'poor Harold'.

When we arrived at the hospital, my father said to the nurse on duty, 'Just come to have a word with my sister's husband, Mr Pegler.'

'Oh dear!' said the nurse. 'I'm afraid you cannot see him now.'

'Why not?' demanded my father, bristling.

'Well, er . . . he died half an hour ago.'

That did not exactly add to our Christmas jollifications. The next morning my father was given the job of breaking the news to Granny. He put on a special death face and tiptoed into her room, to find her sitting up in bed, bright-eyed and smiling. One glance at my father was enough.

'I know what you are going to tell me,' she said. 'Harold's gone. What time did he go?'

Three days later Harold was tucked away in the corner of the grave I used to visit with Granny when I was a child, sharing it with W. D. Lewis, late of the parish of Llangattock, who had been waiting for twenty-four years for my granny to join him there. After the funeral my aunt announced that she and Granny were going to live in London.

*   *   *

One morning during the Summer term at Goldsmiths', I arrived late to find a group of students talking in hushed voices.

'What is it?' I asked.

'Denton,' one of the girls said, 'he has had a terrible accident. They don't think he will live.'

Later we learned that he had been bicycling down to Surrey to visit his uncle and aunt when a woman motorist banged into him, crushing him against a lamp-post. His spine had been injured and his kidneys irreparably damaged. But he did not die. After months in hospital, he was taken to a nursing-home at Broadstairs. Eventually, partially recovered, he was well enough to move to a flat in Tonbridge, where his former landlady, Miss Sinclair, came to look after him.

The lady motorist panicked and left for the continent that very day. She was eventually brought back to face a County Court case. They did not even endorse her licence, though Denton was awarded heavy damages.

The judge said at the time: 'But what is money to a young man whose future is so uncertain.'

It took him thirteen years to die and during that time he wrote five books. Edith Sitwell wrote a short foreword for *Maiden Voyage*, Denton's first book, in which she said, 'Mr Welch may easily prove to be, not only a born writer but a considerable one.' It was Herbert Read who spotted its quality and saw it through the press for the publisher Routledge.

In the summer of 1935, Goldsmiths' put on a quite remarkable show for those days. It was an exhibition of what is now described as 'Graphic Design'. One of the themes was a shop called 'Trojan Toys' for which much of the display was carried out by Ian Hennessy-Smith. Billie produced a very elegant set of cosmetic packages and I showed a series of coloured gouache illustrations for a sentimental tale about a Bohemian family called *The Constant Nymph* by Margaret Kennedy. These illustrations were designed to be reproduced by a then little known (and by now quite unheard of) process called Jean Berté. This involved the use of relief rubber plates and water colour inks. Needless to say the illustrations were never reproduced by it, or by any other process. However, they were seen by a friendly clergyman who worked for the Society for the Propagation of the Gospel. It was he who had commissioned the poster of the Borneo fisherman. As a result of this, I received my first substantial commission. This was to paint a series of large, for want of a better word, 'murals', of the various far-flung outposts of empire where the society propagated the gospel. They could not afford to send me on a world trip, but provided me with sheaves of photographs as references for the paintings.

Unwisely, I allowed myself to be persuaded to leave Deptford and to join my aunt and grandmother, who had by this time moved to a spacious if rather gloomy flat overlooking Battersea Park. It was not a happy arrangement. As a parting present, Douglas Robb sold me the Riley for £20, about a tenth of its true value.

5. Freelance Illustrator

I WAS STILL at Goldsmiths, but felt I could not paint the SPG murals there and there was certainly no suitable room in the flat at Battersea Park. Faced with this problem, I turned to Rowland Hilder. He offered me the use of a large attic room in the high Victorian House into which he had only recently moved. It was in Kidbrooke Grove, Blackheath. The SPG pictures were fun to do. I painted them as if they were posters in flat oil paint, which I bought from Screeton's in New Cross. It was rather like using gouache, for one had huge tins of flake white and small tins of vividly coloured stainers. The subjects ranged from Eskimos to Hawaiian maidens. The SPG suffered from no false modesty about naked breasts. One of the many subjects I painted was of the Rocky Mountains, with snow-covered peaks, a totem pole and a solitary Athabaskan Indian brave sitting on a piebald pony. In 1942 when I crossed the Rockies by the Canadian Pacific Railway, there, in Kicking Horse Pass, was my picture, complete with the same blue shadows on the snow, the same totem pole and even the same Athabaskan Indian (or one very like him), but this time sitting on a white horse.

The only positive benefit of living in Battersea was that Ralph Cusack and Stafford Palin were living just across the river in Pimlico. Ralph had married a dark-haired little Russian girl called Kira whom he had met in a kind of *Constant Nymph* situation in Bavaria. Ralph by this time was an ardent pacifist and stoutly left in his politics. He introduced me to *The News Chronicle*, stating that no one under forty should read *The Times*, and no one with any claim to progressiveness should be seen dead reading any of the other London dailies.

Until that time I had never given politics a thought. Belatedly I started thinking and I became a pacifist. Stafford Palin, who had no interest in such matters, was a dental student at Guy's Hospital. He was also married, to an elfin-faced girl called Haidee, who as well as being pretty appeared to be a model housewife, managing to feed Stafford well and to dress herself beautifully all on no pounds a week. Stafford was spending most of his time inventing his automatic gearbox.

Ralph was working at Lloyds and hating every minute of it. One morning he telephoned me in great excitement.

'I've got some news for you!' he shouted down the line. 'I'm packing in this beastly City life. We are going to live in the South of France. I'm going to paint. Come and celebrate!'

That evening we all got mildly drunk. Ralph's mother, who had died while he was still at Charterhouse, had left him her little villa at Menton-Garavan. The tenant had now died quite suddenly and that was where they were going.

'As soon as we are settled in, you must come and stay with us. By the way, do you want any furniture? I've got no use for this kitchen table and these two chairs.'

The next day I hired a hand cart and trundled these household goods across Chelsea Bridge to Prince of Wales Mansions. My father and mother by chance happened to be there. My father was furious at my demeaning myself by this barrow-boy act, which struck me as rather unreasonable.

I was still commuting daily in my Riley 9 from Battersea to Blackheath and friction was beginning to build up with my aunt, who did not approve of Billie or any of my other girlfriends. The abdication of Edward VIII, who as Prince of Wales she had idolized, quite unhinged her.

'You are just as bad! All your girls are whores!' she shouted at me.

In as dignified a manner as I could summon, I replied stiffly: 'If that's how you feel about things, I had better go.' The same day I moved all my chattels down to Blackheath.

On the strength of the SPG commission, which seemed to be open-ended, I left Goldsmiths'. I had been there three years and one term, which by present day standards does not seem quite adequate; of course it was not, but I had already wasted over two years at Bart's.

Just before I left Goldsmiths', a friend of my mother's gave me an introduction to Jack Beddington at Shell. I was shown into his office, which was just below the clock in the Shell-Mex building on the Embankment. I found Beddington rather terrifying when I first met him. He was a flamboyant figure, dressed in a pearl grey suit and wearing a cravat and a jewelled tie-pin. He was heavy jowled with elegantly curved moustaches and deep bags under his eyes. His younger brother Freddy was a neighbour of my parents in Farnham.

Jack Beddington's fierceness disguised a very kind nature. He was most generous to young artists and commissioned me to do numerous drawings, none of which he ever used. On one occasion, I delivered some sketches to Shell to find that Jack was in the United States and a youngish man called John Betjeman was holding the fort for him. All I can now remember of our conversation was that he was adamant that Shell should pay me more than they were doing. I argued the point with him and said I thought three guineas was an ample return for drawings that would probably never be used.

To help me further on my way, my father engineered another introduction to an aged peer called Lord Marshall, who was the Chairman of a large book distribution house. Lord Marshall very kindly wrote me six letters of introduction to six publishing houses. As far as I can remember, most of the recipients were either dead or, in the case of

John Buchan, who was one of them, had been ennobled and had retired from publishing. The only one I made any positive contact with was Ivor Nicholson of Nicholson and Watson and he told me that he never bought art work directly from artists.

'Who *do* you buy it from?' I asked in all innocence.

'An agent, of course,' he replied rather testily.

'Which agent?' I persisted.

'Oh, Miss Boland; you'd better go and see her, she may be able to help you.'

I did go and see Miss Boland and found there were two of them called Kathleen and Judy. They came from Belfast. Kathleen, the elder, had shining blonde hair and looked as hard as old nails; she was, in fact, the kindest person with the softest of hearts. She did much for me, providing me with a steady trickle of little jobs for magazines I had never heard of, and publishers I would never have met.

In the 1930s Charing Cross Road was packed with second-hand booksellers. There was also Foyles and – most important of all – Zwemmers. This shop, presided over by the intimidating figure of Mr Zwemmer himself, was a gateway to the continent and the modern art movement. Practically every week I bought some book there on contemporary painters or with illustrations by modern artists and never paid more than five shillings for any of them. I had been collecting books – particularly illustrated books – since my childhood. At Zwemmer's I found a children's book called *Macao et Cosmage* written and illustrated by Edy Legrand. This French artist had a profound effect on my work and later I bought several of Legrand's other children's books.

In the spring of 1936 Ralph Cusack invited me to come and stay with him at Menton for a month while Kira was away in Austria visiting her family. The return fare, third class, from London to Menton was only £5 10s 0d. I dozed fitfully through the night as the train travelled southwards. At first light, gritty eyed, I was glued to the window in the corridor looking at the sun rising over the distant Alps. By the time we had passed Avignon, we had entered the new and, as far as I was concerned, magical world of Provence.

Ralph's villa was on the coast road into Italy. It was a little white house overlooking the sea and the railway. In fact it was almost the last house before the frontier. Menton itself had a quiet, Edwardian appearance, but the old town was very different, almost Moorish in character. We spent our days painting and drawing there or down by the harbour. One afternoon we had gone out to Cap Martin. I was earnestly recording the scene. Ralph seemed to be having some trouble with his painting, when suddenly he flew into a rage and flung his canvas far out to sea. It went skimming a full forty yards before coming down onto the water. There it floated for the rest of the afternoon as he sat watching it morosely. Apart from these periodic outbursts, he was still the best of companions. He had a tremendous sense of fun.

On one glorious day we took a bus over the mountains to Sospel. The bus seemed to be as full of livestock as it did of passengers. When we at length arrived at Sospel, we sat down to paint the little double-arched bridge with the toll house in the middle of it. Behind it was a great backdrop of mountains with jagged peaks, some still snow covered. After a while, it grew too hot to paint, so we wandered through the narrow streets until we found a little café. We sat in the shade of the house on a terrace and I drank *pastis* for the first time in my life. We then lunched on crisp new bread and salami, olives and rough red wine. There was a smell of garlic in the air, with a faint undercurrent of drains. On that day there was nowhere I would rather have been in the whole world.

Towards the end of my visit we went over to Monte Carlo to watch the Monaco Grand Prix. It had started raining before we left Menton and by the time our bus had dropped us in Monte Carlo, it was pouring down. However, we found a good place from which to see the race. We had a view right over the harbour road, the one place where the cars could get up to their maximum speed.

'I think we are going to get pretty wet before the end of the day,' Ralph said. 'Let's buy a bottle of brandy. That'll keep us warm inside.' So we did just that. By the time the race started we were in a blissful state of mind. It was a most exciting race with all the great drivers of that time taking part. Rudolf Caracciola was driving a huge Mercedes; Hans Stuck was in a curiously shaped rear-engined Auto-Union; the two local heroes were Louis Chiron, the Frenchman, who was at the wheel of a little Bugatti and the Italian driver Tazio Nuvolari, who was driving a red Alfa Romeo.

The racing cars looked like motorboats as they hurtled along the rain-soaked harbour road, leaving trailing wakes behind them. At the end there was a hairpin bend and at one stage Nuvolari in the Alfa passed Caracciola in his much more powerful Mercedes on the inside of the bend. At the end of the day, however, Stuck's Auto-Union was first past the flag. In spite of Nuvolari's brilliance, his Alfa was out-classed for sheer speed if not in roadholding and cornering, by the big Mercedes and the Auto-Union; Chiron's little Bugatti, notwithstanding the crowd's support, was nowhere. As we soddenly made our way to the bus, Ralph put the brandy bottle back into his mackintosh pocket. It slipped through and smashed to pieces on the road.

'Better get another one,' he cheerfully muttered, 'fortunately there wasn't much left.'

By the time we reached the Villa Irlanda the second bottle was almost finished. We had hot baths and fell into our beds; we both slept solidly for twelve hours. We awoke none the worse for the experience.

That first visit to the south of France was the beginning of a love affair with Provence. I had a quite irrational feeling of coming home;

43

that I belonged to this Mediterranean countryside. Ever since then I have always had a particular affection for Menton, which is practically the only place on the *Cote d'Azur* that is protected from the Mistral, that searing cold north wind that blows off the Alps. I later verified the truth of the saying that if a Provençal murders his wife while the Mistral is blowing, he is automatically pardoned.

Just before I left the Villa Irlanda a postcard arrived from Rowland Hilder saying: 'Edith has done it at last. We have a son and we are calling him Anthony.'

I returned to London after that first visit as a confirmed Francophile. After a month in Menton I felt quite cosmopolitan.

The attic room at 5 Kidbrooke Grove made an excellent studio. It was light and airy with a view right across south London. The night the Crystal Palace was burnt down, I had a grandstand view of this pre-blitz bonfire. Across the landing I had a little bedroom and some primitive cooking arrangements. Cedric Rogers had the other large attic. Very soon Edith Hilder had taken us under her wing and at all times of the day, or night, the cry 'John! (or Cedric!) Cup of tea!' would echo up the stair well. They were kind and generous and broadminded as well, a characteristic that old Mrs Hilder, who lived on the first floor, did not share. The bathroom at 5 Kidbrooke Grove was typical of Rowland's sense of humour; slanting up the wall above the bath was a flight of pottery ducks with one plunging headlong down into the bath. Leaning up against the lavatory cistern was a twelve-bore shotgun.

As well as everything else, I was still painting the SPG murals and continued doing them right up to the outbreak of war. Rowland was a great talker and a great theorist. At one stage it was Marx, at another Freud and always it was anti-establishment. Even in those days, he had a feeling that his considerable abilities had not had the recognition they deserved, in spite of the fact that at Christmas time every mantelpiece in Britain was covered with his cards.

It was a very happy household, with people coming and going and Rowland permanently working at his drawing board. On one occasion, he invited Edward Ardizzone for the evening. Cedric, who even then must have been slightly deaf, was a great Ardizzone fan, so Rowland brought him up to the top floor to meet him. Cedric's behaviour was, to say the least of it, somewhat boorish, so Rowland moved Ardizzone on into my room. I was thrilled to meet this warm-hearted, snuff-taking man. Later Rowland tackled Cedric about his cool reception of Ardizzone.

'Who did you say it was?' Cedric gasped.

'Ardizzone, of course!' Rowland replied.

'Christ! I thought you said it was someone from your Badminton club!'

Cedric Rogers, a gentle and kindly creature, spent most of his waking hours practising the clarinet. His skill was limited. Cedric's parents, Stanley and 'Frank', as his mother was called, lived on Sydenham Hill.

Both parents were artists, though Stanley also wrote books about the sea and ships. When the war came, Cedric's gentle appearance was belied by his heroic career as a Spitfire pilot. He flew more missions in Spitfires than any other pilot in the service, first as a fighter pilot, then as an instructor and finally, as a result of increasing deafness, he was transferred and became a test pilot.

One weekend in February I drove out from Farnham to have tea with the Radcliffe-Wilsons. Their daughter Anne had warned me that she had a friend staying with her, a fellow student at Farnham Art School.

'Her name,' Anne said, 'is Griselda Rideout – her brother was at Charterhouse with you – and she has a perfectly horrid mother who treats her like a slave and never smiles.'

When I arrived at Crondall, Anne and Griselda were having difficulty in manoeuvring Griselda's very small car, a 2-seater Morris 8, into the garage alongside the Radcliffe-Wilsons' SS Jaguar. I offered to help and we finally got it inside by lifting it bodily. After this display of manly strength I took stock of this ill-treated damsel; she was a pretty girl, with a mass of dark brown hair, a fair complexion and rather telling blue eyes. Her most distinctive feature was her voice, which was pitched in a very low key. She also had a faint likeness to her brother whom I knew only slightly and did not particularly like.

After tea we played racing demon and Anne reported back to me later that Griselda had said I had cheated and was a rotten loser. She had also said, 'Why does he wear that awful hat?' in reference to a mole-coloured Homburg that I was rather proud of.

'It is no good you going after her,' Anne said firmly. 'She's got a boyfriend called Guy who she is quite dotty about. They go botanizing together.' Not being able to cap that, I did no more about her. But from that day I stopped wearing hats.

Through Miss Boland I illustrated some books on Basic English. She found me a regular spot in a ladies' magazine called *Eve's Journal* and I illustrated a book about England for Methuen. In the same week that Methuen commissioned these drawings the Craigs invited me to visit them in Madeira.

Charles Craig pointed out that it would only cost me a few pounds to get there as the Royal Mail Line had cut the price of their first class return tickets in order to put some rival out of business. Wanting the best of both worlds, I took the manuscript of this book about England and a sheaf of references out to Madeira with me. Each morning in a garden room at the Craigs' villa at Funchal I worked away on a really dreadful set of illustrations. At noon Charles would take me out to the English Rooms for a drink before lunch.

On Sunday afternoons Clara Craig would invite various young people to the *thé dansant* at Reed's Hotel. The Portuguese girls were all severely chaperoned. I was very attracted by one of them. Her name was Teresa da Camara and she was barely sixteen. She had a complexion

45

like a ripe nectarine. Unfortunately I never saw her alone.

Funchal in the 1930s was not so different from when my father visited it in 1905. The English colony was headed by the families of the great wine firms, the Blandys and the Cossarts. Most of the English people never went further than a few miles from Funchal. One day Teresa's brother drove me to Sao Vicente, a village on the north of the island. It was a hair-raising drive over the mountain passes. When we reached the village, I sat down to do a drawing. I was soon surrounded by a crowd of fishermen.

'Don't be alarmed,' Martin da Camara said, 'you are probably the first Englishman they have ever seen.'

It was all very strange. Life seemed to be suspended in a kind of vacuum; I suppose the existence of the well-to-do English there was much the same as at Menton, or any other place under the sun. The Portuguese that I met seemed to be so very much more interesting than the English. It was, however, a completely feudal society.

I had sailed out in the Royal Mail ship, the *Asturias*, which in company with her sister ship, the *Almansora*, provided a shuttle service to Rio de Janeiro and Buenos Aires. I rejoined the *Asturias* on her return from South America. I found myself sitting next to a nice old lady whom I had met on the outward voyage.

'I don't know what has happened to my sister,' she said. 'We spent the day at Reed's and we had rather a lot to drink. I think she may have gone to lie down.'

She had done no such thing. She was at that moment in the bar of the *Almansora*, probably saying the same thing. It was not until she went to her cabin to change for dinner, and found it occupied, that she discovered she was on the way back to Rio. The wireless waves fairly crackled as this saga was flashed over the Atlantic to us. By this time we were more than a hundred miles apart. There was nothing for it. Back to Rio she had to go.

When I arrived back at Kidbrooke Grove, there was a letter from Miss Boland telling me of the work that was lined up for me. *Vogue* wanted some drawings for a special Christmas number and there were some illustrations for a book of verse called *Such Things Happen* for Herbert Jenkins. When I had completed these drawings, they showed distinct traces of Heath Robinson's wobbly line.

Judy, the younger of the Boland sisters, was, to look at, a retiring little person. In fact she had a core of steel and was a much tougher nut than her elder sister. I grew very fond of them both. The last job I did through them was a number of drawings for Odhams. These were to illustrate books with such titles as *The Fifty Greatest Horror Stories* or *The Fifty Worst Detective Stories*. I never saw them for sale anywhere. They were sold not through the book shops but by door-to-door salesmen, and sold by the yard as furniture for the 'front room'. I discovered this during the war when I was billeted in Chester on one of their salesmen.

He peddled these books around the back streets of Manchester and throughout the Black Country. There they were, in his 'front room'. That man made more out of publishing than any publisher I ever met and he was barely literate.

By the time I had returned from Madeira, Billie was working for Milner Gray and Misha Black in Bedford Square. I went to call on her one day to take her out to lunch. She introduced me to an elegant, very French-looking young man.

'This is Heine Henrion,' she said. 'I'm afraid I've promised to have lunch with him, you don't mind, do you Johnnie? We're working on a job together.' I did mind, very much, at the time. And that was the end of that. They soon set up house together and over the years I came to know Henri well and to become very fond of him. With the coming of war, his name Heine was transposed to Henri. By the end of the war he had become a leading light in the graphic design world. Billie had left him and had moved on to fame and fortune on the stage.

Quite a lot of water had run under quite a lot of bridges when I next heard Anne talking about Griselda. 'She's broken it off with Guy, so now's your chance if you're still interested.'

I made at least a dozen telephone calls to Griselda's lodgings before I could get in touch with her. She sounded surprised to hear me, but when I asked her if she would care to come out into the country for a picnic on the following day, she said she would. I told her that I would meet her by the 'clock that tells the time all over the world' in Piccadilly Circus Underground Station. I always used to meet my new girlfriends by that clock.

I went to the delicatessen counter at the Coventry Street Lyons Corner House and bought roast duck in aspic, French bread, Cornish butter and fresh strawberries and cream. From a pub I bought half a dozen bottles of beer and loaded this into the Riley, which was parked in Leicester Square and then, at least a quarter of an hour early, I went to our rendezvous. She was already there.

We drove down to Kent and in a wood near Eynsford I spread out our picnic. I talked and she listened. She was reluctant to talk about her family, but she did tell me her mother's brother was a writer called Gilbert Cannan, who had run away with J. M. Barrie's wife. I was impressed by this.

Our love affair progressed by fits and starts, but I soon realized that here was a girl it was a joy to be with, who shared my interests and even might be willing to share my life. Her main interests were in flowers and wildlife. Apart from Guy, she had had two other boyfriends who were naturalists. She used to go hawking with them with merlins and goshawks on Salisbury Plain and sometimes with an eagle over Hoo marshes. She had no interest in games; tennis was anathema to her, but she had done some canoeing and had been to Arosa for winter sports, mostly for *l'après-ski*, it seemed.

In the autumn of 1938 with the Munich crisis, my pacifism evaporated and I tried unsuccessfully to join the RNVR. A couple of months later my grandmother died; she was ninety-four and she had a peaceful end in the flat in Battersea. She left nothing in her will but the express wish to be buried in the same grave as her husband. Arrangements were made with the Battersea undertakers that she should be conveyed to the cemetery in Abergavenny. To my dismay, my father suggested that we should follow the hearse down to Wales. I had visions of never getting my much loved Riley 9 into top gear. It did not turn out quite like that.

It was a bright crisp November morning when the hearse drew away from Prince of Wales Mansions. The crew, or whatever the collective term is for four top-hatted mutes, were sitting rigidly upright as if they had been carved out of basalt. We had not reached 30 mph by the time we picked up the Great West Road at Chiswick. Here the hearse came to a stop.

'Probably going to have a prayer meeting,' my father remarked with unbecoming levity. 'They're all getting out,' he added rather obviously. The mutes were slowly removing their top hats and their black over-coats, then reaching into a compartment underneath my granny's coffin – it was a very small coffin – they dragged forth raincoats and check tweed coats and caps. As soon as they had transformed them-selves into what looked like a party off to the races, with cheerful waves to us they climbed aboard again and the hearse shot off like a Grand Prix racing car. I did not catch up with them again until we were coming into Henley-on-Thames. Once past Oxford, the hearse really took off and roared through Witney and Burford and other pretty Cotswold villages with my grandmother in her coffin bouncing about as if it was on a trampoline. On the long stretch of Roman road after Cirencester, the Riley was hard pressed to keep up with the steady 65 mph of the hearse. Far from slackening speed when we came to the precipitous Birdlip Hill, the driver of the hearse must have thought he was on a bobsleigh. Perforce he had to ease up through Gloucester, and the winding road to Monmouth put a further damper on his perfor-mance. After passing Raglan he managed to get moving again, but about three miles short of Abergavenny, he signalled that he was stopping. The mutes climbed out, stretched themselves, stamped their feet then divested themselves of their sporting raiment. Once more top-hatted and in sombre black, they drove into Abergavenny and up to the cemetery at a dignified 15 mph.

We were met at the gates by the Rev. Luther Evans, a distant relative (as far as I was concerned, the distance could not have been too great).

'Nice to see you Claude,' he said to my father, 'and you too, boy,' looking doubtfully at me, 'even though it is a sad occasion. But she had a good innings, man, we have that to be thankful for. Outlived W. D. Lewis by nearly thirty years. There's widowhood for you. Very dignified your arrival. Have you driven that speed all the way from London?'

'Yes,' I untruthfully replied, 'and stopped for prayers twice on the way.'

'Really now! Fancy that, with London undertakers and all. I always thought they were an ungodly lot.'

The next day we drove back to Battersea. After years of waiting on every wish of my grandmother, my aunt now looked a little lost; however, she had plans for going to spend the rest of the winter on the French Riviera. Her skin had gone a parchment yellow and in fact she was such a bad colour that my father insisted on her seeing her doctor. The doctor arrived and said she would have to go into hospital immediately. Five days later she was dead and once again we had to make the same dolorous journey to Abergavenny. This time we went by train in the company of my father's parson brother, Tom.

We travelled from Paddington in the Great Western crack train, the *Bristolian*. After some urging, my father managed to get his brother into the bar, but not to drink anything more powerful than a small glass of sherry. Whilst we were sipping our Martinis, the guard joined us. My father had a knack of striking up an animated conversation with almost anyone.

'Good morning, Guard, beautiful train this!'

'That it is, Sir,' replied the guard, then taking out a large silver stopwatch from his pocket, he looked out of the window for a few moments, then looked up and said, 'What is more, we are doing 108 mph. That is what you might call travelling, isn't it? Wonderful roadbed we have here. We owe it all to Mr Brunel. And it doesn't spill your drink either!

'It is indeed very smooth. What's the engine?'

'Castle Class, Sir, based on Churchward's design. Fine engines they are and built at Swindon. I don't think there has ever been anything to touch them.'

The only apt comment about my poor aunt's funeral came from the Rev. Luther Evans.

'Didn't expect to see you again so soon. Poor soul, poor soul,' he muttered lugubriously, but then added, 'but it's an ill wind . . .' Whether he was remarking on the pleasure of seeing us again, or the thought of another and unexpected funeral feast, we did not stop to enquire.

*   *   *

It was not long before Griselda was a regular visitor to Blackheath, but old Mrs Hilder's disapproving glances as they met on the landing of 5 Kidbrooke Grove made me consider it might be wise to move. A few weeks after my aunt's funeral I heard that there was a ground floor flat to let in Cheyne Walk. It consisted of one large room and a bathroom-cum-kitchen. The rent was twenty-five shillings a week, so I took it. It was at the slummy end of the embankment, overlooking Lot's Road Power Station. There was not much traffic then. I used to garage the Riley the other side of the river, about seven minutes' walk over the Albert Bridge. I would not have dreamt of leaving it out in the street all night. Griselda had moved on from Farnham Art School and, with Anne, had gone to the Central School of Arts and Crafts in Holborn. At the end of two terms, after a row with her parents, because they had been complaining about the cost of keeping her in London, she found a job at Heals in Tottenham Court Road. There she soon came under the influence of Mrs Maufe, the wife of the architect of Guildford Cathedral. Mrs Maufe was a remarkable lady, who always dressed in skirts that reached the ground and in long black cloaks and wide-brimmed hats. The first time I saw her I thought she looked like the Portuguese hidalgo in the poster for Sandeman's Port. Though the pay was miniscule, Griselda enjoyed herself there.

One evening, returning to Cheyne Walk, we saw a notice on the door 'Flat to let'. This could only have been the top floor flat which had been unoccupied the whole time I had been there. Over supper, Griselda said: 'Might be a good idea if Edwin and I took it. It would be cheaper than both of us paying for digs.' Edwin was her younger brother who had just left Oundle and was studying to become a chartered accountant.

The upshot of this was that on the next day I collected the key from the agent and that evening Griselda and I looked at the flat. It had a little balcony and was worth the rent just for the view of the river. Also it was in very good decorative order.

'I think it's lovely,' she said, then rather shyly, 'You don't think I'm running after you, coming to such close quarters?' I quickly settled her mind on that point.

During the next week, she went through all the necessary negotiations with the agents and finally, with the contract ready to sign, she came along to have a final look at the flat. It was a lovely June evening. The tide was up and Battersea Power Station was bathed in a warm rosy light. We climbed the two flights of stairs and as we mounted higher, I felt as if there was a cold wind blowing on the back of my neck. Griselda unlocked the door and we went inside. The room was filled with the reflected light from the river, yet it felt as cold as a refrigerator. We did not speak; she looked round and then turned to me and said in a low voice, 'Let's get out of here.'

We hurried downstairs and it was not until the door of my flat was tightly shut that we spoke.

'What was it?'

'God! What a horrible feeling!' She grasped my arm. 'Johnnie! Nothing, nothing would make me go inside that flat again. I have never felt anything so awful.'

We talked round it for hours, never coming to any sensible conclusions. Then, just as it was getting dark, the telephone rang, but there was no one on the line. Suddenly a painting I had done of a reclining nude, which was on top of a bookcase leaning up against the wall, came flying across the room and crashed at our feet.

'After that, we had both better have a drink.' I poured out a fairly hefty dollop of gin, added a miniscule finger of tonic and handed it to Griselda. As I did so, there was a spitting noise behind me. I turned to see a huge jet black tom cat in the middle of the carpet. I stepped towards it, but with a hiss it was off, hurtling round the room and clawing at the closed windows. Griselda pushed up one of the bottom sashes and this very unwelcome visitor shot out into the night.

'Where the hell did he come from?' I gasped.

'Hell itself, I should think,' Griselda replied. 'There was no open window through which he could have come in.'

After that nothing more happened, apart from the telephone ringing once more, and once again there being no one on the line. Our pulses seemed to slow down and our fears to vanish. The only reference we made to the top flat was when Griselda said: 'I will tell the agents tomorrow that as far as I am concerned, it's all off.'

About a week later Mrs Hand, my daily woman who had been off sick for the previous three weeks, returned. I told her quite casually that Miss Rideout had been thinking of taking the top flat.

'Oh! Laws, Sir, don't you let her do that. No one ever stays there more than a few weeks.'

'But the previous tenant had it for two years.'

'Yes, but she never lived in it. She was a lady doctor and had got a job out in Egypt. Took the flat just before she went abroad.'

'What's wrong with it?'

'I don't rightly know, but I don't like even going up the top stairs.'

So I told her of our experiences and that Griselda had decided against it.

'I should think so too! All I ever heard was that somebody died there nastily. But whether they was murdered, or done themselves in, or had an accident, I never did hear tell. It happened before we came to Blantyre Street and that's nearly twenty years ago.'

For the rest of the time I lived in Cheyne Walk that flat was never occupied and now the house has been demolished.

*　　　*　　　*

I still saw quite a lot of Rowland.

One evening he rang me up and said: 'Do you want to buy a boat?'

I answered, guardedly: 'I'd love to, but how much?'

'Only five pounds – it's my old punt. Ted Baker, the builder, has her down on the Medway. She needs a bit of paintwork, but I think it's a gift at that price.'

'Can I see her?'

'Of course. Come down tomorrow afternoon and I'll drive you down to Gillingham.'

And so I became a boat owner. I have written elsewhere about this little boat;[1] sufficient to say, then, that when I first saw her she did not look very promising. After we had taken her down to a little dock on Oare Creek, off the Swale, had made such modest repairs as were necessary and had rubbed her down and painted her, she became to my eyes a thing of beauty. Her memory is still very precious, for she was part and parcel of the first holiday Griselda and I ever shared.

It was the summer of 1939; we slept in a tent at the back of a little cottage belonging to an old man called Captain Waters. He looked after the sluices that drained the marshes and also looked after a few boats, including from that moment onwards, our punt. It was a blissful month. We were joined by Stafford Palin, whose marriage to Haidee was breaking up. He had a 12 ft National dinghy and often sailed in company with us. We used to sail out into the Swale and over to Seasalter where Rowland had a beach hut or, if it was too windy outside, we would turn up Faversham creek for wonderful cream teas in that charming old town.

It was this holiday that made both of us decide that as soon as I could support her we would marry. It also turned me into a confirmed 'messer about in boats', with all the time wasting that that involves.

Just before we had set off for our boating holiday, Denton had arrived quite unexpectely at 9 Castle Street. He was looking deceptively well. He had brought with him a very handsome Siamese cat who followed him everywhere, like a well-trained dog. I determined one day to own one. As a reaction to my father's dogginess I had had a series of cats, the favourite being a one-eyed tabby called Richard Coeur-de-Lion. Denton's cat seemed to be in a different league.

During the same week, when I was back in Chelsea, I had a visit from J. R. Darling, my one-time form master at Charterhouse. He was by this time headmaster of Geelong Grammar School in Australia. His visit was to invite me to go to Geelong on a temporary basis, while his art master had a two-year sabbatical in Europe. I leapt at the offer. The travel allowance was a first-class steamer ticket to Melbourne. By visiting one or two travel agents I found that I could save quite a lot of money on that by getting a berth on a Holt Line ship that only carried twelve passengers. The voyage via Panama and Tahiti took six weeks and the price was £28!

This two-year stretch in Australia was the only cloud that hung over our trouble-free holiday. By the time we had returned to Cheyne Walk there was an even more formidable cloud gathering; it seemed that at last there was really going to be a war.

The next morning I had a note from Darling to say that he took it, that because of what would seem to be an imminent outbreak of hostilities, our arrangements were at an end. So much for Australia.

I paid my customary weekend visit to Farnham and found my father in a war-like mood.

'What are you going to do about it?' he barked as we took a rather unaccustomed stroll round the town. I muttered something about still wanting to go into the Navy.

'You didn't have much success last time, did you?' referring to the abortive attempt I had made to join the RNVR at the time of the Munich crisis. 'Now, what do you think of that?' He had stopped outside the doors of the local drill hall. An H. M. Bateman-like sergeant was putting a group of pale-faced recruits through bayonet drill practice. To his encouraging roars, they were charging at sandbags suspended from the roof.

'Not quite your thing, eh?' snapped my father. I weakly admitted that it was not. 'The best thing you can do is to join a new anti-aircraft battery they are forming here. That will keep you at a decent distance from the enemy.'

The next morning I signed on and accepted the King's shilling. Three weeks later we were called up. To celebrate these dramatic happenings Griselda and I became engaged. First, I had to ask her father's permission. His reactions were not what I expected.

'Do you really mean you want to marry her?' he asked me.

'Yes, of course I do,' I answered.

'All I can say is, I hope you don't have as awful a time with her as I have had with her mother!'

'I had a temperamental cook.' Illustration from *Such Things Happen*, 1936.

6. Camouflage

CAMOUFLAGE HAD BECOME a recognized subject during the First World War. It began with some French artists who were serving with their artillery. They formed a *Section de Camouflage* with the object of concealing their gun sites and other military positions. Their success led, in 1916, to the establishment of the British Camouflage Service as part of the Royal Engineers.

Various artists were included in this service and they soon arrived at a practical understanding of the subject, particularly against air observation and photography. Camouflage nets came into use and track discipline was soon enforced. The greatest camouflage successes in the First World War were at sea. Norman Wilkinson, landscape painter and poster artist, was serving as a Lieutenant in the RNVR on coastal patrols. He was struck by the fact that most of the transports were painted black, which made them a perfect silhouette target for submarines. It was obviously impossible to paint a ship so that it could not be seen, but Wilkinson thought it might be feasible to disrupt its shape. By the means of dazzle painting the enemy might be confused both as to the actual size of the vessel and also as to the course on which she was steaming. His schemes proved most successful.

By the time the Second World War was looming up, Norman Wilkinson approached the Admiralty. He was rudely brushed off with the excuse that, as all vessels would be travelling in convoy, it was quite unnecessary to paint stripes on them. When the war started Wilkinson was appointed by the Air Ministry as Inspector of Camouflage. They gave him the almost impossible task of trying to conceal air fields.

In 1939 camouflage was non-existent in the army. At the end of the First World War when the camouflage experts (mostly artists) left the army, camouflage was virtually rejected in favour of spit and polish and other forms of what the soldiers called 'bullshit'. In 1939 there was no solid information on the subject. Fred Beddington (Jack Beddington's younger brother) who lived at the top of Castle Street in Farnham and was later to become a Director of Wildensteins, the Bond Street art dealers, was appointed to run a new camouflage department.

Major R. McLean Buckley MC, a New Zealander by birth, was chosen to run the camouflage courses; he was an Etonian by education and in camouflage by chance. His only connection with this uncharted subject was that in the First War he had been, for a short while, a liaison officer for the 1st New Zealand Division and had some casual dealings with a

54

camouflage unit. The first course had consisted of friends of Bed-dington's who had been at the Slade with him. There was Tom van Oss, who was to be the first fatal casualty among the camouflage officers, Gerry Gerrard who was Professor of Sculpture at the Slade, Godfrey Money-Coutts, John Churchill who was a nephew of the Prime Minister, the Hon. Ian Campbell-Gray, Edward Seago and an elderly and rather bibulous illustrator called Joseph Gray, whose greatest claim to fame was that later on he nearly burnt down Farnham Castle, which had become the Camouflage Centre. Lastly there was Dr Hugh Cott, the only one among them who knew anything about the subject. He was a zoologist, famous for his book *Adaptive Coloration of Animals.* The book ultimately became a classic but even then was valuable as an aid to personal camouflage.

Early in the war I had applied for a commission as a camouflage officer. I had an interview at the War Office with the fierce-looking Major Buckley. I heard no more about this until one morning in April 1940 I was summoned to my Battery Commander's office to be told that I was to report forthwith to the No. 1 Training Battalion Royal En-gineers at Shorncliffe for the No. 2 Camouflage Course. The message ending with 'Wear civilian clothing pending Commission'. When I arrived at Shorncliffe wearing my one respectable suit I found there were two other fellows in a similar condition. They had also been in Ack Ack. One was called Michael Farrar Bell, the other Gabriel White. The remainder of the Camouflage Course looked like the chorus line of a First War musical comedy. On the advice of the Commandant, they were dressed in the manner of officers in the 1914–18 war in service dress with riding breeches, field boots, Sam Brownes, revolver holsters and water bottles. The shine of their leather and the gleam of their brass was something to marvel at.

At Shorncliffe we were given elementary instruction in the art of soldiering including map reading. Every morning the class, with the exception of the three 'civilians', did a couple of hours of square bashing. One morning we were taken over to the ranges. I was lying next to a tall, handsome New Zealander called John Hutton. The result of my ten shots was one bull, two outers and seven complete misses. Hutton's card caused something of a sensation. He had ten bulls and seven outers. The latter were my contribution. He took it in good part, then modestly admitted he had won a National Championship for rifle shooting 'down under'.

It was not until we had arrived at Lark Hill, where the actual Camouflage Course was to take place, that the three 'civilians' had their commissions confirmed and were able once again to put on well-worn battledresses with stripes removed from the sleeves and single stars added to the shoulders. On my first 48-hour leave I visited Skews, the military tailor at Camberley who had made my father's uniforms in the First War.

Our Camouflage Course was held at the School of Artillery as there was not yet a proper Camouflage Centre. The students on our course slowly resolved themselves into Victor Stiebel (dress designer), Donald Fraser (opera singer), Horace Buttery (picture restorer), Godfrey Baxter, Peter Proud and Geoffrey Barkus (film people), John Hutton who, after the war, engraved the great west window for Coventry Cathedral, D. E. J. Pavitt (War Office clerk), Inky Stevens (schoolmaster), John Merton and Peter Brooker (painters), Cavendish Warrilow (who came from Australia) and the three ex-Ack Ack gunners: Gabriel White who was married to Edward Ardizzone's sister, Michael Farrar Bell, who had been working in his father's firm as a designer of stained glass; and myself. Gabriel was a painter who was one day to become head of the Fine Art side of the Arts Council. He was a most benevolent person and a landscape painter of some ability. He had studied, like many famous artists, under Bernard Meninsky at the Westminster School of Art.

It was a mixed bag of disparate talents, presided over by Buckley whose only peace-time occupation had been to act as the Honorary Secretary of the Royal Ocean Racing Club. It was an experimental, self-help course, with discussions about how to use paint for disruptive patterning or for concealment, and how to weave coloured hessian or burlap strips into netting. We studied air photographs and we flew.

There was a school of artillery air spotting nearby at Boscombe Down. Its pilots took us up in little two-seater open cockpit high-wing Stinson monoplanes. Flying at a few hundred feet above Salisbury Plain in that glorious weather of May and June in 1940 was an exhilarating experience. We experimented with taking air photographs and were loaned some infra-red stock. With this we managed to take some photographs of Stonehenge that revealed far more than could be seen on the ground.

Camouflage netting was still in use in the army, with a woefully inadequate amount of coloured hessian woven into it. It was almost as if the assumption was that the net itself was a cloak of invisibility. The study of air photographs to teach concealment was in its infancy and the ultimate question – what were they camouflaging against – was not being asked.

It was during No. 2 Course that we began to sort all this out. It soon became clear that for the army in the field, it was much more important to control their movements, and therefore the marks they made on the ground, than to paint stripes on their vehicles or to hide under nets. This was certainly true as a protection against reconnaissance and air photography. Buckles, as we soon called him, may not have known much about camouflage but he succeeded in indoctrinating us with a great enthusiasm for the subject. He was an extraordinary man, with a ginger moustache that seemed to be a continuation of his side-whiskers and china blue eyes that looked like boiled winkles. He also had an appalling temper. More than once he smashed up the furniture in his office. As his rage subsided he would burst into tears. We all grew very fond of this intelligent, unstable Commandant.

As I was now commissioned, Griselda and I decided to get married at the end of the course. We thought it a pity not to take advantage of the marriage allowance. We chose July 4th, the American Day of Independence. However, more serious things happened before that. France fell and at the beginning of June the British army retreated through Dunkirk. Coachloads of haggard, dusty, unsmiling troops arrived on Salisbury Plain. They looked as though they had come from another planet.

We were married at Frensham Parish Church by the Rev. L. J. Allen ('Jazzing Judas', the former Davisites housemaster) who had retired from Charterhouse to this country parish. We chose this church because it was exactly half way between our respective homes.

After the wedding we departed for our honeymoon to Frensham Ponds Hotel. There we spent most of our forty-eight hours' leave sailing a little dinghy around the Great Pond. At the end of that short break we drove over to Chatham, where I had been told to report to await my posting.

We stayed at the Sun Hotel and for meals I was accommodated in the Senior Officers' Mess of the School of Mechanical Engineering. The weekly mess bill, including mess guests (not mine) came to almost the whole of my subaltern's pay. There could be no future in this, but before I could do anything about it, my posting as a full lieutenant came through. It was to the 2nd Anti-Aircraft Division at Hucknall, near Nottingham.

The HQ of this Anti-Aircraft Division was in school buildings that had only recently been finished. It was commanded by Lt General Grove-White, who clearly belonged to another, more peaceful, age. I was met by Alec England, the GSO II (Ops), a regular gunner, who took me in to see the General. He was friendly and talked about anything but the war.

At last he said: 'Do you ride a motor-cycle?'

'Not very well, Sir,' I replied.

'I'm very glad to hear it,' he answered. 'I don't like my staff officers rushing about the country like a lot of dispatch riders. See he gets a car, Alec and a pretty FANY[1] to drive him.'

Just as we were going out, he suddenly said: 'Have you got a British Warm?'

'No, Sir.'

'Well, get one and wear it when you visit a unit, they won't know what rank you are. They will probably turn out the guard for you.'

After a few weeks Griselda joined me and we took a flat just below Nottingham Castle. It was hideously furnished and to cheer it up we bought a Staffordshire pot, a figure of a lady sitting on a horse.

The only other addition to our sitting room was a model ship, a West

Indiaman which I found in a junk shop in Nottingham. Her rigging was in tatters, so we spent practically every evening of that winter rerigging her. We also bought a Siamese kitten, who brought a new dimension into our life. We named her Kwan Yin, which was soon turned into Yini. When she was about six weeks old, she was set on by a neighbouring tom cat. The result of this was a broken foreleg. It was set, but out of alignment and for the rest of her not very long life she had a slightly knock-kneed look about her.

We nursed her back to health (after ten days she ate the plaster cast that encased her foreleg). This nursing established a close bond with the little animal. From then on she was our cat and we were her people. She grew into a beautiful animal with eyes of brilliant deep blue. She travelled everywhere with us. The following Summer we even took her sailing in the punt; water had no terrors for her.

*   *   *

One of the first jobs I was asked to do was to camouflage a caravan that the Colonel in charge of the Divisional Medical side was planning to keep in the grounds of Staunton Harold.

'My girlfriend and I hope to go there for the occasional weekend,' he said. 'I thought it a good chance to see what you could make of it. You don't mind, do you?'

I had imagined that someone as white haired and venerable looking as the Colonel would be past such junketings. He must have been at least fifty, which seemed an immense age to me then. I managed to hide my surprise at such signs of enduring virility and said, 'I would be delighted to, Sir, where is it?'

'Oh, it's with the caravan people down in Derby.'

'What colour is it?'

'A sort of creamy colour.'

'Well, get them to paint it a good dark olive drab as a start and then we will see what we can do.'

'I will certainly do that,' he replied then, pausing for a moment, with a twinkle in his eye he said: 'I have a splendid idea. You and your wife must come for the first weekend we have there. I take it that as you are artists you won't be shocked at my having a mistress!'

A couple of weeks later we drove over in the Riley to Staunton Harold to meet the Colonel and his girlfriend, who appeared to be a lady of immense respectability. We helped them to park the now drably painted caravan in a very inconspicuous position. With some piled brushwood and a tastefully draped camouflage net, it was practically invisible at twenty paces. We then settled down to the first of many uproarious weekends when they fed us almost entirely on a diet of smoked salmon and champagne.

Over Christmas we were snowed up. Someone at Divisional HQ had heard I had painted some murals. The upshot of this was that I was asked by the General to decorate the Officers' Mess for Christmas.

'Hunting scenes or something like that, you know, costume stuff, old coaches, etc., and work in portraits of the HQ staff.'

For the next two weeks I worked out a set of designs with a strong Rowlandson flavour. One of the staff sergeants was a brilliant caricaturist. He painted in portraits of the Divisional Staff on my eighteenth-century figures. By the time we had completed the job, the army hut was quite a colourful place. As far as the 2nd AA Division was concerned, it was not for camouflage work in the field but for decorations in the HQ Officers' Mess that my reputation would rest.

Most of my days at 2nd AA Division were spent in driving round the Midlands or into East Anglia to help camouflage gun sites that were sited near aerodromes or important factories. The AA Batteries spent much energy on draping camouflage nets over their guns, quite ignoring the fact that the anti-aircraft guns themselves were almost invisible from the air. What was painfully visible was the pattern of white concrete roads that had been put down for the easier servicing of the weapons. This same road pattern which was repeated round every aerodrome or important factory was virtually impossible to hide.

Whoever was responsible for civil camouflage had instigated a programme of painting green and brown stripes on factory buildings, so that they were the only noticeable landmarks in industrial wastelands.

Periodically I was sent up in an aeroplane to report on such follies. On one occasion a young Welsh pilot was to fly me over Sheffield for this purpose; the problem was that Sheffield suffered from smog.

'Bound to be pretty shitty over Sheffield,' my pilot said, 'only hope we can find the place. Flying at a bare 2000 ft we plunged into the murk. The first thing I saw was the camouflaged factory. It stood out proudly from its drab surroundings. At that moment the sun broke through the smoke.

'Good grief,' shouted the pilot, 'they've left the bloody barrage balloons up.' We were in the middle of a cage of wires which we could not see, though the tethered balloons above our heads were clear enough.

'Well, we shall just have to go out sideways and hope we don't hit one of their wires.' He turned the old Anson on its side and in a few moments were were clear of danger.

'Bloody balloon barrage corps,' the pilot muttered. 'I warned them we were coming this morning. Second time it has happened, too. I wouldn't be surprised if it was third time unlucky.'

Apart from moments like that, I enjoyed the flying. I also enjoyed being driven over the East Anglian plains by the FANYS. On one particular day my driver was the chief FANY. To discuss some problem I was to meet Oliver Messel, my opposite number from Norwich. When I told my driver with whom we were having lunch she blushed like a schoolgirl.

'Not the stage designer?' she asked with a gasp.

'Yes,' I answered.

'Oh, how exciting! I got engaged after the first night of *This Year of Grace*,' she said. 'He did the décor for it.'

Messel charmed the old dear. He went out of his way to be nice to her. He was small and neat with sparkling brown eyes. In addition to his skills as a stage designer and camoufleur he was a brilliant cabaret artist.

One evening at Farnham Castle which had become the Camouflage Centre, he did his act of a young English Officer visiting a Viennese brothel for the first time. We sat in the mess room with the lights out and Oliver performed under shaded lights behind a half-opened door. We could see nothing except moving shadows. The dialogue between the eager but embarrassed Englishman and the little Viennese tart was a masterpiece.

Oliver Messel's skills as a camoufleur were so considerable that long after any fear of invasion had passed, Eastern Command was still building pillboxes for him to convert into haystacks, ornamental fountains and Greek pavilions.

In the following May I was posted to HQ 12th Corps at Tunbridge Wells. My sybaritic life in Ack Ack had come to an end. I took over the GS03 job from D. E. J. Pavitt, who had moved on to South Eastern Command. I was told that I was to operate under Cavie Warrilow who had got a roving camouflage commission from GHQ, which gave him some scope for what I soon discovered were his less than reputable activities. Just before the war, Warrilow had come over to England from Australia where, so he said, he had worked as an architect for some years. How he found his way into camouflage was not clear, but he seemed to have known Buckley. He was a tall, fat, rather pig-faced man who enjoyed good living. He seemed to have unlimited access to petrol coupons, nylons and other black market commodities.

He was waiting for me at Tunbridge Wells. He explained the routine work, laying particular stress on a contract for a number of dummy railway guns that were to be parked on various false spurs from the railway lines behind Dover and Folkestone.

'I told the contractors to be in touch with you,' he said. 'They are down in Stepney. They will probably lunch you at the Savoy. You'll find them *very* co-operative,' he added, with what might or might not have been a wink.

'Now for your transport. I've got you a driver, he was Lord Gort's driver, and a big Ford V8 car, but I've also got you a brand new Vauxhall, this is a civilian car. You can use it as your own until such time as I shall want it.'

I didn't like the sound of this.

'I've got a car,' I said. 'I can't do with two cars.'

'Have it your own way,' he replied. 'I expect I shall find a use for it.'

After Warrilow had gone, I sat alone in my office until it began to get dark. I seemed to have been moved into a world where I was likely to be out of my depth.

To begin with, life at Tunbridge Wells did not seem so very different from Nottingham. 'Bulgy' Thorne, the General commanding 12th Corps, was as amiable as Grove-White had been. Griselda and our Siamese cat Yini joined me and we found a little flat on Mount Sion.

Within a week of arriving at 12th Corps, I had a message from Blank & Blank, Plasterers and Scene Builders of Stepney. They said they would be obliged if I would visit them to approve of the dummy railway guns they were just completing. Before going up to Stepney I took the precaution of visiting the sites of the railway guns and their dummies. The actual guns, which were Big Bertha-like relics of the first war, were concealed under 18,000 square yards of wire netting and stuff that looked like grass. It was actually a kind of seaweed chemically known as sodium alginate. The first time a sample was shown to the officer commanding special weapons and vehicles, he pencilled across the file: 'This is BG' (meaning 'Bloody Good'). This was mistakenly read by a literally minded ordinance clerk as some cabbalistic sign and 'BG' it became known in the official army manuals from that time on. It was not all that 'BG', for when the weather was damp it drooped in the manner of any proper seaweed and all its covering capabilities were lost. Sodium alginate found its proper level after the war in the manufacture of ice cream.

I also flew over the railway gun sites. The dummy spurs with their lack of mess and turned-up earth were hard to spot, the exquisitely made dummy guns on their bogey flat-tops were so insignificant from the air as to be of no importance. The only thing that stuck up like a sore thumb was the vast canopy of 'BG' that was meant to be hiding the real guns.

I paid my visit to Blank and Blank, submitted to lunch, not at the Savoy but at the Grosvenor Hotel at Victoria Station, and then politely told them no more dummy railway guns would be needed. They cajoled, hinted at what they might do for me or to me, then departed in high dudgeon. The implication was that a hefty commission had been written into the costs and would be coming my way. In my innocence I was deeply shocked.

'Major Warrilow had no objections,' one of the Mr Blanks said. 'Of course, he was more a man of the world than you are, Captain.'

I had barely returned to Tunbridge Wells before Cavie Warrilow was on my doorstep. He stormed and swore and promised me the direst things, then quite suddenly he burst out laughing.

'You've got a lot to learn,' was all he said.

Somehow he squared Blank & Blank, who later became his main suppliers for a camouflage factory that he started up in the Pennines making dummy vehicles and dummy tanks.

As for camouflage, the army in the field knew nothing about it. After some discussion it was decided to open a Camouflage School for South Eastern Command in Tunbridge Wells. I was put in charge of it. We commandeered the new Town Hall. The success of our courses was assured by having a Mess Sergeant posted to us who had been a chef at the Savoy.

One afternoon I was taking a party of senior officers through a farm to see some demonstrations. We had to walk through a field in which there was a herd of Friesian cows. It was a damp day and the animals were sitting on the grass. In the middle of them was a black and white cart horse. I stopped and counted the cows. There were nineteen of them and the one horse.

'Gentlemen,' I said, 'how many cows are there in the field?'

After a moment or two someone said twenty, and the rest agreed. Before I could open my mouth, the horse got up and walked towards us. I began to realize that the element of chance appeared to be as useful in the army as it is in art.

It was not long after that, that the relative tranquility of life at 12th Corps was rudely disrupted. 'Bulgy' Thorne, our amiable GOC had been pensioned off and was replaced by Lt General Bernard Montgomery. Within twenty-four hours an edict had been issued that every officer had to do PT at 6.30 am and that no wives were to be permitted within fifty miles of Tunbridge Wells. I checked my terms of reference and found that technically I was on the staff of GHQ and was only attached to 12th Corps. On these flimsy grounds I marched into the office of the Brigadier HQ to whom I had originally been told to report. White faced, the Brigadier was sitting at his desk, with his head in his hands. He looked up.

'Well, what is it?' he asked.

'This thing about wives, Sir. It doesn't apply to me, Sir, does it? I'm attached to GHQ.'

'Oh! Are you? No, I don't suppose it does.' And once again his head dropped into his hands.

I crept out of the room. What I had not known was that the Brigadier's career had come to an abrupt end, Monty having sacked him a few minutes before our interview. I don't suppose he knew what he was saying. For the rest of the time I was at 12th Corps, Griselda and I lived in some trepidation in our little flat on Mount Sion. As for PT, I detested it. The only time I attended it, the poor old Camp Commandant, playing leap-frog, fell on top of his bald head and had to be invalided out of the army.

On hearing of this, Monty was reputed to have said: 'Better it should happen here than on the field of battle.'

Monty certainly put the fear of God into everyone. Visiting a gun site very early one morning he saw a cook smoking whilst stirring the breakfast porridge. Monty demanded to see the Commanding Officer.

A tousle-headed young subaltern appeared from his tent, still in his pyjamas. The time must have been about 7 am.

'Had a late night?' Monty asked him.

'Well yes, Sir, as a matter of fact I had.'

'Oh! What were you doing?'

'I was at the Battery dance, Sir.'

'I trust you enjoyed it?'

'Yes, Sir, thank you, Sir.'

'Just as well. It will be the last one you will attend as an officer!'

The most enjoyable course that we ran at Tunbridge Wells was for the Royal Navy. There were about twenty Naval officers and two Marine officers. The names of the marines were Major Alan Durst and Captain John Nash. Alan Durst was a sculptor and John Nash had already achieved some fame as a landscape painter and botanical draughtsman, though he was overshadowed by his more worldly brother Paul. During the week they were with us they came up to our flat on Mount Sion on a couple of occasions. John Nash immediately established a rapport with Griselda because of their mutual interest in flower drawing. It was the beginning of a friendship that lasted until his death thirty-five years later.

A week later I found myself in an MTB going down the river Crouch. The navy had requested that a camouflage 'expert' should inspect some coastal defences that they were concerned about. Presumably someone on that course had suggested I might do. There was no way of concealing those coastal guns that stuck up over the sea walls. The only thing I could suggest was that they should disguise them as oyster packing sheds of which there were a number further up the river.

The navy, in the person of a young Lieutenant Commander, approved and we went below to have a pink gin. It was marvellous to be afloat again. Camouflage seemed a rather poor substitute for this messing about in boats. Later I made some tentative enquiries about the possibility of changing services and joining the navy, but nothing came of it and I returned to my Tunbridge Wells school.

We had one or two visiting lecturers from the Camouflage Centre at Farnham. The most eccentric and the most witty was Leonard Huskinson, whose one speciality was a lecture called 'The Concealment of a Headquarters'. This took the form of a running commentary to a drawing that he did on a blackboard of an army unit moving into a Palladian mansion set in Wiltshire parkland. The story began with the arrival of the first 3-ton lorry knocking a gryphon off the top of one of the handsome gateposts and ended with the desecration of the house, gardens and park. It was a very funny cautionary tale of how the army scrawls its signature across the countryside. On another occasion when Huskinson arrived at Tunbridge Wells station, having lunched well but not wisely with another Camouflage officer called Freddy Mayor, he found his camouflage stores had somehow or other been metamorphosed in the luggage van into a case of ferrets and a dead baby in a coffin.

We did a lot of flying, mainly in Avro Ansons, the most reliable old workhorses. But we also flew in Hawker Henleys and Lysanders and every kind of bomber. On one occasion I was taken up by the oldest Pilot Officer who was still flying. He came of a noble family and rumour had it that the RAF only used him to fly army officers. The aircraft was a Boulton and Paul Defiant. It looked like a Hurricane, but had a machine-gun turret behind the pilot's seat and was a very heavy aircraft. We were flying over Kent at 12,000 feet; the pilot called me up on the intercom and, so I thought, said: 'Would you like to drive?'

Stupidly I said I would, thinking for a moment I was in a Hawker-Henley, which had dual control. All I had was a machine gun, which I was soon hanging on to for dear life.

What my pilot had said was: 'Would you like to dive?'

He pushed the stick forward and pointed the Defiant straight down and opened up the throttle. My ears crackled, my nose started to bleed and I thought my last hour had come. Allotment gardens came rushing up to meet us and just about when I could count the brussels sprouts, he brought her out of her dive. I swear to this day that the wing tips swept up and touched over my head. From this appalling plunge, we swept over the allotments and came straight in to land. The wheels hit the runway and we must have bounced forty feet; we continued to bounce like a flat pebble being chucked across the surface of a pond. That undercarriage must have been built by fine craftsmen. Eventually we came to rest at the furthest extremity of the runway. The engine cut out and all was quiet. I wiped my nose and as I looked out I could see some aircraftsmen running towards us. Rather shakily I pushed back the cowling and climbed down.

'Were you the pilot, Sir,' a sergeant shouted at me.

'No, of course not!' I answered.

'Where is he?'

'Up there, I suppose.'

Getting no answer to his shouts, the sergeant climbed up and opened the cowling.

'Lord love us!' he exclaimed. 'What do you make of that? He's passed out!' And that was Pilot Officer ——'s last flight. A point of academic interest was whether he had passed out before or after we had landed.

One day driving through the Kentish lanes near Hadlow, my driver nearly ran head first into an Austin 7, which had come round the bend on the wrong side. Both cars stopped and I got out. The offending driver was Denton and my wrath evaporated. We hugged each other.

'Johnnie! How lovely to see you. I live just round the corner. Come and have a cup of tea.'

His house, which was called 'The Hop Garden', was a modern

concrete box, designed by F. R. S. Yorke. I felt that it might be possible to blow up a house like that, it certainly could not be burnt down. Denton had always had an eye for pretty things and he had converted that arid little house into a magician's cave. The living room was dominated by a red lacquer Coromandel screen and a Dolmetsch harpsichord. On the mantel-shelf was a stone Etruscan head he had bought for 3/6d. In a clear area at one end of the room there was an easel. On it was a painting of Lord Berners as a child that he was working on. Propped up against the wall was another painting of a pug dog with its feet in a pond, surrounded by irises. There was another painting, a sensitive study of some crassula which he later gave to Griselda.

We talked about the years since his terrible accident. Apart from that afternoon at Farnham, we had not met since that awful day.

'I expect my days are numbered,' he said quite cheerfully, 'but I have a marvellous old girlfriend. Her name is May Walbrand-Evans. She used to model for Lavery, God knows how many years ago. She has some lovely things; you must meet her.'

That evening I told Griselda about this fortuitous meeting. She was intrigued and suggested we asked Denton over for the following Sunday.

'He might bring his old girlfriend as well,' I said.

Denton and Mrs Walbrand-Evans arrived in time for lunch. The lady, at first meeting, was a little intimidating. She must have been at least seventy, but she was still a very good-looking woman. Griselda immediately struck up a close friendship with Denton.

'It was like being with a nice girl,' she said afterwards.

Denton was bubbling over with excitement. He told me he had just visited Sickert.

'He showed me a tiny daguerreotype of his mother and said, "What do you think of that as a subject for a painting?" I answered that I thought it was a bit small. "A bit small!" he shouted, "Why, I could square that up and make a painting of it eight feet high!" I must say, he was a marvellous old chap. I've written up the visit and sent it off to *Horizon*. I doubt if they will publish it.'[2]

It has been said that Denton Welch turned to writing as a result of his accident, but in the end he would probably have written anyway. His paintings were not of any great account, they were a reflection of his eclectic taste, but by painting he learnt to see. It is this power of acute observation and sensibility that gives his books such a special quality.

Over the next few months we often saw Denton and May Walbrand-Evans. Her house was indeed full of pretty things, including some very handsome Staffordshire and Leeds pottery figures. It was seeing these that inspired us to add to our small collection of pottery figures , which had begun with a wedding present from Hugh Radcliffe-Wilson and the chance purchase of the flat-back of the lady on the horse that we had bought in Nottingham. Tunbridge Wells was a good hunting ground for such things, as well as for old furniture.

On a day in early Autumn, I was inspecting some coastal gun sites with 'Goldie' Gaskell, who was GSO 3 Camouflage at South Eastern Command. 'Goldie', so named because of his very fair hair, was a bow-legged little man who looked like a retired jockey. In peace time he was the main art buyer for the advertising agents J. Walter Thompson. He also had an eye for good furniture.

We were driving through Rye when he said: 'Let's go and see if old Bragge is in his shop. He's got a watercolour I would quite like – it might be a Bright; he usually has some nice things.'

'Old Bragge' was in. His shop, which was a bit like a warehouse, was packed to the ceiling with furniture. Whilst Goldie was arguing with Mr Bragge over the price of the watercolour, I pottered round the shop. I noticed, tucked away in a gloomy corner, on the top of a tallboy, two painted shield-back armchairs. They were delicate and subtly shaped.

When Goldie had finally settled on a price and bought his picture, I asked Mr Bragge about the chairs.

'Oh! You like those, do you? Hepplewhite, that's what they are and they've been in the same family ever since they were made. But they are very fragile.' He lifted one down. I could see through the grime that they had been painted grey or possibly even white with a pattern of leaves and flowers.

'I think they're beautiful,' I said. 'How much are they?'

'You wouldn't be able to afford them!' Mr Bragge snorted contemptuously. 'They're museum pieces. They ought to be in the Victoria and Albert.'

So that was that, I thought.

We looked at various other things, then Goldie said: 'By Jove! It's getting late, we ought to be going!'

As we moved towards the door, I turned to have a final look at the chairs.

Mr Bragge, in quite a different tone of voice, said: 'You do like those chairs, don't you?'

'I think I have never liked anything more,' I answered.

'How much can you afford?' he asked.

I took out my notecase. 'I've only got five pounds,' I said.

'Five pounds! I might as well give them to you!' He paused for a moment, then almost as if he was talking to himself, he added: 'What's the use of keeping them here, something may happen to me. Take them!'

I handed over my fiver and, with Goldie's help, packed the chairs into the back of our utility truck. Griselda and I spent the rest of the week cleaning them. It was like picture restoration; though much of the paint was missing they emerged from the shadows in gleaming white, with pale pink roses and mossy green leaves.

Two weeks later Rye was bombed and Bragge's shop suffered a direct hit. Everything was destroyed. Fortunately Mr Bragge himself was not there. Those two Hepplewhite chairs are still with us. I have enjoyed looking at them every day since I bought them.

Gerry Gerrard, in peacetime the Professor of Sculpture at the Slade, was another camouflage officer who lived near Tunbridge Wells. One weekend he invited us over for lunch. He was showing us round the stable block that he had converted into a house. We came to some double doors.

'This is the garage,' he said, throwing open the doors. There was Gerrard's old car and alongside it, under a dust sheet, was the gleaming Vauxhall I had been offered on my arrival at Tunbridge Wells.

'What's that?' I gasped.

'Oh, Cavie Warrilow asked me to house it for him,' Gerry answered.

I did not pursue the matter and it was not until eighteen months later that I heard the next step in the Vauxhall saga. Apparently it was still on the Ordinance books and they started making enquiries. Warrilow, on hearing about this, promptly despatched a lorry to the Gerrards' house at Groombridge. In the lorry was an effective piece of camouflage, a collapsible dummy Sherman tank. This was fitted over the Vauxhall and she was towed away to the camouflage factory in the Pennines.

That was not the end of the story. A Royal Engineer Lieutenant Quartermaster, an ex-ranker Regular with over twenty years' service, had been seconded to Warrilow's camouflage factory. One week when Warrilow was away on business, the Lieutenant Quartermaster had a notification that there was to be an Ordinance inspection. He panicked, drove the Vauxhall over to Kendal and sold it to a bent garage proprietor for £50. His trouble was, he was no judge of character. The garage proprietor was not bent enough and came to the conclusion that the car was too hot a property. The result of all this was that the unfortunate Lieutenant Quartermaster was reduced to the ranks and sent to prison.

Warrilow's comment was: 'The silly dolt. I could have got £500 for it and no one would have asked any questions.'

In camouflage there was one rather special job which quite a number of people were after. This was to start a camouflage school for the Canadian army in Canada. It was a job I would have loved to have had. First of all there were rumours that Oliver Messel was to have it, then Edward Seago was actually appointed and only at the last moment was his appointment cancelled. A couple of months later I was summoned to the War Office. Victor Stiebel was in charge of camouflage postings. I had liked Victor from the moment when I met him on our course at Lark Hill. He had a beautiful face, with fine drawn features, surmounted with a mop of crinkly grey hair. Up until the war he had been one of the best-known dress designers in the country. He made the transition from *haute couture* to army life without any apparent effort. He, like Oliver Messel, made no concessions. They just remained the people they were and the generals and brigadiers under whom they served liked them all the more for it.

It was a bright, sunny morning when I presented myself at the War Office.

'John, you are in luck. You've got the pick of the jobs,' Victor said in his soft voice. I expressed my gratitude and asked how on earth that had happened.

'Because of Tunbridge Wells. You impressed some high-ups on a course you ran for senior officers.'

My mind flashed back to the day of the Friesian cows. It must have been that timely black and white horse!

'I have arranged for a congenial young man to go with you. His name is Tony Rhodes. He has just had a book about Dunkirk published. He should be here any minute now.'

He then went on to brief me and to tell me when I was to go and to whom I was to report when I reached Ottawa. He had barely finished when Tony Rhodes was announced. At this first meeting, I thought that he was a slightly reserved young man. He had been trained as a regular gunner and had passed through Woolwich.

'Before we go and have lunch,' Victor said, ' I must take you to see the General.'

A few minutes later we were in the presence of Victor's Commanding Officer. Victor seemed to regard him with some awe.

'Captain Lewis and Lieutenant Rhodes,' the General read out from some document he was holding. 'This seems a nice job you've landed. I'm sure you will do us credit. Anything you would like to ask me?'

I took a deep breath then, greatly daring, said: 'Yes, Sir. Don't you think the Commandant of the Canadian Army Camouflage School should have Field Rank, and that Rhodes should be a Captain? Rank does help . . .' I ended somewhat lamely.

There was an embarrassing silence. Victor looked horrified.

The General said nothing for a moment or two then slowly he smiled.

'I think you have a point there, you should not have had to ask, but I am glad you did. I think you will make a go of it. Stiebel, see me about this later. Meanwhile you can put up your crown and you, Rhodes, your extra pip.'

When we had returned to Victor's office, he said: 'You've got a nerve! I would never have dared to ask for such a thing.'

The day before I left Canada, Denton telephoned us. His apparently indestructible concrete box of a house had been burnt to a blackened shell and all his lovely things with it.

'The fireproofing round the boiler caught fire,' he said. Then, quite cheerfully, 'May is going to put us up until we can find something else.'

7. War in Canada

I HAD SOME hours to kill before meeting Tony on the night train to Glasgow. To fill in the time, I bought a stall ticket for a musical called *Lisbon Story*, in which Billie, under her proper name of Valerie White, was starring with Albert Lieven, a refugee German actor. At the end of the show I went backstage to see her. She kissed me warmly.

'Johnnie darling – to think of you as a soldier and a brand new major at that! Won't your father be proud of you?'

She was still the same Billie, but she had come a long way since Goldsmiths'. I still felt rather young and foolish when I was with her. We talked about many things but at last I had to drag myself away from her to catch the train to Glasgow.

I found Tony Rhodes at Euston. We were sharing a compartment.

'You can have the upper bunk,' I said establishing my rank. Tony was clutching a new novel. 'What are you reading?' I asked.

'I'm not reading it, I wrote it. Tomorrow is its publication day.' The book was called *Sword of Bone*, the title a quotation from Milton's *Samson Agonistes*. It was about Tony's experiences in France and at Dunkirk. It had a striking black and yellow jacket, lettered by Berthold Wolpe, who was one day to become a friend and colleague of mine at the Royal College of Art.

The boat train arrived at Gourock on a drizzling, grey wet morning. We waited about in the rain, standing by glistening railway lines. At last a Transport Officer invited us into the canteen, a very small room already packed tight with American naval officers. Tony and I seemed to be the only British there. After a long wait, an invisible voice ordered us out on to the quay.

As our tender bucked a flood tide, the *Queen Elizabeth* loomed up out of the murk. She looked enormous. There were numerous tenders and lighters tied up to her, like so much flotsam along her waterline. Just upstream of her a convoy was assembling.

When war broke out, the *Queen Elizabeth* had not been delivered to Cunard and her interior was only partly finished. Her first-class lounge, where we sat, was a hideous room, decorated in an Art Deco Odeon Cinema manner. We talked, we read and we played simple card games and we drank a lot of Pepsi-cola, for it was a 'dry' ship. There were one or two celebrities on board, including the film actors Edward G. Robinson and Douglas Fairbanks Jr, the latter in the guise of a lieutenant in the American Navy. He seemed a rather gloomy, slightly self-conscious naval officer.

On the last night of the voyage, Edward G. Robinson, who was only about five feet high, addressed us, beginning with the words: 'We regard you as soldiers of destiny,' which, as most of his audience were either civilians, navy or airforce officers, Tony and I felt was probably meant for us. At the end of his speech we loudly applauded him. It was a long voyage. To avoid the U-boat packs we changed course every twenty minutes. We zig-zagged north of Iceland and then sailed down to Bermuda before we finally came past the Nantucket Light Vessel. It had taken us over eight days. We had no convoy; we were travelling faster than any U-boat could move either on top of the water or below the surface.

As we neared the coast under a troubled watery sky, there was poor visibility at sea level. The sun came out then suddenly and high above the cloud bank, looking like tenuous grey spears, we could see the skyscrapers of Manhattan. A few hours later our tugs edged us into a jetty opposite 89th Street. The *Queen Mary* was in the same basin and the *Normandie* in the next one. We were given no time to explore New York but as soon as we had disembarked, were hurried across to Grand Central Station to catch a train for Montreal. We had time to see the newspaper posters, which, no doubt inspired by our belated arrival, splashed the headline '*Queen Elizabeth* sunk by U-boats.' New York had seemed quite warm but by the time we reached Montreal, where we changed into a train for Ottawa, we were well in the grip of a Canadian winter. The air smelt of cold iron.

Our briefing came on the day after our arrival. Jean Carrière, the French Canadian GSO 2, who was responsible for us, said: 'Not very good news. As you are Royal Engineers, the Commandant of the Canadian Royal Engineers says you must base your school at their training centre. It's a place called Petawawa in Northern Ontario. It's a dump – under ten feet of snow for most of the year. For a short while in summer it's not bad.'

'That doesn't sound very promising,' I said, 'isn't there anything we can do about it?'

'Not before you have taken a look at it. If you can make a strong enough case they may listen to you. They took no notice of my protests. Anyhow, the better news is we want you to go west to Vancouver, stopping off at various places to interview potential camouflage officers.'

'That sounds grand – but I'd like to get this Petawawa business settled first. When can I go up there?'

'Tomorrow, if you like. Oh, just one other thing. We take a fews days leave at Christmas, so if you want to slip down to New York, that will be your chance.

Petawawa was all that Jean had said. It might well have been Solzhenitsyn's labour camp in Northern Kazakhstan. By chance, the

General commanding the Canadian Engineers was also there at the same time. He summoned me to his presence.

'Now, Major Lewis, do you think you can get a Camouflage School going up here?'

'No, Sir,' was my blunt answer.

'No! How's that?' he said, looking a bit put out.

'Well, Sir, your boys are going to fight over the green fields of Europe and as the major part of our course is practical work in the field, all this white stuff is hardly relevant. It would be all right if we were fighting the Russians up in the Arctic Circle.'

He paused for a moment, then in a rather grudging manner said: 'You'd better go to the other side of the Rockies. They don't get much snow there. Go back to Ottawa and tell them I leave it to you to pick your site.'

Jean Carrière arranged our itinerary to the West Coast.

'I'm sending you out by the Canadian National Railway and bringing you back by Canadian Pacific. It'll add a bit of variety. You go west from here and cross the prairies to Winnipeg and Saskatchewan, then up to Edmonton and over the Rockies through Jasper National Park to Vancouver – and finally to Victoria on Vancouver Island.'

'That's fabulous!' Tony said.

'Nice trip,' Jean admitted, 'but we want you to see a bit of the country.'

*　　　*　　　*

I grew to love the long train journeys. The doleful wail of the whistle as the train approached open crossings was like the hoot of a tawny owl. That sound and the call of the Great Northern Diver, which I heard many years later, evoke memories of Canada more than anything else.

We were given a compartment to ourselves. At the back of the train there was a parlour car with comfortable arm chairs and large windows. Unlike England where the scene changes every few miles, in Canada there are basically three different views. The first, which lasts for a day and a half is made up of fir trees and little lakes, scattered in their thousands across Ontario; the next, which lasts for another day and a half is the prairies, with limitless horizons and a repeating pattern of identically similar farms and barns. Finally the day-and-night-long climb and descent over the Rockies, the Selkirks and the Coast Range.

We stepped out of the train at Winnipeg. The cold hit us across the face like a slap from a wet duster. It was 40° below. In company with some local would-be camoufleurs we stood for a moment in a howling wind at an intersection of the two principle streets. It was the corner of Portage and Main, which all Winnipegians claim to be the coldest spot on earth. We took their word for it. I certainly could not conceive anything colder, but on the next day I left the train at Saskatoon. The platform was deserted. It was very still and the steam from the great express locomotive was going straight up in the air. Suddenly I was hailed by the coloured station master, who had popped out of his office. He had turned that curious green colour that coloured people tend to go in extreme cold.

'Don't you stand there, Sir, you'll lose your nose and your ears!' I must have looked surprised, for as he bundled me back into the train he said: 'Do you know what the temperature is? It's 54° below, and that, Sir, is 86° of frost. That's plenty cold enough.'

The corner of Portage and Main had seemed far colder.

For the climb over the Rockies two gigantic 4.10.4 oil burning steam locomotives were hitched on to our train for the 1 in 40 gradient up to the Glacier Summit. These locomotives were nearly 100 feet long and weighed well over 300 tons. A changing pattern of black fir trees and snow covered peaks with caribou and moose perched on impossible precipices kept us rushing from one side of the parlour-car to the other.

We arrived at Vancouver at breakfast time in thick fog. A taxi drove us to the Vancouver Hotel and the elevator took us up to a room on the 12th floor.

'Can't see a bloody thing,' Tony said, peering out of the window. It was not until we had unpacked and settled in, that the fog thinned, then quite suddenly it rolled away and the most stupendous scenery unfolded. It was a breath-taking view of snow-covered mountains and Mediterranean blue inlets; the mountains looked so close we felt we might have leant out of the window and touched them.

Vancouver is one of the most beautifully sited cities in the world and one of the few places where you can go for a swim or a sail in the morning and go skiing in the afternoon.

We were on the point of leaving our room for our formal visit to Pacific Command Headquarters, when the telephone rang.

'We have a Captain Marcel Godfrey waiting for you in the lounge,' the hall porter said. I replied that I would be down right away.

'Sounds like a hairdresser,' Tony said.

Marcel was not a hairdresser. He was a nephew of the Marquis of Reading and had been born Marcel Godfrey-Isaacs, but because of his father's involvement in the Marconi scandal, the family name was changed. Marcel was a comfortable looking man, cultivated and, as we found out later, permanently at war with his masters. He was the camouflage officer for the Pacific Coast.

I told Marcel of the possibility of our school being in Vancouver and he promptly said: 'I know just the place for you. It's a tea-shop – or at least it was one, on the campus of the University of British Columbia. Let's go and have a look at it.'

Our first impression of Vancouver as a modern North American city was soon dispelled as we drove out to the University. Away from the centre, where even then there were only two buildings with more than a dozen floors, the Marine Building and the Vancouver Hotel, Vancouver proved to be something of a frontier town with single storey clapboard buildings soon replacing the brick, stone and concrete of the business section. Street cars on rails seemed to dominate the roads along which we were driving. But one only had to look over the tawdry fascia boards of the shops and the run-down shacks to see the mountains that lay beyond.

The campus of UBC[1] was set fairly high up on a plateau that topped a promontory jutting out into the Strait of Georgia.

'That's the place,' Marcel Godfrey said, pointing towards a group of buildings that might have been in any Surrey suburb, 'the half-timbered one, it's called "The Gables" – that's the one.' This unlikely structure served our needs perfectly; like the school at Tunbridge Wells it even had a gallery from which students could look down on the landscape models.

That evening we dined with Marcel and his wife Louise. Over the meal I told her that Tony and I, after completing our tour of Canadian cities, were planning to take our Christmas leave in New York. I said I had one introduction and Tony also had one.

'Well, here's a third,' Louise said. 'It's to an old boy-friend. He is an author called Hendrik Willem van Loon. He wrote *The Story of Mankind* and Lord knows how many other books. He is a lovely man. He has a suite at the Algonquin. Have you fixed where you are staying?'

We admitted that we had not. 'In that case, you *must* stay at the Algonquin. It's on West 44th Street and you will see all sorts there. It is where *The New Yorker* holds its round table. Thurber is always there. And stage people. But it isn't smart, you'll just love it.'

Our return to the East by Canadian Pacific Railway was even more spectacular than our outward journey. Our last stop before Ottawa was Toronto.

I had been told by the National Defence Headquarters at Ottawa to get in touch with a certain Colonel Holloway. This I did and on seeing him, did not need telling that he was Stanley Holloway's brother. He had the same large nose and, not surprisingly, was known as 'Beak'.

We had not been with him for many minutes when he said: 'I've got just the chap for your Camouflage School. He's a portrait painter called Cleeve Horne. He's a remarkable fellow, he has a look of that witty actor William Powell in those *Thin Man* films. He also has an extremely pretty wife, she's a sculptor.

The Hornes lived in a large rambling Edwardian house on Balmoral Avenue that might have been built (though it was not) by Charles Rennie Mackintosh. It was panelled throughout in dark wood. Over the years I grew to know that house well. Cleeve was tall, dark-haired, well brilliantined and black moustached. He and his wife Jean had more than their fair share of adrenalin. Their enthusiasm for painting and sculpture, for modern art, for lost causes or for camouflage and above all for Canada, was unlimited. There was no question but that he would make an admirable candidate for our course and a possible future commandant. We signed him on immediately.

Cleeve was a most ebullient, teasing and lovable man. As much as anybody, he made our Canadian Camouflage School a success. In 1942 Toronto was known as 'Toronto the Good' and was under the heavy hand of the Scottish Presbyterians. Anybody found with a bottle of whisky in his automobile was liable to be locked in the town gaol for the night. Yet it was in Toroto that we had a more amusing time than anywhere else in Canada. This was all because of the Hornes. It was with them that we heard the first heartening news of the war – the 8th Army victory over Rommel at El Alamein.

A few days before Christmas we were back in Ottawa; from there we went east to Montreal and then took the night train to New York. We arrived at the Algonquin in time for breakfast. As soon as the shops were open Tony went out to find a book store.

After a leisurely morning, I put on my British Warm and stepped out into the winter sunshine and 44th Street. I had not walked a dozen paces before I heard the sound of gun fire. People rushed past me or flattened themselves on the pavement. I felt that the honour of the British army was at stake, so I straightened my back and marched smartly on. Across the road I saw someone running, with others chasing him. It was a boy carrying a gun. He suddenly turned and fired at his pursuers. There was another fusillade of shots and the boy dropped on the sidewalk I have the evening tabloid still – the headline runs: 'Teenage kid holds up candy store. First gun battle in New York for fifteen years.' It was the first time in the war that I had heard shots fired in anger.

On that first afternoon Tony took me with him to see the American publisher of his book. He was an exuberant, friendly man called Frank Morley, who had been born in Woodbridge in Suffolk where we were destined one day to live.

The air was sparkling and clear. All along 5th Avenue there were bars and restaurants with striped awnings. After the drabness of London in the black-out and the provincialism of Canadian cities, New York looked more like Paris than anything American.

The Algonquin Hotel was friendly and a little antiquated. Our bedrooms were comfortable, with Rowlandson prints hanging on the walls. The hotel was run by Frank Case and his wife. On the one evening I was in New York that I did not have a date, they insisted on my dining with them and when on the last morning I called for my bill, there was nothing on it except the cut-price rate for bed and breakfast for 'enlisted men'.

When I had pointed out to the cashier that I had numerous meals and drinks, all he said was, 'That's OK, Major. Mr Case would like you to have the rest on us.'

My first sight of Hendrik Willem van Loon was when he summoned me on the house telephone to come up to his suite. I banged on the door of his sitting room and a loud voice shouted: 'Binnen komen!'

I entered. There, across the room, standing in his shirt sleeves, was an enormous pear-shaped man.

He beamed at me. 'So you are little Louise's friend. Any friend of hers is a friend of mine.'

After I had answered his questions about my movements over Christmas, he said: 'You will come down to Old Greenwich, to my home overlooking Long Island Sound for the day after Christmas. The house is called 'Nieue Veere', after the little Dutch town in Zeeland where I used to live; the taxi drivers know where it is. Take a train to Old Greenwich and just ask for the Van Loon home.'

The morning after Christmas Day, I took a train to Old Greenwich, but by mistake got out at the wrong station and had a long and expensive taxi ride to Van Loon's house. I was met at the door by Mrs Van Loon, who looked like a little old Japanese doll. Her Eton-cropped grey hair stuck out like a sweep's brush.

'We have a house guest staying here. Her name is Elizabeth Riley. She's a publisher, a partner in the firm of T. Y. Crowell. I'm sure you will like her.' As she was talking, she was leading me through a Vermeer-like hall into a large sitting room lined with books.

Mr Van Loon was looking larger and more benign than ever.

'I wish I was welcoming you to our house in Veere. I built this one to remind me of it.' He pointed out of the window. 'That's Long Island Sound, it would be nicer if it was the Veersegat or the Zaandkreek.'

After lunch, Van Loon suggested that Elizabeth and I should walk down to the water's edge. It was a brilliantly clear afternoon, with quantities of wild fowl flying low over the marshes. We walked for a while along the edge of the Sound.

'Have you known Mr Van Loon long?' I asked.

'Oh, a good few years. They've been very kind to me.'

'Tell me something about him. He was just a name to me until I met him at the Algonquin.'

'He was born and educated in Holland – at the University of Utrecht, I think, then he came over to the States. He was teaching at Princeton and writing rather stodgy books when he married his present wife. She was a journalist and she started him off on his fantastic career.

'She said to him one day: "Haan, you tell very funny stories. You're a born raconteur, but you write the dullest books. Why don't you write history in the way you talk?"

'He did not like the idea and said: "I doubt if people would take me very seriously if I did."

' "Who wants to be taken seriously?" she replied. "You will reach a market a hundred times bigger than any 'serious' historian ever does."

'The result of all that was *The Story of Mankind* and all its successors.'

'He must be a best seller?'

'Best seller! He's probably the world's best seller. His books have been translated into fifty languages, including Urdu. And he is still a dear un-spoilt old Dutchman.'

It was turning cold, so we hurried back along the seashore. On our return Van Loon took me into his work room. There was a large pile of thick yellow-jacketed books on the floor.

'This is my new book – it's called *Van Loon's Lives*,' he said. 'I would like to give you a copy.'

He picked up one of the books, opened it at the fly-leaf: 'What shall I write in it?' He paused for a moment and then wrote with a spluttering pen: 'To John Lewis with what his fellow Canadians call "a water ticket". Hendrick van Loon'.

I was puzzled by the term 'water ticket' until Mrs Van Loon said: 'It's Haan's way of saying "a rain cheque".'

We talked until late, at least Van Loon talked, much about his native country and of sailing through the Zeeland estuaries.

'You are interested in boats and sailing?'

I said I was.

'I've got some etchings and drawings I did of boats somewhere.'

He scrabbled about in one drawer and then another and finally dragged out a pile of old prints and etchings.

He looked through them, then said: 'Here, you take the lot. I'd like you to have them. Perhaps one day you will sail over to Holland in your own boat. If you go to Veere they may still remember me there.'

*   *   *

'Veere'. Etching by Hendrik Willem van Loon.

As a result of our visits and interviews across the continent, we finally assembled a course of potential camouflage officer-instructors who were mostly architects, painters or naturalists. In addition to Cleeve Horne, we picked another likely member for the school staff in a young architect called Johnny Porter, who proved to be as great a success as Cleeve. We also collected a staff of other ranks, including two very fine model-makers.

To begin with, Tony and I lodged with an exuberant Austrian refugee in North Vancouver, but early in the New Year we found an apartment down on English Bay. The day we moved in I had a letter from Griselda telling me she was on a BBC course for Technical Assistants at Lime Grove and that she hoped to get posted, after another month's course in Daventry, to the Penrith transmitter, because a girl on the course who lived up there had invited her to lodge with her family; she seemed to like this idea. She also told me that Guy Stretton-Smith, her previous and much loved boyfriend had been killed operating a midget submarine in the Mediterranean. Griselda's letters had been barometric in their ups and downs. There was no joy for her in this war-time separation.

Six weeks later I heard that she had been ill off and on ever since joining the BBC. The girls involved in this work were on shift and working in hot and confined conditions, then they had a five-mile bicycle ride over the icy fells to their lodgings. One early morning someone found Griselda lying unconscious by her bicycle. She was very ill, but the doctors could not explain it. That was the end of her BBC career. Her parents came up to Penrith and took her home to Grayshott.

*   *   *

In April Tony and I and our new instructors, Cleeve Horne and Johnny Porter, visited the American army Camouflage School at Fort Belvoir in Virginia. We soon became friendly with an architect called Leslie Cheek, one of the few who had a grasp of our subject. In peace time he had been Curator of the Baltimore Museum and Art Gallery. He was a large dark-haired reassuring man. At the end of this visit we were asked to make certain recommendations. Apparently as a result of this a lot of things happened at Fort Belvoir. The most gratifying was the appointment of Leslie as the Chief Instructor; and the most surprising was a demonstration of a complete infantry division marching up and down the parade ground with that curious sloping gait common to American soldiers, all decked out with 'personal' camouflage, with bits of foliage stuck about their persons and black grease-paint on their hands and faces.

We broke our journey to Ottawa at New York and I had lunch with Van Loon at the St Regis. A feather-hatted lady seated at the next table inspired him to produce a minute paintbox and a three inch long brush, which he dipped into his glass of Chablis. In no time he had immortalised the lady on the back of his menu.

The purpose of our visit to New York was to visit the Pratt Institute in Brooklyn. This famous art school was running an independent camouflage course under the direction of James V. Boudreau, a powerful publicist. From my point of view the interest of the visit centred on a bushy haired little Pole called Alexander Kostellow who had been a student at the Bauhaus. The hours I spent talking to Kostellow taught me more about design education than anything I ever heard before or since. His theories were largely those of Gropius and Joseph Itten. However, the enthusiasm with which Kostellow expounded this practical dogma was peculiarly his own.

We returned once again for our last term in Vancouver. The school was thriving and the new staff an unqualified success. On the way back to the West Coast. I left the train at Banff, for two weeks skiing up at Sunshine Lodge. It was late in the afternoon when I arrived but the sun was still shining. There was no one out on the slopes, but there were still a couple of hours of daylight left. I changed quickly, donned my skis and plodded up to the top of the nearest hill. It took me longer than I thought and when I reached the top the sun had already dropped below the peaks. All form had gone out of the landscape.

I stood at the top of the slope. The ski lodge looked like a tiny model chalet, the kind of thing one used to bring back from Switzerland. Nervously I gave a push with my ski sticks and started slowly off downhill, with a distinct wobble in my knees. Slowly as I gathered speed, confidence came. I tried a little 'tailwag' christy. It worked. I began to think 'This is the life!' I was by this time hurtling downhill. Intoxicated by the speed, I did not see, in the flat light, a small hummock ahead of me. It could not have been more than a couple of feet high. I shot over it and landed quite fairly. The next thing I knew, the points of my skis had disappeared and I was doing a somersault over them. Without realizing it, I was skiing on ice-crust that forms late in the season after the sun has gone off the snow. That was why there was no one about on the slopes. When I had picked myself up, I found my face was bleeding from at least a dozen cuts and my collarbone was feeling very uncomfortable. I had gouged out of the snow a large hole, nearly twenty feet long, mostly with my face.

At the ski lodge, a Czech airforce doctor strapped up my collarbone and cleaned up my face.

'You'll be OK now,' he said, 'sure, you can ski tomorrow – but come in before the surface freezes up.' I did not need telling twice.

Skiing in the Rockies was quite unlike skiing in Switzerland, one only had to go out of sight of the lodge, maybe only over the next ridge, to realise there was nothing between oneself and the North Pole, except perhaps a few grizzlies. No comfortable little Alpine huts to serve steaming glasses of glüwein, no St Bernard dogs with little casks of cognac strapped beneath their chins. It could be a very lonely place.

At the end of a fortnight, burnt as dark as a Red Indian, I made my way down to Banff to rejoin the train for Vancouver. I was met at the station by Cleeve Horne, wearing tropical kit. Summer had arrived on the west coast.

For the next few weekends we borrowed a Star Class boat and went sailing through the islands and up Howe Sound. It all seemed very remote from war-weary England.

As far as our military masters were concerned, the time for Tony and me to hand over and return to England was coming near. In July I heard from Jean Carrière at NDHQ.[2] His final act of kindness was to arrange a trip for me to go down to California, to visit March Field, the Air Corps Camouflage School. From there I was to cross the continent to Washington DC to visit Fort Belvoir once again. Tony, meanwhile, was to cross to the East Coast and establish a camouflage school at Bedford, in Nova Scottia.

At last, after a series of farewell parties, I left Vancouver. I got off the train at Oakland and in the automobile of a friendly surveyor, whom I had met on the train, crossed the eight-mile-long Bay Bridge and explored the city of San Francisco, or at least as much as we could see of it through a thick sea wrack. We made the obligatory visit to the 'Top of the Mark',[3] where there was a huge bar occupying the top floor. They refused to serve me anything stronger than beer, because I was in uniform.

March Field was on the borders of the Californian desert and the midday temperature was 110° in the shade. As a respite from that I had weekends at Beverly Hills and visits to the Warner Brothers and Disney Studios. When my tour of duty was finished, I took a train to Chicago and another down to Washington DC. After a spell at Fort Belvoir I travelled up to Nova Scotia.

My last few days in Canada were spent with Tony Rhodes at Bedford, near Halifax. One afternoon I was driven down to Lunenburg, where they were still building Grand Banks schooners. I managed to track down the foreman of the gang that built *Bluenose*, the most famous of all the Grand Bankers. From him I came away with an unfinished model of *Bluenose*.

On the drive back to Halifax, my Canadian driver said: 'Beats me, Sir, how you can want something like that. Seems to me that's just kid's stuff.'

My return to England in the *Queen Mary* looked as if it was going to be more uncomfortable than my outward voyage. This time we had 20,000 troops on board including an entire American Division and also Mr Churchill's staff from the Quebec Conference. In the 18-berth cabin to which I had been directed I found I was the nineteenth. I made such a fuss with the Purser about this that I was given a state-room that had been reserved for some VIP. The voyage took less than four days.

I sent off a telegram to Griselda and before I had left the ship I had a reply; it said 'Waiting for you at the Piccadilly Hotel'.

When I arrived at the hotel I found Griselda sitting with her mother. She looked frail and hollow-eyed. Her mother, at the best of times not a very forthcoming lady, said: 'I will leave you now, I expect you'd like to be alone.'

*   *   *

I had been away for less than a year. For me it had gone all too quickly but to Griselda it had seemed like a lifetime. She had not fully recovered from her illness and her doctors did not seem able to diagnose the problem.

The next morning Griselda returned to her parents' home in Hampshire and I reported to the War Office. Victor Stiebel greeted me with: 'We want you to go out to Italy, to report on some special devices the Americans have made. Actually they are dummy tanks and it is up to you to decide which, if any of them, we should put into production. Can you be ready to fly out after the weekend?'

I managed to get a lift down to Hampshire in an army truck. In the late afternoon it dropped me off at the end of the lane that led up to Griselda's parents' home. As I walked towards the house, I saw our Siamese cat sitting on a windowsill washing herself. I must have been about forty or fifty yards away when I shouted her name. She stopped washing and looked up. I shouted 'Yini!' again and she immediately jumped down and came galloping across the grass and jumped into my arms. I have never been so flattered.

What Griselda wanted was her own home. She had heard of an old cottage for sale at Tilford. It was a dear little house. We bought it and Griselda spent the next few months decorating it and turning it into our first home. It was quite near Lowicks. Not long after we had moved in Marjorie Kerr rang up to say they were selling their house. She asked if we wanted any furniture as there were various things that were going to be sold. The house stripped of furniture and pictures looked very forlorn. The garden was weedy and unkempt. It presented a very different picture from how it had looked when I first stayed there when I was ten years old. Sadly we came away with a set of bookshelves and a copy of a Boulestin cookery book.

8. Secret Devices

AIR TRAVEL IN wartime was made up of short flights and long delays. I left Prestwick, after a day's wait, for North Africa and Marrakech. After a day there I flew on to Algiers to visit Allied Forces Headquarters. Our branch consisted of one officer, Lt Col The Hon Ian Campbell-Gray, who was playing the part of GSO 1 (Camouflage). He was one of the survivors of the first camouflage course. He did not seem pleased to see me.

'No one told me you were coming,' he said petulantly. 'What a nuisance! I can't think why they sent you here. I believe you've got to report to a Colonel Strangeways at 15th Army Group at Bari. I'm afraid you will have to make your own arrangements, I'm far too busy. I'm just off to a sherry party with the Governor-General.'

Somewhat ruffled, I found an aeroplane to take me to Tunis where, after yet another delay, I was airborne once again in a DC3, and flying over an erupting Stromboli. At length we reached the Italian coast and started to climb. After we had crossed the mountains I could see miles of olive groves unfolding before us, then suddenly the Adriatic came into view. The DC3 circled over a neat geometrical town, with a harbour full of fishing boats and little sailing schooners. This was Bari, and our destination. We made two circuits over the flying field, then gently came down on the tarmac runway. The plane came to a stop in front of the Station HQ, the door was opened and we stepped out on to what had been until recently, enemy soil. I felt rather excited and wondered if any hostile Italian would try to shoot me.

As I was collecting my bags from the aircraft, I felt a touch on the shoulder. I turned to look into the face of Horace Buttery whom I had not seen since the course at Lark Hill.

'I heard you were coming, old boy, so I thought I'd try and meet you before Colonel Strangeways got hold of you. This is Dugald McLauchlan.' He turned to introduce a lantern-jawed young man who was wearing a Tam-o'-Shanter. We shook hands and muttered inconsequential how-do-you-dos.

'15th Army group HQ is quite near here.' Horace broke in, 'You will stay with us for a few days, won't you? After we've fixed you up at the mess, I'll have to let Strangeways know you are here. But we must have a *good* talk.' He looked at me meaningly. We climbed into his utility truck and I sat wondering about this Colonel Strangeways. He seemed to have made an impression on little Buttery. On our arrival at the mess Horace found a message for us from Strangeways.

'He wants to see you at 9 o'clock tonight,' Horace said. 'I think I had better come too. You know, he's very difficult. I am rather frightened of him. He's a clever man really, Alex wouldn't have him unless he was. You know Alex calls us his hand-picked staff, all 3,500 of us!' Horace puffed out his little chest and went into a eulogy about General Alexander.

After dinner, we visited Colonel Strangeways who, to my surprise, looked very young and was quietly agreeable. He confirmed the instructions I had already been given, but told me that the devices had not yet arrived from the USA and it looked as if they would not be arriving for some weeks.

'Run away and enjoy yourself,' he ended, 'go and look at the war!'

When we were outside the door, Horace mopped his brow saying, 'What a blessing he was in a good mood, sometimes he just makes mincement of me. Anyhow, I'm glad that at least I know what you're here for. My goodness, they are TOP SECRET!'

We walked back to the billet and discussed what I should do. I thought it would be a good idea to follow up Strangeways' suggestion by going up to the forward areas. Horace was not too sure about this.

'I know what we'll do,' he said, 'I'll take you up to 8th Army and we will see Brian Robb, the camouflage officer there. He may have some ideas. Brian is a marvellous person. We'd better take McLauchlan with us; I think he would welcome a change, he's found it a bit of a strain working for Strangeways.'

In peace time Horace Buttery was one of the foremost picture restorers in England. His office was in Bond Street and his speciality was Italian Renaissance painting. He was a quietly spoken, kind man with a happy sense of the ridiculous, and precise in his ways.

The next morning we set out for 8th Army Headquarters at Lucera. It was a long slow drive. We arrived at Molfetta just as a German plane, a three-engined Fokker, flew low over our heads and did a belly landing on the quay. By the time we reached it, three smiling Italians had emerged. They had escaped from a concentration camp and stolen the aeroplane. We delayed for a while to hear their story until the Carabinieri arrived and took them into custody.

We drove on until we reached Barletta where we stopped the car outside a wine shop, as Horace said it was the done thing to take a bottle or so of vermouth when visiting a unit. The proprietor asked me to taste it first before buying any. He picked up a glass and held it to the light to see if it was clean. It did not satisfy him, so he selected another. Then, picking up a piece of black rubber tubing from the floor, he bent down and inserted one end into a vast basket-covered flagon, the other end he put in his mouth. After sucking hard, with a concentrated expression on his face, he compressed his fingers over the end of the tube, removed it from his mouth and held it over the glass. Releasing the pressure a thin golden jet shot into the tumbler. He handed me the glass of wine – it was excellent and I bought four bottles.

From Barletta we turned north-west for Foggia. In the far distance through the haze I could see the peaks of the Appennines. They looked both ethereal and two-dimensional, as if painted on a distant backdrop. After we had passed Foggia we lost our way twice, before finding ourselves back on the road to Lucera. On that day, as I first saw it, Lucera, with its battlemented walls, looked like a fairy-tale city. Nearer to, it lost some of its magic.

We drove through the town leaving the battlements on our right and turned towards 8th Army HQ. A dusty, bumpy road brought us to their lair which was in a grove of cork oaks. Tents and trucks were scattered about in an area of about half a mile, making ineffectual efforts to hide themselves beneath the stunted trees. A few had faded camouflage nets draped over them, modestly but ineffectually trying to hide their nakedness. We found Brian Robb waiting for us.

At 8th Army, so Horace told me, War Office visitors were not welcome. They had a reputation of coming, criticising and going; I was not sure what kind of reception to expect. Brian Robb I had known by reputation before the war as a humorous draughtsman. I knew also that he had served with the 8th Army in the desert campaign and had been at El Alamein. As my own operational experience was nil, I went to meet him with a feeling of some inferiority.

Five minutes after meeting Brian, all my complexes disappeared; he made me feel that I was the one person in the world who should have arrived at that moment. He was not very tall and prematurely bald with a high forehead. He laughed readily yet had a certain reticence and often took refuge in a prolonged ceremony of lighting and relighting his pipe. He never seemed to smoke it! Brian Robb's name had been a household (or Unithold) word in the Middle East because of his drawings of the 'Little Known Units of the Western Desert' and 'Rigours of the Cairo Campaign' that appeared in the pages of the 8th Army paper *The Crusader*. He was also responsible, with one or two others, for the camouflage and deception plan that played such a large part in the El Alamein victory.

Brian took us along to his mess. The first person I saw there was Ted Ardizzone who I had last seen at Blackheath.

He greeted me with: 'How nice to see you again. Have some wine?'

He handed me a glass and topped up his own. He looked older and plumper than the last time I had seen him. His hair had been cut short, in deference to the army. Even in uniform he had a Dickensian aura and could well have been cast for one of the Cheeryble brothers. I asked him about his work as an Official War Artist.

'I find it a bit exacting,' he answered, 'certainly more demanding than being an Ack-Ack gunner. You know my sister's husband Gabriel White, he was on your course, wasn't he?'

I nodded. 'Gabriel and I were in the same battery. We had an easy time of it compared to all this.'

I asked Ardizzone how he worked.

'Oh, they give me a pretty free hand. It's just a matter of not getting in the way of people who are doing more important things. I have been soaked through every day this week, but have done some stuff that is not too bad. If you would like to see it, I will show it to you later on.'

At lunch next day, Ardizzone said: 'Would you really like to see some of the work I've done? I have been given a room to paint in, in a nearby farm. We could go along there later, though I warn you, it's unbelievably cold.'

After lunch I went along with Ardizzone to see his makeshift studio. He picked up a cylindrical cardboard shell case and, opening the top, pulled out a large roll of drawings. They were watercolour and gouache drawings portraying various happenings and places in Italy.

'I think they're marvellous,' I said. 'I didn't know you did this kind of thing. I thought of you as a black and white draughtsman. The first time I ever saw your work was that beautiful set of drawings you did to advertise Johnny Walker whisky.'

'They were my beginning and my undoing,' he replied. 'I got the job through Crawford's Advertising. They paid me £400 for those drawings. It was on the strength of that cheque that Catherine and I got married.'

'It sounds like a fairy story,' I interrupted.

'It didn't end like one,' he replied. 'Johnny Walker hated the drawings, Crawfords lost the account and I didn't get another job for five years. Catherine had to go out to work to keep me. My sister Betty was doing the same thing for Gabriel. We shared a house in Maida Vale. I did the housework, Gabriel the cooking and the girls earned the money.'

The most noticeable thing about the people at 8th Army was the effect that the desert campaign had on them. Nothing would ever again be quite the same for those who had fought in the Western Desert. They had achieved the kind of cameraderie that my father had known in the first war, but fighting under conditions that were far less severe than the muddy trenches of the Western Front. I had learnt at 2nd AA Division that Regular officers were much less formal than amateur soldiers, calling each other by their Christian names, irrespective of rank. This informality had spread in every direction at 8th Army, including to their clothes, where khaki shirts were often replaced by ones of a dusty duck-egg blue and ties by multi-coloured scarves. 'O' mess, of which I had been made a temporary member, was a microcosm of life in 8th Army. It was a privilege to spend even a little time in their company.

Monty, who had seemed such an abrasive little man at 12th Corps in Tunbridge Wells, had turned into every man's hero at 8th Army. It was

Canadian National Railways locomotive.

Commandant and Chief Instructor, Canadian Army
Camouflage School, Vancouver.

Brian Robb.

Southern Italy, 1944.

Refugees were travelling southwards.

Death of a peasant girl on the road to Aversa.

Homage to St Michael, shrine at Giovannezza.

Dead horse on the road to Montecilfone.

Foggia, entrance to a mausoleum.

Refugees with a puncture.

The wineshop at Barletta.

Farnham Castle Gatehouse watercolour drawing.

Lynton Lamb. *Photograph by Edward Morgan.*

Drawing of set for *Let's Make an Opera.*

Sir Cedric Morris, Bt and Stuart Rose.

John Brinkley and Blair Hughes-Stanton.

Cowells' party at The Old Neptune. *Photographs by John Tarleton.*

Henry Moore and Jan le Witt.

Griselda and Denis Wirth-Miller.

14

Harry Newman, Barbara and Will Carter.

John Minton and Edward Ardizzone.

Cover for *A Handbook of Printing Types.*

Illustration to *Genesis* by Henry Moore for *A Handbook of Printing Types.*

not quite the same at 15th Army Group where Horace Buttery and the other members of Alexander's staff regarded Monty as a mere upstart in contrast to their incomparable Alex.

It took us a week to get clearance to go down to Naples to see the American 5th Army and then to go on to the British 10th Corps at Giuliano. In Brian's Jeep, accompanied by Dugald McLauchlan, we set off on a clear over-bright morning. In the distance the battlements of Lucera still looked like the castle walls of Camelot. We drove south to Foggia, through the horrible shambles caused by our bombing. The road was good and the traffic, though heavy, was mostly going the other way. As we left the southbound road and turned west to the mountains, the sky clouded over as if warning us that our lighter moments were past. It began to rain.

After numerous detours, caused by 'blown' bridges, we reached Naples in late afternoon. It was a sad and bedraggled town, with silent men standing about in groups, or queuing for food or clothes. We hurried on, for we still had some miles to go. It was then getting dark and the rain was pelting down. Night had long since fallen when we arrived at Giuliano. The rain was still coming down with unabated fury and the road was a sea of mud.

'I don't see much joy in pitching tents in this,' Brian said. 'Let's see if we can find the Field Security Section, they've usually got something on the locals,' he remarked cryptically.

We at length found the Military Police Headquarters and in a short time Brian came out accompanied by a very small Field Security corporal. We drove into the village square and stopped outside an imposing building. Our guide jumped out of the car and, in voluble Italian, started addressing the night. We thought he had taken leave of his senses, but out of the darkness emerged a group of Carabinieri. They flung open the massive door of the Town Hall (as the building proved to be) and proudly led us to a chamber which was in pitch darkness. After a further discussion between our guide and the Carabinieri we began to unload the car.

Someone produced a candle and we started laying out our belongings. The possibilities of 'brewing up' still did not look too good, until a very old man appeared carrying a great armful of kindling which he threw into the open fireplace. He set a match to it and huge flames flew up the chimney; within a few minutes the room was so thick with smoke it was practically uninhabitable. The old man was in no way daunted and, opening all the windows, he threw more and more kindling on the fire, soon creating a vast furnace. This had the desired effect of burning all the obstacles out of the chimney. The smoke cleared and dimly, with watering eyes, we could see one another once more. We were in a large and lofty room.

Many villagers had been coming and going and I was on the point of trying to drive them away, when to my amazement I saw that they had brought eggs, bread and wine, in great profusion. I turned to thank them and try to settle with them, when one of the Carabinieri stepped forward and said: 'Pliz, I spik Englis, tomorrow pay, goodnight.'

With that he saluted and they all departed except for the old man who kept returning with more and more firewood. He also found an excellent pressure oil lamp for us that practically turned our night into day.

Whilst Brian and I had been doing nothing very much except get in the way, McLauchlan and the driver had been preparing our meal. In a very short time we sat down to heaped-up plates of eggs and bacon with crisp new bread and good red wine.

Outside the rain still beat down, but we were safe and warm. We talked until the warmth and the wine made us drowsy, when we unrolled our sleeping bags, climbed into them and were soon asleep.

The next morning we were awakened by the old man relighting our fire. An hour later we had finished breakfast and were ready to depart. The policeman who had spoken English turned up and I asked for the bill.

'It is nothing, no. It is nothing to pay.' And he kept repeating this, so we thanked him and slipped the old man 40 lire. When we went down to the car we saw, to our astonishment, quite a large crowd. As soon as we appeared they cheered. As we drove off, a guard of honour of Carabinieri saluted us and the crowd cheered once more. Never have I had such a send off, and never such spontaneous hospitality.

McLauchlan introduced a harsh note by saying that Field Security must have had a lot on them, for us to get so much. We finished our official business at 10th Corps by midday. It was the only British Corps then operating with the American 5th Army. From there we drove to 5th Army Headquarters. It was situated in a beautiful rococo palace not far from Naples. In comparison with the 8th Army it all seemed very formal and orderly. After paying our respects, we returned without mishap to 8th Army Headquarters.

For our next visit to the front line Brian, McLauchlan and I started off in the early hours of daylight in Brian's Jeep. This time we were making for the forward areas. Brian's driver was sick, so I drove. Either because of that or because there was a lot of traffic on the road, we made very poor time. We reached Termoli about midday and, after looking at the harbour, we pulled in to the roadside for lunch. Termoli was not much damaged, but round about there were many signs of recent battle. At one point we counted eleven burnt out 'Tiger' tanks and at another several Shermans in the same condition.

After lunch we took the road to Pescara, but were turned back by Military Police. We drove on for some time without incident, except that we were the unwilling witnesses to a tragedy which was being repeated all over Italy. The Italian peasant seemed woefully lacking in traffic sense, and on this occasion we saw a pretty young girl run out from behind an ambulance straight in front of a gigantic American lorry. She didn't stand a chance. For a moment she raised herself on one arm and a dark stream of blood began to trickle from her mouth. As some onlookers rushed to her assistance, she fell back, dead.

Later we came to a place where there was a curious heavy smell. I asked what it was.

'Death,' Brian replied. 'There was a road in Sicily much like this, that smelt of death for weeks.' There were no corpses in sight, but as it was some time since we had passed any of the Graves Commission's little wooden crosses, we concluded that there were still unburied dead lying in the roadside ditches.

At a village called, we thought, San Giacomo, we stopped and asked a group of soldiers if the road was clear; they told us that it was, but only as far as Montecilfone, so we drove on. The road was now quite deserted and everything seemed very quiet. At two places we passed dead horses lying by the roadside in grotesque and inflated attitudes. In the distance we could hear a gun firing, it sounded like a 3.7 anti-aircraft gun. Then, rounding a bend, the road dropped into a cutting where we came upon a Bren-carrier platoon parked close up against the bank. They looked at us rather curiously. At the time we wondered why. We drove another few hundred yards and, leaving the cutting, came to a shell-pocked stretch of road. I had to drive off the road to pass a Bren-carrier, practically burnt out, with wisps of smoke still eddying from it. At last we reached a little village on a hill that we took to be Guglionesi. It seemed almost deserted, though one or two figures in khaki were flitting about in the shadows. We drove through and on down a winding hill. We were following some red and blue telephone lines that ran along the verge; McLauchlan said that as long as they were there, there must be troops ahead of us. Suddenly a gun started firing away on our flank and somewhat behind us. We could hear no shells going over.

All this time McLauchlan had been fussing over the map, twisting and turning it and muttering to himself.

'Bluidy Hell!' he suddenly exclaimed. 'That was not Guglionesi. The last place we just came through was Montecilfone, which is our forward position!'

I took that to mean we had gone too far, so I turned the Jeep round and we streaked back up the hill down which we had driven so sedately, passing within fifty yards of a German gun crew with their backs to us, grouped round an 88 mm gun. Within a quarter of an hour we were back in Montecilfone.

Brian remarked, with unaccustomed acidity, that it was as well to check on the nationality of telephone wires before using them as guidelines. We parked the Jeep and went up to a sentry to ask him where his OC was.

'There he is now, Sir, just coming out of that door.' He pointed to a house a few yards down the street. We walked up to the officer, but before we could speak, he asked us quite pointedly what on earth we thought we were doing. We told him and explained as best we could.

'I heard you'd gone through,' he continued, 'the Carrier Platoon called me up, they were full of admiration for you; thought you were part of Popski's Private Army.'[1]

We hastily swept aside any claim to such heroics and McLauchlan asked him the position of the enemy.

'Oh, they're about three hundred to five hundred yards away, on three sides of us. The only way out of here is along the road on which you came, and that is being shelled intermittently. You probably heard their 88 mm banging away.'

We admitted not only to hearing it, but to having been right behind it.

'Come and have a look at our mortars,' the Company Commander said. His 4.2 mortars were in the process of lobbing bombs into a wood about a quarter of a mile away. He told us that his company had taken Montecilfone thirty-six hours before; how the Germans had made a strong counter attack, but with the aid of these redoubtable mortars they had been repulsed, the German casualties numbering about sixty. 'They don't like these heavy mortars,' he continued, 'they sent a strong patrol into the village last night and walked off with one of them and the crew. Come to think of it, it's a pity you didn't bring in that 88 mm gun crew. That would have evened things up!'

All this time we had been walking up the main street; it was steep and winding and had a cobbled surface. We turned to the left between two houses and, squeezing between a carrier and the wall of a house, we came out on to the crest of the hill. Below us lay open country, a mixture of cultivated fields and small spinnies. In the middle distance a truck was driving along a road; I had to look twice to realise that it was German. On the rim of the hill were four machine gun posts, dug well into the ground. In the sector in which we were, this was the foremost outpost, a salient flanked by Germans, but it was difficult to believe that we were not in a peaceful bit of English countryside.

Our guide showed us points of interest. 'Those three farms are all occupied by the enemy. We're going out tonight to mop them up. They always go for farms, just living off the country. Of course they kill all the poultry and livestock that they can lay hands on, the peasants hate them for it. In one place there was a dispute over a pig: as a result they shot twenty-five Italians. The peasants keep filtering in here, they're doing all they can to help us. When the German Unit opposite to us were here they carried off the grand-daughters of the old woman who lived over there, the house with the broken shutter, the poor kids were only about fifteen or sixteen; they used them as a mobile brothel, then, when they wanted to move on, they just shot them. As you can well imagine the peasants took a pretty dim view of that.'

Brian broke in with a remark about atrocity stories being much exaggerated.

The Company Commander looked thoughtful for a moment and then said: 'Well, perhaps they are, but when we were down in the south we came across the body of a young girl that they had used, then killed and not content with that, had disembowelled her.'

Another officer joined us, he was red-eyed and unshaven, we were introduced to him as visitors from the 8th Army HQ. Everyone was very formal and polite. He apologised for his appearance, saying that he had not had any sleep for three nights. I felt that if I had been in his place and had been bothered with visitors, I should have very quickly sent them about their business.

While he was talking we had remained by the barn. To the left we could see a bit of open ground with the machine gun posts. A door in the house opposite opened and an old man came out. He did not look up, but started to hoe his small patch of garden. Removing weeds seemed to him of more importance than the possibility of being hit by a stray machine gun bullet.

As it was getting late, we said goodbye. Just as we were going, the Company Commander turned to me and said: 'Didn't you run that Camouflage School at Tunbridge Wells?

I replied that I had.

'I thought I remembered you,' he said. 'We still talk about that course, what splendid food you gave us!'

We made two more visits to the forward areas, to Vinchiaturo, where the Canadians were fighting and to Campobasso where we saw a terrific artillery barrage.

Eventually the time came for me to return to Bari and 15th Army Group. After a riotous night in 'O' mess, I left Lucera and arrived at Bari to find a message from Strangeways saying that the devices had been lost at sea, and a telegram from the War Office saying: 'Return forthwith'.

With feelings of some frustration, I went off to fix up my passage to Algiers and home. Having done this, I had the remainder of the day in which to amuse myself. Horace suggested we should drive up to Molfetta, have a picnic lunch and do some painting there. Having left word where we were going, we drove off up the Adriatic road. Passing through Giovanezza, we reached Molfetta in about thirty minutes. We ate our lunch and then, in a particulary smelly corner of the shipyard, we sat down to draw. The inevitable crowd gathered round, but remained fairly quiet until rudely jostled by an intruder, a grimy sapper subaltern. He bent down over my shoulder and whispered something in my ear.

'What!' I shouted.

'Psst!' he hissed; and then in a low tone, 'Go at once to the Cathedral at Cerignola. There on the steps you will be met by a guide. Don't waste time.' And with that he was gone.

Mystified, we packed up our things, bundled into our car and drove off to Cerignola. We arrived there soon after two o'clock and stopped at the Cathedral. Standing on the steps was Strangeways' batman, Pott.

He saluted and said: 'Will you follow me, Sir?'

We asked him to where, but her only put his finger to his lips, then he saluted again and ran down the steps to a 15 cwt truck, which immediately set off at great speed. We were hard put to it to keep him in sight as he dodged through narrow streets and back alleys. Twice we were blocked by peasant carts, nearly losing him each time, but at last we were clear of the town with Pott's truck about two hundred yards in front of us heading down a narrow country road that stretched in a straight line for twenty or thirty miles. It must have been built by the old Romans, but we had no time for musing on its history for all our attention was fixed on Pott, who was rapidly gaining on us and becoming a cloud in the distance. Suddenly his dust cloud increased in size, billowing masses of brown dust went up into the air, and then through the haze we could see the truck rolling over and over off the road and on to a ploughed field.

'Poor devils! They must have hit a mine!' Horace said briefly.

Within a few minutes we had pulled up at the scene of the accident and rather gingerly made our way across the ditch and up to the vehicle which lay on its side, one wheel still slowly spinning. On the ground, on the other side of the truck, was Pott. He was sitting holding his knee and cursing softly. The driver, with blood running down his face, was bending over him.

'Are you badly hurt?' asked Horace anxiously.

'No, Sir, I reckon we were lucky. I just banged my knee, Sir, and the driver only got a cut on his forehead.' Pott replied as he was helped to his feet. 'I've been on that road dozens of times without touching that mine off, the road and verges were checked weeks ago. Monty drove over it yesterday.'

'I hope there aren't any more like that,' Horace said. 'You'll just have to come along with us, Pott. Driver, you had better stay with the truck. We will send help.'

As we helped Pott into the back of the utility, it started to rain, large heavy drops that hit the dusty road like marbles. We scrambled into the car and, with Pott to guide us, drove on. Within a very short time, rain was pouring down. After about half an hour, Pott began peering through the side window.

'Here we are, Sir, turn in at the next gate on the left.' I could not imagine how he knew where he was as our visibility through the rain was only about ten yards.

We reached the gate and I turned in and drove up to a white farm building. A sentry stopped us, but recognising Pott, directed us through into a courtyard. We dismounted from the car and Pott led us into a large paddock; the rain poured down and we plodded miserably along through long wet grass. At last, rounding a thorn bush, we came upon Strangeways, surrounded by a respectful, if damp, audience of senior officers.

He greeted us in a perfunctory manner, then moved up a steep incline, his audience trailing behind him. We reached the top of the slope; Strangeways stopped and with a dramatic gesture said: 'Gentlemen, there they are!'

And there they were, three more or less recognizable tanks.

'I thought that they had been lost at sea!' I gasped.

'I know you did,' Strangeways said. 'All part of the plan. We don't want everybody to know about them, do we? Least of all that nincompoop in Algiers.'

It took me no more than half an hour to complete my assignment. Two of the dummy tanks would not have lasted any time in the hands of the soldiery, but the third looked indestructible. It was built like an inflatable dinghy and was just what we needed. On my return to HQ I sent my recommendations to the War Office in the form of a brief signal.

On the way to the mess that night we were treated to a wonderful 'Brock's Benefit' firework display. This was very fitting as it was the night of the fifth of November. The whole of the sky to the south of us was filled with streams of red tracer firing at some German plane and moving across the sky in gentle parabolic arches. Above the clouds, flashes of exploding heavy AA shells could be seen, then a long time afterwards we could hear the distant rumblings of the explosions. When shell caps began to fall around us, we retired indoors. In a very little while the night was made hideous by a nearby Bofors starting in on the fight. It sounded as if some demented giant was beating an enormous carpet. This went on at intervals for most of the night, but never a bomb did we hear.

The next morning I said goodbye to Horace Buttery and to the faithful McLauchlan. After a series of delays at Bizerta, Maison Blanche at Algiers and Marrakech, I boarded a C54 for Prestwick. Twelve hours later I was back in Scotland.

On my return I reported to the War Office. I was met by Victor, who said, with rather a grave look on his face: 'I'm afraid the General wants to see you about your report. What on earth did you say?'

'I haven't written a report!' I gasped.

Before he could answer we were interrupted by a summons to present ourselves to the Director of Special Weapons and Vehicles.

'Come in, Lewis,' the General said. 'I just wanted to have a word with you about this report of yours.' He ruffled through some papers and withdrew a signal form. 'Let me see now, what did you say? Ah, yes, here it is. You say "Type 2" and nothing else. Is that all you have to say?'

Nervously I cleared my throat. 'Yes, Sir, Type 2 was the only possible

one – and it was more than possible – it looked just like a Sherman tank –
it met with all our requirements.'

The General looked at me over the top of his glasses.

'Little known Units of the Western Desert', by Brian Robb.

In Limbo

ON MY RETURN to England, I was posted to the Camouflage Centre at Farnham Castle as an assistant instructor under Talbot Kelly. He was a bird-like man and birds were his main interest. Both kinds. He was a dedicated ornithologist and the paper birds he made were brilliant creations. A nuthatch that he painted for Griselda also revealed that reptilian quality that so many birds have and so few artists capture.

TK, as he was always known, had been the art master at Rugby School and his forte was his ability as a lecturer. His subject – apart from camouflage – was military history. It was a revelation to watch a class of very senior officers listening, open-mouthed, like a bunch of school-boys as TK took them through the battle of Flodden Field or described how Burnham Wood came to Dunsinane.

At the Camouflage School, it all seemed rather *déja vu*, but there were compensations. It was within a few hundred yards of No 9 Castle Street and Freddy Gore was attached to us for a short time. He was the only son of Spencer Gore and had been brought up in the shadows of the Camden Town Group.

Freddy Gore had started at the Westminster School of Art under Meninsky. Later he moved on to the Slade. While he was there he was living above Cedric Morris and soon became part of the circle that surrounded that charismatic and wonderful painter. Freddy Mayor showed Gore's work and he had a number of exhibitions at the Redfern Gallery, both before and after the war. His final triumph was the big Retrospective Exhibition at the Royal Academy in 1989. He certainly added to the cultural tone of the Camouflage Centre, as did Lynton Lamb, a painter who was also an illustrator and a typographer. I owed much to Lamb, who pointed me in the direction I was ultimately to take.

Freddy Mayor (Huskinson's friend), who had an art gallery in Cork Street, was mess secretary and had used Farnham Castle as a storehouse for his pictures. Hanging over my bed was a beautiful little study by Rouault for the head of a clown. Freddy Mayor was the son of a painter, also called Fred. He had been born in 1903 at Montreuil. His gallery was the most *avant garde* in London. Freddy was gregarious, but had a very barbed wit. He loved good food and good wine and made a first class mess secretary.

It was a time when soldiers who had been badly wounded were being repatriated. Blair Hughes-Stanton was one of the first of them. He arrived unannounced at Farnham Castle. Blair, who was a GSO 3 Camouflage, had been captured in Crete, something he was very bitter about.

'We could have easily got away,' he said 'but we were under orders not to try to escape.'

Whilst in a prisoner-of-war cage he had been shot through the mouth by a trigger-happy sentry.

'I had gone up to the wire fence to buy some fruit from a peasant, when the idiot shot me. I was lucky, we had a New Zealand surgeon with us, who was an expert on facial surgery. He wired up my jaw so that I could only drink through a straw. I was like that until we reached Germany, six weeks later.'

'It must have been very painful,' I interjected.

'Uncomfortable rather than painful. The worst thing was when flies or bluebottles crawled in through the wound in my cheek and started buzzing about in my mouth.'

'How horrible! What did you do?'

'Swallowed them, of course.'

It was some months later that Talbot Kelly retired and I became Chief instructor. The Camouflage Centre had moved from Farnham Castle to Pierrepont House, a monstrous, half-timbered Norman Shaw house near Frensham. It was only a couple of miles away from our cottage at Tilford.

This was our first settled home and we began to make friends. Victor Stiebel and Freddy Mayor were frequent visitors and Basil Spence even more so. At that time Basil was almost unknown as an architect outside Scotland. He had built a mock Scottish baronial castle for a wealthy American lady. As she was left handed he had made the spiral staircase twist the wrong way so that she could defend her honour with a sword in her left hand. Basil used to describe how, when he first qualified, he worked for Lutyens, who always referred to him as 'Scotch boy'. He also told us that for his first job Lutyens sent him out to draw the steps of the Albert Memorial.

As the first British troops landed on the Normandy beaches, Griselda, who had again been very ill, was undergoing a major operation in a London nursing home. The operation was successful but they left a swab inside her; for eight days she hovered between life and death. Her temperature chart look like a profile of the Alps. Once they had removed the swab she slowly recovered and returned to convalesce in our cottage. Her doctors had still not got to the bottom of her trouble.

The development side of things at Pierrepont was run by a genius called James Gardner, appropriately assisted by W. Heath Robinson's eldest son, Oliver. Gardner was known as 'G'. Oliver Robinson was a jolly, smiling man with a strong look of the many round-faced infants in his father's drawings. G's other assistant was Basil Spence.

I sold my beloved Riley 9, thinking I would be able to replace it with a new car as soon as the war was over. As a temporary measure, I bought a 1929 Austin 7 from one of my sergeants. This was just to ferry me back and forth from our cottage to Pierrepont House.

On the day I started my job as Chief Instructor, the first flying bomb, a V.1, flew over Tilford. We were out in the garden talking to our neighbour as the thing came over.

'Ugh! I hate those nasty things,' she said. 'You do miss the human touch!' As she spoke the engine suddenly cut out, then coughed, spluttered and started up again. It finally plunged to earth on Frensham Common, hurting nobody.

We were soon training our soldiers for jungle warfare. Ostensibly our job was to teach them the principles of personal camouflage. In fact what we found necessary was to teach them to see and to interpret what they saw. It was not many months before even that became irrelevant.

As the war drew towards its end, the Camouflage Centre became rather like a transit camp. Buckles retired and was replaced by a kindly man called Colonel Burn, who urged me to make the Army my career. Freddy Mayor was still mess secretary and made sure we were well fed and generally kept happy.

There was one sad note and that was the death from feline enteritis of our dear, wayward Siamese cat, Yini. There were no antibiotics available then.

*   *   *

Nagasaki and Hiroshima had been blasted by atomic bombs and we were celebrating VJ Day in the Camouflage Centre mess at Pierrepont House. The talk was of how quickly we could get out of the army and what we would do then. Victor Stiebel was going back to his dress designing. Freddy Mayor to his gallery in Cork Street; James Gardner and Basil Spence to design the 'Britain can Make it' Exhibition and other even more prestigious things. Blair Hughes-Stanton was returning to teach at the Central. Freddy Gore and Lynton Lamb were establishing themselves as painters; Freddy had a teaching job at St Martin's and Larry a job at the Oxford University Press. They all seemed very sure of themselves. I suddenly began to feel rather insecure. My brief experience as a mural painter and a free-lance illustrator before the war did not seem much of a foundation on which to build a career.

Larry Lamb, who was sitting next to me at dinner, must have sensed something of this, for he suddenly said: 'Illustration is not the only way you might earn a living; you might follow my example. As you have illustrated books and collected books all your life, why don't you design them?'

'Design them! How do you do that?' I asked.

'It means knowing about typography, about printing and book binding. If you could manage it, the best thing would be to go and work with a printer and a book binder.'

I was about to ask him some more about this when our conversation was interrupted by someone suggesting we all went down to the village pub. But the seed was sown and later on I thought about what he had said.

At breakfast a week later, James Gardner shouted across the table to me: 'Do you want a job in printing?'

'Why?' I asked.

'I've just had an offer from the printers who did my Puffin books. They're up in East Anglia. They want to start a design studio. The job's no good for me – but I thought it might suit you.'

'Why?' I asked again.

'Well, you like sailing, don't you? Lots of water up there.'

'That's an idea,' I said, 'tell me more.'

After we had finished our breakfast, we wandered out of the mess and into the garden. 'G' lit his pipe.

'The reason I thought you might like this job is because the other night I overheard Lamb talking to you about book design. If that's what you want to do, I shouldn't think there's a better place to learn about that sort of thing than a print shop.'

'Tell me about the printers. Who are they?'

'It's a firm called Cowells in Ipswich. It's an old-fashioned outfit. They run a shop and a wine business as well. They're basically lithographers and bloody good colour printers. Geoffrey Smith, one of the bosses, is dead keen on turning them into book printers – I reckon that's something you could do for them.'

'But I don't know anything about book printing.'

'Nor do they. You can learn together!'

A couple of weeks later Griselda and I drove up to Ipswich in our old Austin 7 to meet Geoffrey Smith. I wondered if the tyres would last the journey. In the meantime I had an interview with Eric Hanson, the other managing director of the firm. This meeting was in some offices off the Strand, as he was still working for the Board of Trade. He was a shy man with heavy eyebrows and a somewhat overbearing manner. He spent most of the interview drawing a chart of the River Deben, showing me how to negotiate the bar and shingle banks at the entrance.

'We can only offer you £600 a year,' he said, just as I was going. 'That must be a lot less than you are getting paid as a staff major.'

I said it was, but that I would come for nothing if I could have afforded to. He must have thought I was a simpleton.

Before visiting Cowells, Eric Hanson had suggested I met Noel Carrington, the editor of Puffin Picture Books. Cowells was the first printer of these books.

Carrington, the younger brother of Dora Carrington, was a sympathetic and helpful man. I told him about myself and my complete lack of knowledge of printing or of running a printer's studio.

He listened patiently and then said:

'I think it's because you know so little about this job that you can be the most use to Cowells. The kind of person they *must* not have – and I told Geoffrey Smith this – is a 'Commercial artist', who is set in the ways of advertising studios. As a virtual amateur you can come in with a fresh eye. Also, you might show them that little book you did for Coles.

Adlard Coles, an accountant friend of my father's and a famous sailor, had started a small publishing concern. He had commissioned me to write a book in his 'Careers Series' on *Commercial Art and Industrial Design*. The fact that I had hardly started on my career as an illustrator when the war came along in no way inhibited me. I had written the book in the last days of the war and John Mansbridge, who had been one of my tutors at Goldsmiths' and was also in Camouflage, had decorated it with some very lively little designs. I had even persuaded Milner Gray, one of the founders of the Society of Industrial Artists and Designers, who I had also known since Goldsmiths' days, to write an introduction. Adlard Coles did me another good service. He published my first piece about boats in *The Yachtsman*. It was an article called '*Bluenose*' based on my visit to Lunenburg, just before I returned from Canada.

Our Austin 7 just about survived the journey to Ipswich. I had left Griselda sitting in the car while I made my way through Cowells Store, which seemed to specialize in perambulators, chamber pots and other nursery equipment. A lift took me up to top floor of the building where, under a huge skylight and around the well that lit the shop floors below, were rows and rows of desks. It looked like an American newspaper office of the 1920s.

I was shown into Geoffrey Smith's office. He was a large clean shaven smiling man. He apologised for what he considered to be his cousin's somewhat intimidating manner.

'He's very shy, you know. He was very much under the thumb of his father – a very domineering man.'

The fact that Geoffrey had been in awe of his equally formidable mother (who was Eric's father's sister) I did not discover until later. Eric was actually a brilliant accountant and, as I was to discover later, had very considerable entrepreneurial skills.

'We will have some lunch. You have brought your wife?'

I said I had.

'Good, she can join us then. Beresford, who has been helping me throughout the war, will come with us as well. Very useful man, but . . . well, you'll see him shortly.' He looked at his watch. 'Where is your wife?'

I told him I had left Griselda in the car.

'Good gracious! That's not very nice for her; let us go and collect her.'

Griselda was sitting in the Austin 7, patiently knitting a pullover. I introduced her to Geoffrey Smith. Once again he looked at his watch.

'I think we've just time to go over to the litho studios. We have an artist visiting us, working on a job for Harling. Do you know Harling?'

I said I did not.

'Amazing fellow, you must meet him.' As he talked, he was leading us through a warren of corridors. 'I think our artist friend is in here.' He pushed open a door. 'Ah, yes, come in.'

A tall, thin, hollow-eyed man of indeterminate age rose to his feet.

'Forgive me for interrupting you,' Geoffrey Smith said, 'but I would like you to meet John Lewis and his wife, er . . .'

'Griselda,' I said.

'Ah, yes, Griselda. John may be joining us as our studio manager.'

I looked enquiringly at Geoffrey Smith.

'Oh, of course, this is Mr Mervyn Peake, who is working on a lithograph.'

'What is it for?' I asked.

'For *Bleak House*,' Peake answered, 'it's meant to be a portrait of Joe the crossing sweeper.' As he spoke he was looking at Griselda.

'We met in Sark,' she reminded him. 'You did drawings of my brother and me. I must have been about fifteen.'

They continued to talk about the Channel Islands until Geoffrey Smith interrupted them.

'Come along, we have things to discuss. We must leave Mr Peake to finish his lithograph.'

To my lasting regret I never saw Mervyn Peake again. For some reason or other John Murray, who had commissioned the drawings, didn't publish his *Bleak House* illustrations, though the lithograph of Joe appeared in the first number of Robert Harling's magazine *Alphabet and Image*.

I showed Geoffrey Smith the few examples of my work that I had been able to collect. I also handed him the little book I had done for Adlard Coles.

'Do you mean to say you wrote this?' he said, turning over the pages. 'Most interesting, most interesting!'

If it was not Noel Carrington's kind words about me, then it must have been that little book that clinched my appointment.

We found Beresford waiting for us outside the studio. Laurie Beresford was a sallow, rather plump man who spoke with a marked Lancashire accent. He was blunt and I liked him. I soon discovered that if anyone knew anything about printing in that firm, it was he. What he made of me I never found out. I think at that stage he lumped me in with Mr Geoffrey's 'arty' friends.

Before we had finished lunch and a half-pint of bitter Geoffrey Smith confirmed me in the job. There was the proviso that I should spend six weeks at the London School of Printing.

I did not feel I could learn much about printing in six weeks, so when in due course I arrived there, remembering Larry Lamb's words about book binding, I spent all my time re-binding some of my books.

As we drove back to Tilford, Griselda had said: 'Are you sure that this is what you want to do? I'd hate to think you were taking a full time job just to support me.'

I reassured her.

'But Johnnie, you've never been in a full time job except for the army, and you can't count that. You've always said the one thing you wanted was to be your own man, to work free-lance.'

'So it is,' I answered 'and one day, God willing, so I will.'

'Well,' she answered, 'I only hope you know what you're doing.'

NOTES

Part 1: *Life Class*

3.1. Long after I had given up medicine, I kept in touch with Teddy Smyth who, apart from being a successful orthopaedic surgeon, later became a renowned Alpine climber. In fact he actually climbed Mont Blanc a year after having a severe heart attack.

4.1. *Carel Weight.* Mervyn Levy, Weidenfeld and Nicholson, 1986.

4.2. *Commercial Art and Industrial Design.* Robert Ross, 1945.

5.1. *A Taste for Sailing.* Adlard Coles, 1969. Second edn, Terence Dalton, 1989.

6.1. First Aid Nursing Yeomanry.

6.2. Cyril Connolly, an admirer of Denton and editor of *Horizon*, did publish the Sickert article in August 1942.

7.1. University of British Columbia.

7.2. National Defence Headquarters.

7.3. The Mark Hopkins Hotel.

8.1. 'Popski's Private Army' was the Italian version of the Long Range Desert Group, who spent the bulk of their time behind the enemy lines.

FAMILY TEA,

Coffee, and Spice Warehouse,

NEW MARKET LANE,

BUTTER MARKET, IPSWICH.

———

S. H. COWELL

Begs very respectfully to acquaint his Friends and the Public, he has opened a Shop, adjoining his present business, for the Sale of GENUINE TEAS, COFFEE, and SPICES. At the last Sale it is well known a great reduction took place in the price of Tea, and S. H. C. has been enabled to purchase his Entire Stock, direct from the East India Company's Warehouses, on the most advantageous terms. He pledges himself to give the full benefit of it to the consumer, who has now an opportunity of purchasing Tea, cheaper than has been offered to the public for the last 15 years. S. H. C. solicits attention to the following Prices, for Ready Money only.

	Per Pound. s. d.		Per Pound. s. d.
Good Bohea	3 8	Very Fine Souchong	10 0
Good Congou	5 0	Strong Caper	8 0
Fine Rough ditto	5 4	Fine Pekoe	11 0
Ditto	5 8	Fine Bloom	7 6
Ditto	6 0	Good Hyson	8 0
Good Souchong	6 8	Fine ditto	10 0
Fine ditto	7 0	Super ditto	12 0
Ditto	8 0	Strong Gunpowder	13 0
Good Plantation Coffee	2 0	Sir Hans Sloane's Chocolate	6 0
Fine Jamaica ditto	2 6	Best Plain ditto	5 0
Ditto Berbice ditto	3 0	Plain ditto	4 0
Fine Turkey ditto	3 6	White's Cocoa	3 4

Spices of every description on the most Reasonable Terms.

☞ No Credit Given.

S. H. Cowell notice, 1827.

Part II

The Printer's Devil

An illustrated scenario

The Printer's Devil: 'The press-man has a boy
to take the sheets, as they are printed off the
tympan, these boys do in a printing house
commonly daub themselves, whence the
workmen do jocosely call them devils.'

Mechanick Exercises   Joseph Moxon 1683

1. Life in a Printing House

IT WAS ON the first of January 1946 that I joined Cowells. I was dressed in my pre-war suit, a clean shirt and a new tie. I felt I looked the part of an office worker but I had a slight feeling of hollowness as I took the lift to the top floor.

I asked for 'Mr Geoffrey' the name by which my employer was known to his staff. I was told that he had not yet arrived, but would I wait. I sat rather apprehensively in a little windowless waiting room, next to the lift and about the size of a clothes cupboard. There were two framed pictures hanging on the wall. One was a wash drawing of the front of the premises, which must have been drawn in the 1880s; it showed a pleasant early nineteenth-century façade. Across the front of the building was painted in Tuscan letters 'Steam Printing Works'. I wondered if Cowells was still a technologically minded concern. The other picture was a little bill dated in pencil 1827, in which S.H. Cowell begged very respectfully to acquaint his friends that he had opened a shop next door to his existing premises for the sale of genuine Teas, Coffees and Spices (and what was more, they were cheaper than they had been for the last fifteen years). At the foot of the bill, printed in bold type were the words 'No Credit Given'. I supposed that on such sound business principles the firm had prospered.

I had been sitting there for nearly an hour when the door was flung open and 'Mr Geoffrey' was beaming down on me. Dressed in chaps with a five gallon Stetson on his head, he would have made a passable double for John Wayne.

'Good gracious me! Haven't they showed you into your office? It's next door; it used to be the ladies cloakroom.' He swept through a group of gossiping order clerks and threw open a door with frosted glass in its upper half.

'Here is your office, and what's more, your staff as well.' A pretty little blonde was standing nervously in the corner.

'Now, let me see, you are Irené, aren't you?'

'No,' she replied in a whispery voice, 'I'm Ireen.'

'Oh, yes, of course. Well this is Mr Lewis, the studio manager. And this, er- John, is er- Ireen. I'll leave you to get settled in, but come and see me at half-past eleven when I can discuss a job I want you to do.'

Geoffrey Smith had picked out Ireen from the vocational class at the Ipswich Art School, I'm sure more for her looks than her talents.

When it was time for my appointment, I walked across the office to

Geoffrey Smith's room.

'Come in, come in! That'll be all, Mary, I'll ring for you later.' This to his secretary, a comely bespectacled girl of uncertain age.

'Now – about a spot of work. What do you say to doing a type book for us?'

'A type book!' I exclaimed. 'What sort of a type book do you want?' I added playing for time.

'Oh, something to show we are in the book market – the *illustrated* book market. A chap who was coming to us has done a little work on it. Here are his proofs. This will give you something to get your teeth into.'

He handed me a sheaf of type proofs.

'See what you can do with those.'

As I was going through the door, Geoffrey Smith said, 'We don't want the expense of adding to our list of Monotype faces. Make the best of what we've got.'

I set to work. My knowledge of typography was minimal, but the word 'illustrated' gave me hope. To further my understanding of typography, I visited the composing room which was next to the office. With its ranks of type cases, it had not changed since the 1850s. The overseer was an elderly bulldogish figure with beetling black eyebrows. His name was Schofield and he came from Manchester. At first he regarded me with some suspicion, then with quizzical amusement and finally with what might almost be called affection. I asked him if I could be allowed to handle type. His response was instant.

'If you come in here and pick up as much as a single piece of type, the whole floor will be out on strike!'

'How am I ever going to learn, if your chaps won't help?'

'Oh, you want to learn, lad, do you? Well, that's a different matter. I'll see what we can do about that.' He then gave me a run down on their work. After about twenty minutes, he said, 'I can't sit here doing this all day. Come and have a word with my clicker[1], Bob Cooper. He's a patient fellow, even if he is a bit deaf. He'll help you.'

He led me out of his office across the floor of the composing room, threading our way between cases of type. We passed a burly man locking up a forme of type.

'That's 'Arry 'Ogger,' Schofield said. 'Best stone hand I've ever had – that is – up to lunch time. In the afternoon that's a different matter. He likes his beer, does 'Arry.' I discovered later that in the morning Harry Hogger ruled up his imposition sheets with a 6H pencil, with impeccable precision. After his beery lunch a much relaxed Harry used to use a pica wide carpenter's pencil for his anything but precise impositions.

Schofield looked round the room then seeing a group of men in conversation, he called out: 'Bob, when you've finished your mothers' meeting, come over here.'

A sandy-haired, frail-looking man detached himself from the group.

As he came up to us Schofield said, 'This is Mr Lewis – Mr John Lewis. He's the new studio manager and he wants to learn about what we do. Perhaps you can help him.'

Then turning to me, 'Don't waste too much of his time, but the more you learn about this department, the better we shall understand each other. Those idiots in the sales office – they don't know a thing about it!'

Bob Cooper, speaking in the flat tones of the very deaf, explained the simpler facts about marking-up copy and what leading and point sizes meant. At length he said, 'Now John – you don't mind me calling you John do you? If you ever want to know anything, at any time, come straight up here and ask me, or if I'm busy ask Tom Nunn.' He called to a military looking individual who was working at a case nearby. 'Tom, here a minute. This is Mr Lewis – John – he is the new studio manager. He doesn't know much about typography or composing, so I've said we'll help him – you and me.'

Tom Nunn looked doubtfully at me, but before I could say anything, he rapped out: 'You were in the army?'

I nodded.

'Thought so, what unit were you in?'

'Sappers,' I answered.

'So was I – shake.' We shook hands. I did not know then but it was the beginning of a life-long friendship with Tom Nunn and was the first step to a happy relationship with the 'works'. Thirty years later, Tom and I were sailing together in the Western Isles.

In addition to commercial work in their offset department, Cowells were printing Puffin books for Penguins such as the *Orlando* books by Kathleen Hale, *The Battle of Britain* by James Gardner (the same Gardner who had introduced me to Cowells) and *Moorland Birds* by Talbot Kelly. They were also printing for the Oxford University Press the first of the *Little Tim* books by Edward Ardizzone. The first offset book I was involved in was *Hunting with 'The Fox'* a collection of aphorisms from Jules Renard's *Histoires Naturelles,* with lithographs by Henri de Toulouse-Lautrec, published by an emigré publisher called Bruno Cassirer.

I was soon on as friendly terms with Fred Fenner and his photo artists as I was with Mr Patrick, the litho machine room overseer. I was beginning to find the printing trade, at least from the actual production side, quite fascinating.[2] It took me much longer to come to terms with the 'office'. There I soon learned that I would have to tread pretty warily.

I had my first brush with one of the older order clerks. He was a lay reader called Mr Pell. A small job that had passed through my hands had gone wrong. Mr Pell was in a terrible state.

'Look what has happened to it,' he said to me pointing at some wrongly scaled reproductions. 'I don't know what the customer will say!'

'One thing is certain,' I replied, 'it's entirely my fault.'

'What did you say?'

'I said it's my fault.'

'Do you mean to say you will take the blame?'

'Of course I will.'

'Oh, well, that's a different matter. We'll see what we can do to cover it up.'

Meanwhile I started work on the type book. I read what I could find in the Cowells' library about the origins of the various type faces that the firm held, then I began to look for suitable texts. I worked away at my layouts and designed a very fanciful title-page, with a variety of type faces and swashes and cursive ornaments. Inspired by Freddy Mayor, I had become a snuff taker and only the week before had bought a little box of 'Prince's Mixture' from Fribourg and Treyer, the tobacconists in the Haymarket. Its richly engraved label was the inspiration for my idiotic title-page.

One Saturday morning, when I was working on this design, Robert Harling walked into our design office. (We worked on Saturdays until lunch time.) He looked at my layouts, picked up my title-page and, without saying anything, re-titled the type book and in ten minutes had re-laid it out in the form in which it was finally printed.

Cowells' London office was then in Holborn and was run by a very austere old man called Mr Cooper, who dressed in subfusc clothing and a high winged collar. His weakness, apart from being a chain-smoker and a chain-drinker as well, was falling asleep in his chair and dropping his lighted cigarette into the waste-paper basket. On more than one occasion the fire brigade had to be summoned to put out the blaze. Mr Cooper's second-in-command was Mr Reggie Watts, whose domed bald head surmounted a sad face with washed-out blue eyes. This rather weak appearance was more than compensated for by his mordant tongue. The London office soon moved to an attractive house in Percy Street, off Tottenham Court Road.

Two other members of the office were Geoffrey King and George Bodley-Scott, whom I had met when he was commanding an A.A. Battery. George was a fresh-faced, moustached, soldierly-looking man and a descendant of both Gilbert Scott and G.F. Bodley, the architects of Liverpool Cathedral. He came from a family of doctors – his brother Ronald was to become the Queen's physician. Geoff King had been in the Navy. He was an extrovert East Anglian and in many ways had modelled himself on Geoffrey Smith. They were being groomed for higher management, which was probably one of the causes of the acid view of the firm taken by Mr Watts, who had been passed over for such preferment, and the resolute way in which he refused to call them by their Christian names, no matter how much they Reggied him. He always referred to the directors as 'our Masters'. The higher echelon of Cowells' London office was completed by Colonel Champion whose battledress jacket, with its red tabs and SAS insignia used to hang over the back of the chair by the side of his bed in the flat he had in Percy Street. It was as if he was eternally waiting a call to arms as a release from his task of selling print to book publishers, a thing he did with considerable success. The management was as wary of him as it was of me. He did much for Cowells over the years, but he was never given a seat on the board.

After my first visit to the London office, I lunched with Geoffrey King. He was a friendly, talkative man. Later that afternoon I made my way to 4 St James's Square to see Gabriel White, who had left camouflage to work for the Arts Council.

I told Gabriel about my type book and asked him if he knew the addresses of the artists I ingenuously thought I would like to use in it. He did and he gave them to me. Thus armed, I returned in triumph to Ipswich. The next morning I told Geoffrey Smith of my plans for illustrating his type book. He looked embarrassed.

'Of course, I don't know anything about art, but aren't they rather modern?' I said they were, but that they were very distinguished artists as well.

'You say they are distinguished; well then, perhaps it's all right, though I don't see why we have to have Henry Moore. We were asked to print his *Shelter Sketchbook* but turned it down. We didn't think the drawings were very nice.'

'But Henry Moore is the greatest living sculptor!' I almost exploded. 'Don't you want Cowells to be seen to be a *modern* house?'

'Oh, yes, of course; I'll take your advice. That's what you are here for.' So I wrote to Moore, Sutherland, Piper and Bawden and also to John Nash and Blair Hughes-Stanton. In due course I met each of them, and none of them thought the reproduction fee of twelve guineas that Cowells was offering was a despicable sum.

The second time I met Henry Moore (it was in the Tate Gallery), he handed over his sketches. We had decided to use one of his shelter drawings to illustrate Psalm 23, and two studies for his sculpture group 'The family' to go with the first chapter of *Genesis*. Later, when I returned this drawing to Henry Moore, I asked rather nervously if I could buy it.

'Yes, of course,' he said, 'but wouldn't you rather have the small bronze maquette of the same subject?'

I gulped and said I doubted if I could afford it.

'I think we could let you have it fairly cheaply,' he said. 'Anyhow, you may not like it. Let's have some tea and I'll take you to see it.'

We had tea and we talked about his work and he told me about his love for Turner. After tea we took a taxi to the Berkeley Gallery which was run by a dear old man called Ohly. In a glass case there were four or five little bronzes.

'That's the one.' Henry Moore picked it up and handed it to me. 'I'll just have a word with Ohly.' This meant, I supposed that he was telling him make a special price for me. He did – most generously – and I bought it. That night I put it on the mantelpiece of my rather mean lodgings and felt that I had bought a stake in the future. I sat on the iron bed, looking at it with some satisfaction.

Graham Sutherland and John Piper were just as accommodating about their pictures. Edward Bawden, whom I had not seen since I was a student at Goldsmiths' agreed to do a drawing for *The Tempest* but jibbed at a passage I had chosen from *The Water Babies*.

'I have got an idea for a book on snails. Wouldn't one of those drawings do?' he asked.

I said I was sure it would. His sense of the macabre was shown in a drawing of a tomb, inscribed 'Here lies Lady Mary Anne', with a graceful statue of a young maiden and below wonderfully caparisoned snails climbing over her skull and scattered bones.

Drawing on various sources, I compiled a short text and was then faced with the design of the cover and the jacket. Wandering round Ipswich one day, I found in a junk shop an old map of Suffolk. This gave me the bones of an idea. I measured it. It was the exact proportions of the cover of the book. Apart from the fact that Ipswich was in Suffolk and Cowells was in Ipswich, this did not have much bearing on printing. How to combine printing with the John Speede's Suffolk map, came to me in the middle of the night. I think I must have dreamed it. I would place a composing stick across the map, with the title set up in the stick. With careful lighting, the shadow from the stick could point at Ipswich. It worked and we printed it in full colour on the cloth cover and with a reduced number of colours on the jacket. The book was almost complete when Geoffrey Smith sent for me.

'I've been talking to Noel Carrington about your type book. He approves of your choice of artists, but thinks you ought to have something by Barnett Freedman as he is a lithographer, in fact, so Noel says, the best lithographer now working. Do you know him?'

I said I did not, but that I knew his work.

'You'd better go and see him – here's his address. While you're about it, you'd better go and see Stanley Morison as well. He's the great authority on types. He was kind enough to say you could call on him.'

Barnett Freedman lived in a flat in Canning Place in South Kensington. He invited me into his immaculately tidy studio. On his drawing desk his pens and pencils were lined up as if they were on parade. Barnett was a stocky, short-legged figure with a massive head. His face was fleshy, his eyes small and twinkling behind the thick lenses of his steel-rimmed glasses. He spoke with a marked East End accent.

'What's all this about doing a lithograph for some type book?' he asked in a severe voice.

'Geoffrey Smith said you might be willing to do one.'

'Yes! I'll do one but you tell Geoffrey Smith his offering me twelve guineas is an insult. I'd rather do it for nothing.' I said I would pass on his message.

'I shouldn't be surprised if he didn't accept my offer!' Barnett said with a grin. 'Now, you tell me about yourself. When I heard about you, I guessed you were some sort of playboy, dabbling in print. How much do you know about printing and typography?'

'Painfully little.'

'Have you got a set of *Signatures*?'

'No, what are they?'

'What's *Signatures*! Oh, tut, tut! You've got a lot to learn. You must get them, they are a veritable bible for typographers. I'll just ring up Stanley Smith, he's a bookseller I know, and I think he's got a set.' He turned to the telephone, checked the number from a list on the wall and dialled. 'Hullo, is that the Beauchamp Bookshop? Is that you Stanley? It's me, Barnett. Yers, I'm orl right. Stanley, have you got a set of *Signatures*? . . . I thought you had. How much? . . . . . . That's a bit steep . . . . . . Yers, knock off a fiver. I've got a young friend who wants a set. I'll send him round. His name is Lewis – John Lewis.'

That was typical of the man and was the first of many kindnesses he did me over the years. Barnett was one of the most life-enhancing people I have ever met. He had been born in Stepney, the child of poor Russian-Jewish parents. As a child he suffered a long and crippling illness. When he was well enough and old enough, he worked first for a monumental stone mason and then in an architect's office. Failing to get a scholarship to the Royal College Art, with dogged pertinacity, he managed to get an interview with Sir William Rothenstein, who was so impressed by this red-headed Jewish boy, that he persuaded the LCC to give Barnett a grant so that he could go to the College.

Barnett told me all this on that first morning and also of his struggle after leaving the College.

'I never actually starved, though I jolly nearly did,' he said as he saw me out of the front door. 'I'll do your lithograph – I think I'll do a subject from Burton's *The Anatomy of Melancholy*. Ever read that?'

I said I hadn't.

'I'll have to take you in hand – you need educating!'

I went round to the Beauchamp Bookshop and bought the set of *Signatures*. Oliver Simon's magazine was an inspiration. There was clearly more to typography than the study of ems and ens and letter-forms. From the Beauchamp Bookshop I made my way to Whitehall Court, where Stanley Morison had an apartment.

Morison was an austere man. He might well have been a Jesuit. That afternoon I nervously told him what I was trying to do with my type book.

At length he said, 'Go ahead! I expect the book will be full of mistakes and it will cost your firm a lot of money, but there is just a chance that by doing something like this, you will learn your job.'

After that he talked at length about himself and how he had worked for Francis Meynell (and had never forgiven him for being his boss!). As I was going, he said, 'One thing more, if you want to be a typographer, go away and read logic.'

Considering the limitations of such paper as was available in 1947, *A Handbook of Printing Types* was well printed and had a very friendly reception from the trade and elsewhere. Geoffrey Smith scattered copies in all directions. One went to John Hayward, a wheelchair-bound scholar friend of T.S. Eliot and the first editor of *The Book Collector*. He returned his copy without comment, but with fifty-seven proof corrections; he had also marked a couple of howlers. I hung my head in shame as Geoffrey went through the corrections. All he said was: 'How good of him to take all that trouble. We can make the corrections for the second edition.'

Within a few months a revised and enlarged edition was printed. It was an improvement on the first attempt. With that slight, imperfect little book as a starting point, the pattern of my future was fashioned.

Eric Hanson had provided us with somewhere to live. It was a flat in a tall Edwardian house overlooking Christchurch Park. We had the first floor. The rooms were large and light and it suited us well. In the mornings and evenings, I could walk through the Park to work and back. The rent, cheap though it was, was something over a third of my salary. During the first winter we were there, there was a heavy fall of snow that did not thaw for a fortnight. Each morning, to the surprise of the local inhabitants, I skied down through the Park to my work. Eric Hanson saw me arriving one morning, which did much to confirm his doubts about my suitability for a life in the printing trade.

The first difficult design job I had to handle at Cowells was an engineering catalogue. It was quite beyond my abilities, so I turned to a young designer called Stuart Rose[3] for help. I had met Stuart through Geoffrey Smith. There had been some question of his taking on the job I now had, but for some reason or other he and Cowells had failed to reach an agreement. With no hesitation, he came into the studio and showed me just what a professional design job should be like.

It must have been quite soon after that, when one morning I was puzzling over a layout. By chance I picked up my fountain pen and started writing out the copy, almost unconsciously changing the weight and size of my writing as the sense dictated. As I finished writing, I saw that the design was virtually done. The scales fell from my eyes and I was filled with excitement. I had in my innocence discovered the key to the art of typographic design, which was to let the sense of the words dictate the form of the design. I imagined I was a fully fledged typographer. Nearly fifty years later, I would make no such claims.

The friendly terms I had reached with the composing room, then with Fred Fenner and his photo-artists, made bearable those early difficult months at Cowells. I took longer to get to know the machine minders, though Mr Patrick, the litho room overseer was a kind and helpful man. Mr Hall the letterpress room overseer was a little tartar and it took him about five years to tolerate my presence near his machines. When at length it dawned on him that I, as a designer, just as much as he and his staff, was part of the production line, he relented slightly. Apart from the composing room, the bindery was the department I most enjoyed visiting. It was run by an old bald-headed man called Mr Steele. He was a real craftsman and had served his time with Sangorski and Sutcliffe in London. He ruled over a large room, mainly staffed by girls who did all the forwarding work. The finishing was done by men.

In those early days at Cowells a thing that worried me was the demarcation between works and office. That a skilled machine minder or compositor should rate lower in the hierarchy than an order clerk seemed absurd. I tried to move my studio-office into the works, so that it could be nearer the craftsmen who did the job, but was told it would not do.

Design jobs began to flow in from London office. It was clear that I needed more help than little Ireen could provide, so with Geoffrey Smith's agreement, I advertised for 'an experienced print designer' – the term 'graphic designer' was not then in common use. We interviewed a dozen or so applicants varying from ex-comps to skilled commercial artists. The last one we saw was a neat dark-haired man with twinkling brown eyes. His name was John Brinkley and he had just come out of the army. Like me, he had been a sapper, first in Army Survey and latterly running a newspaper in Germany. It did not take me long to make up my mind. When I saw the few beautifully drawn pieces of lettering that he had brought, I realized how lucky I would be to have him working with me. He had all the skills of hand that I lacked, but he knew no more about typography than I did – so we would learn together. After Cowells had confirmed his appointment, he stayed the weekend with us. When he had gone I asked Griselda what she thought of him.

'I don't really know,' she said. 'I've got some reservations. He reminds me of some French film actor. He always seems to be playing a part. I'm not sure of him.'

At the time, I thought she had got him all wrong. In fact, as I found out later, the whole of his life was played like a charade.

Each morning when we met, we shook hands and exchanged greetings in French. Whether he spoke French any better than I did, I never discovered. He was a neat dresser and out of doors always wore a small green Homburg hat or a check cap. He was quite a different man at home to the face he presented to the outside world. Yet that was not his true image either. When I first visited him at home, he reminded me of Wemmick, Mr Jaggers' clerk in *Great Expectations*, who changed his personality as he lowered the drawbridge to enter his home at

Walworth. He was a chameleon, taking his colour and his tone from whoever he was with.

When John Brinkley and I started working at Cowells, our knowledge of typography really was very slight. Apart from the help I had from Robert Harling and from Stuart Rose for that engineering catalogue, the first time either of us saw a typographic layout done by someone who knew what he was doing, was when Penguin Books sent into Cowells some layouts by Ruari McLean.[4] I forget what the book was; what I do remember is the effect these beautifully marked-up layouts had on us. They became a yardstick and we both started to emulate Ruari's elegant chancery script.

The first job we did together was a little book for Rolex Watches. I roughed out the idea and John took this a stage further, to what we used to call a finished rough. He could knock in a line of lettering very freely, so well spaced that from a short distance it looked as if it had been printed. For this particular rough, I did the drawings, but felt the book deserved a greater talent, so turned to Lynton Lamb for the finished work. When Larry Lamb saw my sketches, to my surprise he said, 'I can't think why you bothered to ask me.'

The studio was soon increased by the addition of an enormous boy called Jack, who we always referred to as 'the giant'. Ireen left, to be replaced by Annabel, a tall, slender sixteen-year-old girl of fawn-like beauty.

One of the crosses I had to bear was designing labels for Cowells' wine shop. The wine shop, which also had an off-licence and a men-only bar, was yet another facet of this many-sided printing house. This was the only direct contact I had with Eric Hanson, and some of our meetings were very abrasive. In fact, I was rather frightened of him. On one occasion Brinkley and I had done a couple of very pretty labels for rum and gin, for Cowells' own proprietary brands. The dominant feature of both labels was the word RUM or GIN.

'Those are no good,' Eric Hanson said rather brusquely.

'Why not?' I replied, instantly bristling.

'What do you think we are selling?' he shouted.

'Gin or rum, of course.'

'No, we are not! We're selling *Cowells'* Gin or Rum!'

'Do you really think anyone is going to buy gin or rum because it's Cowells',' I answered. 'They are buying it because it is all they can get!'

'If that's what you think, I don't think you and I are going to get along very well. Here, take this away and bring back some new designs next week . . .' Then rather sheepishly, 'I never told you what their names were.' He handed me two bits of paper with the words 'Yard-arm Rum' and 'Priory Gin' on them. While we had been shouting at each other, he must have thought up these proprietary names. Back I went across that awful open-plan office, with a flaming red face to start all over again.

In spite of an outwardly care-free disposition, I had real feelings of insecurity, to which Eric Hanson certainly contributed. Anything I could not face up to, I resolutely swept under the carpet. When things became too much, I used to retire to bed with all the symptoms of influenza. This habit dated back to my childhood. Nearly always, just before the end of term exams I used to run a high temperature and be packed off to the sanatorium. Over the years, how I enjoyed being ill, with trays of food and books to read, insulated against the harsh world, firstly by the loving care of a devoted mother, then by the pretty sanatorium sister at Charterhouse and lastly by Griselda.

During one of these bouts in bed, I had a letter from John Brinkley. It was headed: 'Atelier Brinkley, Much Binding in the Butter Market' and began:

> Cher Ami John
>   I am grieved to hear that you will not be with us for a few days; have you had the Free Doctor in yet with Prescription NHSSA/33. All is well here except GBS wishes to move us into the new building fairly quickly: have you any objection – I couldn't care less . . .
>   Van Krimpen came this morning and I talked to him also some other character.[5] Autrement, tout va bien M. le Marquis et je regrette votre absence énormement. Mais – il y a toujours la belle Annabel pour s'amuser . . .
>   Anything you require – dial 2276 and please ask.
>   Yours John x

At Cowells, John Brinkley began to move away from his background, but it was not until later, when he had become one of Robin Darwin's favourites at the Royal College of Art, that he really blossomed. He was a brilliant and highly inventive story teller, but I had doubts about his tales of successes with the various ladies at the College. Over the years I became devoted to him but never really punctured his armour.

Soon after that attack of 'flu or whatever it was, we moved out of our ex-ladies cloakroom into a room near the top of the new factory, a multi-storey building that had been designed in emulation of a block of flats in Bayswater that one of the managing directors had admired. The top floor, in hot weather, was more suitable for growing tomatoes than for a composing room. We were now 'on the works'. My remarks had not gone unheeded.

Cowells was on the crest of a wave and so we surfed along in their wake. By this time they were one of the best colour printers in England. The work ranged from catalogues for the Arts Council to leaflets, brochures and books for industry. The first Arts Council catalogue I designed was for an exhibition of *Drawings from the Bruce Ingram Collection.* I took immense trouble to get from Monotype some swash capitals to go with the italic Caslon. Looking at it now, I doubt if it was worth it.

Within a hundred yards of Cowells, there were two antiquarian book shops in which I used to spend most of my lunch hours. In one, run by an old man called Wilcox, I found a copy of Stower's *Printer's Grammar*, which, though published in 1808, still contained much information that was of value, for we were still, typographically speaking, in the age of letterpress and our typefaces were cast in metal. On another occasion I bought, for thirty shillings, a copy of the second edition of Somerville's *The Chase* with wood engravings by Bewick, printed by William Bulmer. I was entranced both by the engravings and the typography of this book. A little later I found a copy of *The Castle of Otranto* printed by Bodoni, which, in spite of what Horace Walpole had to say about it, is a lovely book. These two examples of neo-classical typography and a Baskerville Prayer Book became my yardstick and my inspiration. It was an unfashionable choice, at a time when taste on the one hand was led by Stanley Morison and his devotion to Jenson, Aldus and the other Italian and French founding fathers of the trade, and on the other hand by the post-Bauhaus typographers of Switzerland.

During one lunch break I wandered down Silent Street and called in at the other book shop. Mr Cook knew of my typographic interests. Like so many antiquarian booksellers he was a garrulous character, but for once his talk had some relevance to my needs.

'I've got something I would like to show you,' he said. 'It's an old album of press cuttings, letters and bits of printing, a lot of printer's marks and a Baskerville specimen page. I'll get it for you.'

I wondered what I was going to see and even more, if it was of any interest, how much he would want for it. It was some minutes before he returned, struggling with a huge elephant-size folio. He dropped it on the table. A cloud of dust enveloped us.

'Can't have been looked at for quite a while,' he said. 'It came from a sale of the Palgrave family effects – you know, the *Golden Treasury* Palgrave.' He opened the album and further clouds of dust rose up. It contained a collection of engraved title-pages, literally hundreds of printers' devices, pages of vellum manuscripts, proclamations, and playbills (one printed on silk), numerous 'For Sale' notices, some letters, a Papal Indulgence and the Baskerville Specimen sheet. This was loose, so I picked it up and looked at it carefully. It was a plain piece of printing, the type punched into the smooth wove paper as if it had been Braille. The presswork was immaculately crisp.

'How much?' I asked.

'Two pounds,' he replied.

'What, for the Baskerville sheet?'

'No, no, for the whole album,' he replied irascibly.

By the time I had finished looking at it, my lunch hour had long since expired. I paid my two pounds and hurried back to Cowells with this treasure under my arm. I did not do any more work that day, for I spent the whole afternoon looking at the album. Later I showed it to

A
SPECIMEN

By *JOHN BASKERVILLE* of *Birmingham.*

I·Am indebted to you for two Letters dated from Corcyra. You congratulate me in one of them on the Account you have Received, that I ſtill preſerve my former Authority in the Commonwealth: and wiſh me Joy in the other of my late Marriage. With reſpect to the Firſt,

I Am indebted to you for two Letters dated from Corcyra. You congratulate me in one of them on the Account you have Received, that I ſtill preſerve my former Authority in the Commonwealth: and wiſh me Joy in the other of my late Marriage. With reſpect to the firſt, if to mean well to the Intereſt of my Country and to

I Am indebted to you for two Letters dated from Corcyra. You congratulate me in one of them on the Account you have received, that I ſtill preſerve my former Authority in the Commonwealth: and wiſh me joy in the other of my late Marriage. With reſpect to the Firſt, if to mean well to the Intereſt of my Country and to approve that meaning to every Friend of its Liberties, may be conſider'd as maintaining

if to mean well to the Intereſt of my Country and to approve that meaning to every Friend of its Liberties, may be conſider'd as maintaining my Authority; the Account you have heard is certainly true. But if it conſiſts in rendering thoſe Sentiments effectual to the Public Welfare or at leaſt in daring freely to Support and inforce them;

approve that meaning to every Friend of its Liberties, may be conſider'd as maintaining my Authority; the Account you have heard is certainly true. But if it conſiſts in rendering thoſe Sentiments effectual to the Public Welfare or at leaſt in daring freely to Support and inforce them; alas! my Friend I have not the leaſt ſha-

my Authority; the Account you have heard is certainly true. But if it conſiſts in rendering thoſe Sentiments effectual to the Public Welfare or at leaſt in daring freely to Support and inforce them; alas! my Friend I have not the leaſt ſhadow of Authority remaining. The Truth of it is, it will be ſufficient Honor if I can have ſo much Authority over myſelf as to bear with patience our preſent and impending Calamities: a frame of Mind not to be acquired without difficulty,

Q. HORATII FLACCI

Hac ego ſi compellar imago, cuncta reſigno.
Nec ſomnum plebis laudo ſatur altilium; nec
Otia divitiis Arabum liberrima muto.
Sæpe verecundum laudaſti: rexque, paterque
Audiſti coram, nec verbo parcius abſens
Inſpice ſi poſſum donata reponere lætus.
Haud male Telemachus proles patientis Ulyſſei;
Non eſt aptus equis Ithacæ locus, ut neque planis
Porrectus ſpatiis, neque multæ prodigus herbæ:
Atride, magis apta tibi tua dona relinquam.
Parvum parva decent. mihi jam non regia Roma,
Sed vacuum Tibur placet, aut imbelle Tarentum.
Strenuus et fortis, cauſiſque Philippus agendis

EPISTOLARUM LIBER I.

Clarus, ab officiis octavam circiter horam
Dum redit, atque foro nimium diſtare Carinas
Jam grandis natu queritur; conſpexit, ut aiunt,
Adraſum quendam vacua tonſoris in umbra
Cultello proprios purgantem leniter ungues.
Demetri, (puer hic non læve juſſa Philippi (quis,
Accipiebat) abi, quære, et refer; unde domo,
Cujus fortunæ, quo ſit patre, quove patrono.
It, redit, et narrat, Vulteium nomine Menam
Præconem, tenui cenſu ſine crimine notum,
Et properare loco, et ceſſare, et quærere, et uti
Gaudentem parviſque ſodalibus, et lare certo,
Et ludis, et poſt deciſa negotia, Campo.

Baskerville specimen page 1757.

114

Mr Steele, the book binding foreman.

'How can I clean all this up?' I asked him.

'Throw it in the bath,' was his prompt reply.

'Won't that hurt it?'

'Of course not, except for the vellum sheets and the letters. You'll find the printed pages will float off this awful old brown paper. Then I'll show you how to clean and re-size them.'

As I found out, good rag paper and printing ink are practically indestructible, providing you keep them away from fire. This was proved in the flood disasters in Florence when the books of the Laurentiana were submerged in water, mud and oil. Roger Powell and Peter Waters (the Royal College of Art book binders), who were responsible for much of the salvage work there, said that most of the books, after they had been cleaned, re-sized and re-bound, were in better shape than they had been for centuries.

The next stage for me was to try to identify each piece of print. An introduction from Stanley Morison to A.F. Johnson at the British Museum was the beginning of my education in the history of printing. A.F. Johnson was a little gnome of a man, round-shouldered from a lifetime spent peering into old books. The first thing he did was to identify one of the items from my album. It was the Indulgence which, he told me, had been printed by Thierry Martens of Antwerp in 1497; he then provided me with a list of source books and finally he opened up for me the British Museum collections of printed ephemera, particularly that of John Bagford, who in the early years of the eighteenth century had made a huge collection of such trivia.

'He started his collection with the idea of writing a history of printing,' Mr Johnson said. 'He never achieved his goal. I doubt if he ever could have done so. He was no scholar – quite an uneducated fellow. I think he was a shoemaker!'

This observation sowed a little seed in my mind which ultimately led to the production of my book *Printed Ephemera*.

I discovered that the Palgrave album had been compiled by Dr Lodge in about 1820. Dr Lodge was the University Librarian at Cambridge, and a Fellow of Magdalene. Far from despoiling fine books to make this collection, the likely fact is that these pieces of paper came from broken up or defective volumes, or even from inside the vellum or calf covered bindings, for in the first few centuries of printing, paste-board did not exist as a commodity in its own right. It took me over ten years to identify everything in the collection. It was certainly a delightful way of learning.

The job where I learnt my toughest lesson, at least about human relations, was a periodical for a famous chemical firm, which for obvious reasons had better be nameless. This firm was an enormous concern. By the time I came into the picture, they had decided that they might as well use up some of their taxable profits by producing a journal for the medical profession. The idea was that it was to be a highly informative, sober production, without a hint of advertising, apart from the fact that the name of the firm was to be splashed across the cover.

The first I heard of all this was when Reggie Watts summoned me to a meeting at his London Office. I arrived a few minutes before the appointed time. Mr Watts was sitting by himself.

'I'm glad you got here a little early,' he said. 'This is a portentous occasion. This firm is one of our most valuable clients. Their trade, as you must know, used to be fertilizers – but they do other and more profitable things nowadays, including the manufacture of drugs. They were first in the field with hallucinatory drugs – I believe discovered by accident as a by-product from some kind of artificial manure. At least that is what I have been told.' He paused, wiped his nose and said, 'They want to make a real dent in the medical supplies business. To that end – among various other approaches – they propose to publish a magazine – a kind of popular *British Medical Journal*. They, in their wisdom, have decided to call it *Panacea*. It is going to be up to us to suggest the physical form it shall take.' There was a sound of voices. 'This must be them,' he said. The door opened and three strange looking men were shown in. They were an unpromising trio. Watts formally introduced them: 'Mr Whitlow, the firm's advertising manager, Mr Cleary, the editor-to-be of this project I have told you about and Mr er . . .'

'Doolan, Pat Doolan,' the third man interjected in a heavy Irish accent.

'Mr Doolan is our art director, no doubt he will be able to help you over the artistic side of *Panacea*,' Mr Whitlow explained.

'Merely advisory,' cut in Mr Cleary, who appeared to be jealous of his domain. 'We want Cowells to design it,' he said, looking at me.

Mr Doolan looked at the ceiling.

Whitlow seemed a bit out of his depth as he turned to Cleary and said, 'Er – Mr Cleary, perhaps you'll act as spokesman and tell our friends what we are planning to do.'

Cleary, a twisted little man, needed no further encouragement. I heard Doolan mutter something. It sounded like 'We shan't be home 'till morning.'

First, with no possible reference to the matter in hand, Cleary delivered a homily on the importance of his work, and the heavy scientific responsibility of handling such copy as would be coming his way. He talked like a member of the Royal Society. In fact as I learnt afterwards, he had learnt his trade as a police court reporter on the *Kentish Messenger*.

The main drift of his argument was that no sordid advertising tricks would be allowed within the sanctified covers of *Panacea*. Cleary cleared his throat, expectorated into a paper handkerchief and continued,

'The aims are to be lofty and noble. *Panacea* will never pander to public taste, but yet must be understandable to the most obtuse of NHS general practitioners. What is more, it is to have a world wide circulation – that is outside the Iron Curtain.'

'That shouldn't be difficult as we plan to give it away,' Doolan interposed.

'Finally,' Cleary continued, ignoring this sally, 'it must be designed with impeccable taste.'

'Whose taste?' I wondered.

While Cleary was rambling away, Doolan had been fiddling with the ties of a portfolio. As Cleary once again cleared his throat in the most disagreeable manner (he was a man with unpleasant personal habits) Doolan leaped up from his chair and opened his portfolio.

'I have taken the opportunity of preparing a dummy of what I think this magazine should look like.'

This was clearly a surprise turn. Whitlow looked bemused, Cleary horrified. Mr Doolan's idea of what this impeccably designed periodical should look like was a cross between the Book of Kells and a Christmas supplement to one of the popular magazines. We were all struck dumb as Doolan, like some street trader pushing a difficult line, revealed his horrible offering. It was Mr Watts who brought this performance to an end by very tactfully explaining that this was a job for a typographer, not for an artist however talented he might be. He bowed courteously to Mr Doolan. Doolan's hopes of glory vanished. Cleary again hurriedly explained that Mr Doolan's position was only advisory and he would be more than happy to leave such matters to us. Doolan looked as if he would like to dump Mr Cleary in the Liffey.

Inspired by this flood of words, I took my courage in both hands and began to expound my ideas about the magazine, its format and the kind of layout it should have and the process by which it should be printed. I was on the point of saying, 'This is obviously a letterpress job,' when Mr Watts neatly cut me out with, 'Process – only offset lithography will do justice to a periodical of this nature.'

I was about to argue this point, when I caught his eye and held my peace. I concluded Cowells must have told him they were short of offset work or that some of their ageing letterpress machines had broken down. The meeting ended with my being given the responsibility for producing a specification and mock-up based on their somewhat woolly brief.

With no material to play with, I started work, using copy from *The Lancet* for the trial text settings. I set the text in Baskerville (this was before the days of the sans serif Univers). The pages were proofed, printed and bound up into a dummy. Into this I stuck suitable photographs.

The wily Mr Watts arranged for me to take the dummy down to the customer. I was expecting to see Mr Cleary, the editor, but to my surprise found Doolan waiting for me. Somehow or other he had climbed back into the picture.

I nervously unpacked my little offering. Doolan leered at me. Encouraged by this, I passed over the dummy. He turned over the pages, taking care to crumple them in the process. He did not say much, except that the typography was very conservative. He was obviously looking for some excuse to denigrate the design. Looking at the cover, he said, 'Do you really think a typographic solution is worthy of this magazine?'

I said I did.

'Opinions could differ on that.'

Opinions did differ and I was persuaded to think again about the use of hand-lettering. After some thought, I asked Reynolds Stone, an engraver of great skill, to engrave the title. The result was very handsome. Doolan talked his colleagues into liking only part of it and substituted some rather characterful (I use his own word) hand drawn lettering for the main title-line. This was the first crack in the edifice. I should have stuck to my typographic guns. I did not, and I never caught up. However, the basic concept of the design was accepted and the material for the first number was collected.

At some stage or other, it had been suggested that each number should be enlivened with some examples of fine art – on the questionable assumption that doctors are great patrons of the arts. I suggested that they should commission a series of paintings of the East Anglian countryside, where the firm had its main factory, from John Nash, Edward Bawden, Cedric Morris and other East Anglian artists that I knew.

Doolan came to life at this suggestion, but put forward the idea that he should be commissioned to do these pictures. As his speciality in the world of art had been in painting sentimental Christmas cards of coaching scenes, I managed to get that one over-ruled. Doolan retired into the background to re-form for fresh wrecking procedures and someone else on *Panacea*'s board, who was known to have artistic taste, was delegated to choose the artists. His preference was limited to Mr Edward Seago and Sir Alfred Munnings.

Instead of having the copy set first and then ordering the reproduction of the pictures – a normal procedure in magazine production, Cleary wanted the pictures to go for reproduction at the same time as the text for setting. This brought in an element of chance. On this occasion, my casting-off was no worse than it should have been, but nothing fitted. Then I discovered that the editor, without reference to me and at the last moment, had added much additional copy. All the off-set plates had to be re-made. Relations were getting strained. Cowells started breathing down my neck. The editor's additions had bumped the cost of the job up far beyond the estimated price.

The first number came out. It looked dreadful. The design had been mangled, the text did not balance the pictures, the pictures did not fit the format and, as in the last stages, the job had to be rushed, it was not well printed. There were postmortems and recriminations. Somehow the blame seemed to be coming my way.

The second number was worse and everyone was at loggerheads. Then to my surprise Mr Whitlow asked me out to lunch at the Savoy Grill and gave me the best lunch I had ever had. When he had me properly softened up, he leaned forward and silkily suggested that I should take over the running of the entire job, controlling both their side and the printers. All this on a free-lance basis for a handsome fee – and, just when I thought the whole job was falling apart. Cowells, to my surprise, made no objection to this arrangement.

The third number was a disaster from start to finish. I did no less than four complete paste-ups, because of repeated editorial changes; the plates had to be re-made three times and the printer's bill was twice the original estimate. The firm would not pay. The printer produced the costings, they were all there plain enough. Suddenly both customer and printer turned on me, 'Hadn't I agreed to take responsibility . . . ?'

The implications of that lunch at the Savoy at last dawned on me. I could see ruin staring me in the face.

In fact in the end I did not have to pay, because it was obvious I could not and Cowells and the customer sorted it out between themselves. Of course I lost the job, but at least the customer had the grace to sack that inglorious trio. The printing of the magazine, oddly enough, remained with Cowells and a new editor was appointed and was told on pain of death never to alter the design in the slightest degree. Presumably because it had cost so much.

Many years later, I happened to be walking through the bindery at Cowells and came on a freshly bound pile of *Panaceas*. It looked exactly the same as it had done all those years ago. It had a certain period charm.

I still shudder when I remember that awful trio.

Apart from that horror story, there were a lot of other things going on at Cowells, including work from publishing houses. One of the first pieces of book design that we did for a commercial publisher was an edition of *The Forsyte Saga* for Heinemann. Anthony Gross had been commissioned to illustrate the book. The only reason I became involved in this was because James Champion had persuaded Heinemann to let Cowells print Gross's coloured illustrations by their new Plastocowell process.[6]

Tony Gross immediately saw the possibilities of the medium. The result was one of the finest pieces of book illustration since the last war, even if the text of the book was somewhat ill printed. In order that the line illustrations should fall in exactly the right places Griselda and I did a complete paste-up of the book, all 821 pages of it.

The happiest outcome of this was getting to know Tony Gross

Pen drawing by Anthony Gross for *The Forsyte Saga*. 'Jolyon and Irene in Paris', 1950.

himself. He was a slight, balding figure with a slim moustache. He could have been taken for a Frenchman, which was not surprising as he spent most of his life in France. The first time I had heard of him was when I was at Goldsmiths' and saw his cartoon film *La Joie de Vivre*. The fluidity of the cartoon line seemed to spill over into the Forsyte drawings. The frontispiece of *The Forsyte Saga* is a drawing of Irene in Montpelier Square. She seems to be moving across the page and almost walking into the book. We saw much of Tony Gross over the years and it was he who introduced us to the Lot, where he had a house.

Various other books followed this including *A Book of Beauty* for John Hadfield, the first of a successful series of anthologies that Cowells printed. John Hadfield, who was the first Director of the National Book League, had an absolute genius for producing books of this kind. Over the years we worked with him on various projects. My introduction to Studio Vista, which led to the production and editing of a series of art and design paperbacks was due to John Hadfield. We also shared an interest in cricket and in later years watched many a Test Match together on television.

2. Manningtree

GRISELDA AND I decided that if I was going to stay at Cowells, we might enjoy life more if we found a house outside Ipswich. We still had no car, though I was having a little boat built, so wherever it was, it had to be on a bus route to Ipswich and to be near the water. The railway line to London, about ten miles on the Colchester side of Ipswich, crosses two bridges that span the channels of the river Stour where it opens out into the estuary. The little town of Manningtree overlooks this wide river. It seemed worth investigating.

We took a bus to Manningtree on a cold, blustery day in late September. It is a town that is mainly eighteenth-century in character. In those days most of the houses looked in need of a coat of paint. We found one that was part of a reverse crescent, overlooking a triangular green. It needed more than a coat of paint. Every window in its tall, grey-bricked façade was boarded up. We wandered round to the back. In the wildly overgrown garden, a man in shirt sleeves was burning leaves. I asked him if the house was for sale and he told me it was.

'Go inside and have a look if you want to,' he said.

The house was virtually derelict; it looked forlorn beyond belief, yet it had a welcoming atmosphere. It was called 'Cumberland House' apparently after the 'Butcher' Duke of Cumberland.

We bought it for a song and found a local builder to do it up for us. It was far larger than we needed, so we decided to remove the whole of the top floor at the back, which needed re-roofing anyway. We planned a flat roof with a parapet, topped with a stone coping. Also, because of the difficulties in obtaining building permits in those early post-war years of austerity, we found that if we turned the house into two flats, we could spend double the permitted amount on it. So this is just what we did, letting off the ground floor and living in the rest. Will Carter[1] cut a handsome name plate in slate and fixed it onto one of the brick pillars that supported the gate.

We moved into Cumberland House in April 1947. To begin with we camped in one of the attics whilst the builder finished off the rest of the house. The electrician, an emaciated young man, who answered to the name of 'Slim' suggested his mother-in-law would come and 'do' for us, that is, if we wanted any help. We did.

Flossie arrived that evening. She was in no way emaciated. She was a fresh-faced buxom woman and all seventeen stone of her radiated good will. Our furniture blinded us with its scintillating surfaces as the result of her polishing. The house resounded to her laughter as she told one Rabelaisian anecdote after another – or maybe Chaucerian would be a better term. Her turns of phrase were worthy of the Wife of Bath. When one of our neighbours' daughters was getting married, Flossie, who thought little of the young man burst out with: 'I wouldn't have him, even if his arse was stuffed with diamonds.'

As a girl, Flossie had been in service in a very grand house in London. She loved to recall those, to her, happy and exciting days. The

Cumberland House, wood engraving, by David Gentleman.

great moment of the year apparently was when the entire household departed for the Scottish grouse moors.

'Coo!' she would say, 'what times we had, and what didn't we get up to!' With that she would bury her face in her apron, shaking the house to the foundations with her laughter.

From our attic windows we could look over the roofs of Manningtree right down the river to Stutton Ness. When after a few years our first tenants moved out, we let the ground floor again, but this time to Blair Hughes-Stanton. His second marriage had broken up and he needed somewhere to live. It was not long before a third wife arrived. Her name was Annie Ross and she had once been a student of Blair's. She was Australian, with a lovely Australian sense of humour.

We continued to sleep in our attic room. At night, the British Xylonite factory, ablaze with lights, on the Brantham shore looked like a stranded liner. Periodically the hum of the turbines would be overlaid by the call of redshank or curlew, or at first light by the wing beats of a skein of swans flying over the house.

Cumberland House was haunted by a benign ghost. Various people had seen him, and none had been in the least frightened. On the other hand our two cats, a Suffolk cream called Gaily, who came from Cedric Morris and a long-haired tabby called Bolivar from the Hughes-Stantons, could not bear him. Ridge-backed, they spat fury at this usually invisible presence. The first time I saw him, I had been into the sitting-room to fetch a book. As I walked along the landing, turning the pages, I thought Griselda was walking in front of me. I came into the kitchen to find her right across the room at the sink. She was looking over her shoulder.

'I thought you had just walked through into the other room,' she said. That at least was a cross-bearing.

Every morning I took the 8 o'clock bus to Ipswich. My companion on these journeys was called Wilf. He was then a solicitor's clerk, but his interest in life centred on boats. The journey through leafy Suffolk lanes past the Naval School at Holbrook and down along the river Orwell at Freston never seemed to take long as we discussed our ideas for improbable and ideal craft.

The little boat which had been built for me was too small and tender for coastal cruising. After nearly drowning Griselda off Landguard Point, I sold the boat at the end of the season. The idea of being

The ruins of Mistley Thorn church, 1947.

without a boat seemed intolerable, but I had not much money to play with. It was the Porter family who set me on to the idea of lifeboat conversion. Dod Porter was our sweep, but he was also a longshoreman, a wild fowler, an expert marksman and a former professional yacht hand. On an autumnal afternoon, down on the foreshore at Manningtree, he suggested to me that his nephew Bill, who was 'just out of the Navy', might do a conversion for me.

In due course, I bought from a depot for the disposal of small craft, a 26 ft lifeboat, licensed to carry forty shipwrecked persons. Over the next two years, working under a tarpaulin shelter down on the marshes near Mistley Towers, Bill Porter, with a little help from me, turned this unpromising craft into a handsome ketch. I kept a day-by-day diary of the work on this conversion, which by the time she was ready for launching, had become the basis for a book. Bill's charges were 2/4d an hour, though on one occasion he deducted a day's wages from his account.

'What's this for?' I asked.

'Oh! I wasted a day trying to plan how to put that beam in,' he said. 'I can't charge you for thinking!'

I called the lifeboat *Grace Darling* after the Longstones lighthouse keeper's daughter. She sailed quite well, within about five points of the wind, and in her we discovered the joys of cruising. Our normal weekend sail was down to the Walton Backwaters, and for a time we kept the boat at Landermere, a little hamlet at the head of Hamford Water where John Hutton and Basil Spence had cottages.

I completed the draft of the book, calling it *Small Boat Conversion*. It was accepted by Edward Young[2] at Rupert Hart-Davis. He gave Richard Garnett the job of copy-editing it. This was Richard's first job. He questioned the meaning of every sentence I had written. I learnt more about the craft of writing from him than from any other editor I have ever had.

The conversion book sold well. In due course we also sold the lifeboat and on the proceeds of that and the royalties from the book, we had our first proper little yacht built.

The vicissitudes of this boat which was called *Cormorant*, have been told elsewhere,[3] but we had a lot of fun out of her. Anna Hadfield became a regular member of our crew. John, her husband, as a result of being torpedoed and spending some days in an open boat in the north Atlantic, had somewhat jaundiced views about sailing. Anna was a McMullen (a hallowed name in sailing circles[4]) and had spent her childhood summers at West Mersea, crewing for her father. Her father's sister had married Andrew Mellon. Paul Mellon was her first cousin.

Most weekends that Anna was with us, we sailed away from Manningtree on the ebb tide and after rounding Harwich breakwater, we used to bear away across Dovercourt Bay and pick up the flood into Hamford Water. We had a very special anchorage, in a landlocked lagoon, just off the end of Landermere Creek. It was called the 'Bustway', because it had been caused by a break in the sea wall.

Leaving *Cormorant* in our protected anchorage, we would sail up to Landermere in our dinghy, to visit the Spences or the Huttons and later on the Paolozzis. Basil Spence's first sailing boat was a little Shetland 'Foureen', with a sharp bow, sheathed in brass. On one particularly gusty afternoon, he was caught by a squall and careered straight into *Cormorant*, splitting one of her topside planks. He was overcome by the enormity of his crime. Later as we were having supper with them, he explained to his wife Joan, what had happened. 'I fear I gave their boat a sore dunt. I didn't think such a wee boat as mine could have done so much damage.'

The return to my job at the end of each weekend was no great penance. Working with John Brinkley was a constant delight. His wit and humour – and we laughed a lot – helped to preserve our sanity. Working in that little studio with Annabel to keep us happy, we never took anything very seriously, yet somehow we began to build up a reputation as designers. This was very much linked with Cowells' skills as colour printers.

John Brinkley shared with Griselda and me a passion for the works of Charles Dickens. In the studio at Cowells our conversation as often as not, was about Uncle Pumblechook or Trabb's boy, or Captain Cuttle and Mrs McStinger. The days never seemed too long. John Brinkley was happy doing what he did so superlatively. He was a very fine craftsman. I was equally happy, for I felt at last that I was learning a trade.

Very soon after I had met Robert Harling at Cowells, we asked him and Phoebe his wife, to lunch in the Ipswich flat. As soon as he saw our Hepplewhite chairs, he darted across the sitting room and plonked himself down in one. I watched, with my heart in my mouth, as he lolled back, running his hands over the fragile and rather wobbly arms.

Before we were half way through lunch, he had organized us into writing articles for him. Seeing our quite small collection of pottery, he persuaded Griselda to write *An Introduction to English Pottery* for Art and Technics, the publishing firm that he had started with James Shand of the Shenval Press. It was not long before I was writing articles for his new magazine *Alphabet and Image* about artists I knew, such as Lamb and Hughes-Stanton and also on ones I had not yet met, like John Minton.

Griselda's little book for Art and Technics was the forerunner of a series of books on the history of English pottery. The first of these was *A Picture History of English Pottery*, published by the Hulton Press in 1956. This was commissioned by John Hadfield. It was followed by the first edition of her *A Collector's History of English Pottery*, which Studio Vista published in 1969. This ran through four editions and three publishers, finally being published by the Antique Collectors' Club in a much enlarged format, the last printing being in 1992.

We saw more of the Nash's than anyone else. Since we first met John Nash during the war he had moved from the Chilterns to a remote farmhouse in the Stour valley. I had not been in Ipswich for more than a couple of weeks when I heard from him. He invited us to lunch the following Sunday. I explained that Griselda was visiting her parents and that I had no car, for we had sold the Austin 7.

'Don't worry,' he said, 'one of us will pick you up at Colchester station. Bring gum boots.'

That night it started to snow. By the weekend it was lying thickly in the fields. Christine Nash met me at Colchester. She was grey haired and wearing spectacles but had the figure of a young girl. On the drive out to Wormingford we talked of mutual friends. I was amused by the sharpness of some of her comments.

'I'm afraid we shall have to walk from here,' Christine said as she stopped the car by a five-barred gate with the words 'Bottengoms Farm' on it. The track down to Bottengoms led for half a mile between deep embankments. The snow had drifted in places to five or six feet deep and a bitter north-east wind was cutting through our clothes.

The old house had no electricity and the only source of water was a stream that ran through the kitchen in an open culvert. The temperature in that room was sub-zero.

John Nash gave me a warm welcome, saying, 'Come by the fire, my dear fellow.'

I studied his face as he poured me a glass of sherry. He had looked younger in khaki. Now he looked thinner, his eyes more heavily lidded.

He had just poured out our drinks when we were joined by a good-looking, solidly-built young man. John Nash looked up and with a wintry smile said, 'This is the Hog, trust him to come in if there is anything going in the way of food or drink.'

The Hog's real name was John Langston and he had been practically a part of the Nash household since before the war. He had been a school master at Brighton College, but in 1941 gave it up to take some government job. He was a diabetic and as we learned over the years, he played fast and loose with his disease, as he did with his friends' wives! As a result of his disease, he finally went blind. He made little of his disability and with the help of a Golden Retriever called Cinders, every day he would walk from the Ministry of Information over Waterloo Bridge to the Garrick Club.

He would just say 'Come on Cinders, the Garrick,' and she would take him there. On that day at the Nash's he confined his attention to food and drink.

It had been a sunny morning and the glare off the snow was quite blinding. As we were finishing lunch, the sky clouded over, John Nash looked out of the window and then said, 'You must excuse me. Now the sun has gone in there is just a chance of doing a quick painting. I can't bear all that bright light and blue shadows, it kills the colours. Snow art is good for Biz!' he concluded with relish, as he went out into the freezing cold with his sketch book.

John Nash introduced us to various people, including the Cranbrooks and the painter Cedric Morris. Cedric had inherited a baronetcy from an uncle. He came from Sketty, near Swansea and may well have been a distant connection of my mother's, whose maiden name was also Morris. In Wales it is difficult not to be related to people, and in that rather less class-conscious society, they can be in almost any walk of life. Cedric had been at Charterhouse, but many years before me.

Cedric lived with his friend Lett Haines near Hadleigh in a tall, rambling old farmhouse called Benton End. There they ran a school of painting for practising artists and usually with a sprinkling of spinster school teachers. Cedric delighted in shocking them by telling improper Welsh stories, and not only Welsh stories. On one of our visits to Benton End we were discussing a Suffolk eccentric who lived nearby, where every summer he ran a local festival.

'Keeps his ballet dancers locked up in the attic,' Cedric said. 'Just lets them out each summer. Every year their elbows get sharper and their knees more knobbly.'

'Did you hear', someone said, 'that the poor old fellow had been run in for accosting two respectable maiden ladies at 2.0 a.m. in Dover Street? He'd been to the Chelsea Arts Ball dressed only in chains and two small pieces of leather.'

'I wouldn't mind betting he was wearing them as blinkers,' Cedric replied. Cedric's pride was his garden, his speciality the cultivation of the iris. As a painter of flowers (and vegetables) he was unique. He had achieved by the 1930s a *succès d'estime*, but had quarrelled with the London galleries and retired to Suffolk, where he continued to paint, but rarely to exhibit.

Cedric's painting, apart from his success in the 1930s had its first public recognition when a retrospective of his work was held at the National Museum of Wales, Cardiff in 1968. Cedric's work stood up proudly against the superb collection of French Impressionists in the next gallery. Metropolitan recognition came with the exhibition of his work at the Tate Gallery in 1984, sadly too late for him to see, for he had died in 1982.

Though Cedric Morris lacked general recognition, he had a devoted circle of friends, who thought the world of him and his work. There can be no question about it, he was a very original, perhaps great painter. His influences on such artists as Christopher Wood have never been fully acknowledged.

Cedric and I were both born on 11 December. One year while we were still living at Manningtree, Cedric and Lett came over for a birthday dinner. It was a joyous evening. Cedric presented me with a black Jackfield pottery cow with 'A Present from Llandilo' painted on it in gold. He was very proud of being Welsh.

Cedric and Lett made a curious couple. Cedric, lean and handsome, with a mop of wavy hair, dressed in old corduroys, a check shirt and with a coloured handkerchief tied carelessly round his neck, looked as if he was starring in a Western. Lett was in some contrast. As often as not at Benton End he was dressed as the chef he was, in striped apron, his large, full face surmounted by a great bald head, beaming like a contented eunuch. Whatever time of day one arrived there, they always made one welcome.

It was quite soon after visiting the Nash's that I went over to Sandon, a village near Chelmsford, to spend a weekend with the Lambs. Larry was a parson's son and Biddy, his wife, a parson's daughter. It was not surprising that their house had something of the vicarage about it.

'I see you took my advice about going into print,' Larry said with his curious chuckle. 'I hope you won't regret it.'

That night we talked long and late about design and printing. Larry told me about his own career. He had studied at the Central under Meninski and Noel Rooke. In the early 1930s he had joined the Oxford University Press while Humphrey Milford was still publisher.

'I have enjoyed the Press much more since Jock Cumberlege succeeded Milford,' he said. 'Jock is a man of sensibility and has a tremendous sense of fun. Milford was a tuft-hunter.'

As we were going up to bed, Larry turned to me and said, 'Being a typographic designer means occupying a shadowy post. You are always playing second fiddle to authors and illustrators, publishers and printers, yet there is something satisfying about it.'

I continued to see much of Larry. He took me to my first Double Crown Club dinner and lunched me at the Reform Club, where he was as much at home as he was on the village green at Sandon (for many years he played for the Sandon Cricket Club). As a man, Larry Lamb

Drawing by Lynton Lamb for *The Story of Rolex*.

129

was urbane and charming. He looked like a retired cavalry officer and had an infectious, bubbling laugh, like a cork being withdrawn from a bottle. I learnt much from him. He was the kind of person who made one feel better for being in his company.

In September 1947 the piece that I had written about Lamb appeared in *Alphabet and Image*. Harling, who could never leave well alone had switched my text round so that the article began: 'I should say that Lamb was a slow starter . . .' and he had finished off my article with a quotation from Emerson which I had always thought was by John Donne. In spite of that Larry and I remained friends.

I knew little about the Double Crown Club when Larry invited me to be his guest at Kettner's. It was the 94th dinner. The club had been founded in 1924 by Oliver Simon 'for the exchange of ideas on good printing'.

I was elected to the Double Crown Club a couple of years after my first visit, with Larry as my proposer. Over the years the fortunes of the club waxed and waned. Some excellent (and some not so excellent) papers were read. My own contribution, 'Trial by Teaching' was summed up by John Dreyfus, that year's President, as 'broad rather than deep'. In 1969 I was due to become Vice-President, when Charles Ede (the founder of the Folio Society), the President-Elect suddenly withdrew. So, without warning, I became President. The year was notable for nothing except a witty talk by Richard Usborne on misprints, and a good summer's dinner with especially fine wine at the Apothecaries' Hall.

The Club continues, its dinners no longer held in the familiar if slightly frumpish atmosphere of Kettner's Restaurant but within the pretentious décor of the re-built Arts Club.

3. Painters and Musicians

In July of 1948 Geoffrey Smith went over to France with Brenda Rawnsley and Raglan Squire, who between them ran a little publishing concern called School Prints. The object of this outing was to try to persuade four or five of the most famous of the modern painters of the school of Paris to co-operate in a series of pictures for children. The reason Mrs Rawnsley and Squire were taking Geoffrey with them was because of Plastocowell, the new autographic process that Cowells had pioneered and that Tony Gross later used so well for his *Forsyte Saga* illustrations. Squire had been at my prep school and was the son of J.C. Squire, the editor of the *London Mercury*, who when I was at Bigshot took me out to tea with his two sons.

Brenda Rawnsley must have been a very persuasive lady, for by the end of August, Braque, Léger, Matisse and Dufy had all completed lithographs for her. Picasso was the only one from whom they had heard nothing. This is where we came into the picture. Griselda and I had planned to have our first post-war holiday abroad. A small hotel called La Mirasole at Rocquebrune had been recommended to us by Marjorie Kerr. Geoffrey, on hearing where we were going, told us we could combine business with pleasure by calling on Picasso. 'Tell him we can't wait much longer,' he said. 'Edmund Kapp lives at Rocquebrune, he knows Picasso. Incidentally Kapp is called "Peter", he will tell you where to find him.'

I must have looked a bit doubtful, for he added, 'If you want an excuse, we have some long metal cylinders in which he can pack his rolled up drawings to send to us. You can take one with you.'

It was nearing the middle of September when we arrived at Rocquebrune, to find a message from Peter Kapp saying that he would call on us that evening. The Mirasole was run by a man named Lorenzi. It was a friendly little inn. Lorenzi's brother used to help in the kitchen. He was a convicted murderer and a mild and pleasant man. He had killed his wife while the Mistral was blowing, which in Provence is considered an understandable aberration.

Peter Kapp arrived with his sister Helen and they soon put our fears at rest.

'You'll find Picasso on the beach at Golfe Juan – he holds court there. Don't be put off by the crowd of people round him, just march up to him and say why you have come. The girl he lives with – Françoise Gillot – will be there. She's referred to as "Madame Françoise". She speaks better English than I do. Could you go and see him in a couple of days time?'

'Of course,' I said.

'I'll drop him a card to say you will both be on the beach at noon on Thursday.'

Thursday was a grilling hot day. We arrived at Golfe Juan soon after eleven o'clock and had a bathe. The sea was like hot coffee. After we had dried off, we went in search of Picasso. We found him sitting under a striped umbrella surrounded by such a bevy of brown-skinned young men and pretty girls that we got stage fright and walked past. When we had got our breath, I said to Griselda, 'This is too silly, here we are, and here is the *rouleau* for the drawings. The worst he can do is to say "Go away!" '

As we approached the group, a beautiful girl got up and walked towards us. 'You are Peter Kapp's friends from England,' she said. She took each of us by the arm and led us up to Picasso. She said something rapidly in French to him.

He scrambled to his feet and shook our hands and welcomed us most kindly. I stumbled hesitantly through a few sentences in French when Françoise came to my rescue and acted as interpreter. Griselda said something about her interest in his pottery. Picasso's eyes lit up. I told him that on Kapp's recommendation we were going on to Antibes to see his work.

'We will take you there, but first you will have lunch with us. Henri Laurens – you know, the sculptor – he and his family are joining us.'

I demurred, muttering 'trop gentil' and said surely we would be intruding on such a big party.

'Oh, them!' Picasso with a sweep of his arm dismissed the brown-skinned young people. 'They are mostly my nephews, but I don't have to feed them all!'

While we were waiting for the family Laurens, Picasso talked. He had a voice of a lighter timbre than I would have expected. He told us what an intolerable bore American visitors had been that summer. 'They come unannounced, sit themselves at my feet and expect me to entertain them as if I was a performing monkey!'

I apologised for our intrusion.

He grinned and brushed this aside, saying: 'Pas la même chose. Nous avons le même métier!'

I watched Françoise as she struggled into her dress. She was a very lovely girl, solidly built, full-breasted, firm-limbed and flat-thighed. Her long hair hung damply over her shoulders. At that time she was twenty-eight and Picasso was forty years older. Yet she seemed the older of the two.

'Before we lunch, I think I will have one more swim,' Picasso said. He entered the water and swam sedately out to a bathing raft, rested there for a moment and then swam back again. After he had dried himself

T HESE snails are called
LOVELIES because
they crawl over and caress
the bones of girls who have
died of love.

They live in tombs, mau-
soleums, and in catacombs.
Like Emperors, Kings and
Cardinals, the snails are

sumptuously clothed in rich colours, in Tyrian purple and Alizarine crimson and Monastral blue.
Search for them in burial places, and go armed with

'Caparisoned snails'. Drawing by Edward Bawden for *A Handbook of Printing Types*.

Stanley Morison and C. W. F. Nordlunder at All Souls', Oxford, 1959.

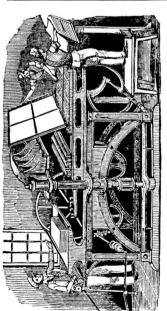

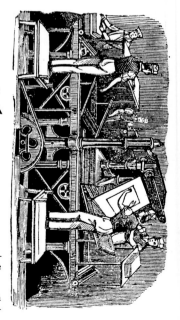

W. S. COWELL LIMITED

announce that

the publication date of

A
HANDBOOK
OF
PRINTING
TYPES

will be about

MAY 23rd, 1947

The Handbook will be obtainable
from the distributors
Messrs Faber and Faber Ltd London

W. S. COWELL LIMITED BUTTER MARKET IPSWICH AND 329 HIGH HOLBORN LONDON WC1

Advertisement for *A Handbook of Printing Types*.

Barnett
Freedman.
Portrait by
Robert Buhler.
The Tate Gallery.

Robert Harling
at Meadow
Cottage.

'Flossie'. *Photograph by Phillip Glasier.*

John Nash fishing. *Photograph by Kurt Hutton.*

Double Crown Dinner at All Souls', Oxford, 1957.

From left to right: Vivian Ridler, John Lewis, John O'Connor, Charles Pickering, David Bland, Lynton Lamb, Eliot Viney and Ellic Howe. To the right of near row, Stuart Rose talking to Will Carter.

Picasso and Françoise at Golfe
Juan, 1948.

Ruari McLean at the time he
was editing *Motif*
Photograph by John Hedgecoe.

Basil Spence by his Shetland boat at
Landermere.

Richard Guyatt.
Photograph by John Hedgecoe.

The Royal College of Art Painting School, 1950, by Rodrigo Moynihan. *The Tate Gallery.*

From left to right: John Minton, Colin Hayes, Carel Weight, Rodney Burn, Robert Buhler, Charles Mahoney, Kenneth Rowntree, Ruskin Spear (on couch) and Rodrigo Moynihan.

Robin Darwin,
by Richard
Guyatt.

23

Oak Timber.

TO BE SOLD

At the GLOBE, in NETHER STOWEY,

On WEDNESDAY the 19th, Day of APRIL Inftant,

BY FOUR O'CLOCK,

FORTY
Large Oak Trees,

LOT 1. No. 1 to 10, both inclufive.
  2. - 11 to 20, ditto.
  3, - 21 to 30, ditto.
  4. - 31 to 40, ditto.

THE TREES are in HOLFORD WOOD, near STOWEY, 3 Miles from COOMBWICH; 6 from WATCHET, and 12 from BRIDGWATER.

☞ JOHN WEBBER, of *Holford* aforefaid, will fhew the TIMBER.

Dated 12th, *April,* 1815.

PILE, PRINTER, NORTON.

To be SOLD, in Fee,
BY AUCTION,
AT THE
White Hart, in *Glastonbury,*
On Wednesday the 10th Day of January Inft.
By 4 o'Clock in the Afternoon,

In 1, 2, or 3 LOTS,
Two Gardens,

ADJOINING to, or near NORTH LOAD STREET, in *GLASTONBURY* aforesaid, late in the Possession of JOHN FRY REEVES, ESQR.

☞ MR. WILLIAM GODFREY, of NORTH LOAD STREET, or his SON, will shew the GARDENS; and Particulars may be known of MR. HANCOCK, of FORD, near *Wiveliscombe.*

Dated 2nd. JANUARY, 1827.

Piles: Book-sellers, Norton.

Two Guineas Bounty
In Addition to His MAJESTY*'s*
Will be given immediately by the
Corporation of BRIDGNORTH
To the Firft Fifteen *VOLUNTEERS,* who fhall
Enter with
LIEUTENANT WILL^M ROSS,
At his Rendezvous the *TUMBLING SAILORS,* for
the Service of the

Royal Navy.

Bridgnorth March 10th. 1795.

---

3 *Guineas*
REWARD.
WHEREAS
A SHEEP

Of **MR. Hancock,** of *Ford,* was in the night between the 14th and 15th instant, **STOLEN** from *Horridge Down,* in the parish of *Milverton.* The Person or Persons who shall give such information, as may be the means of apprehending and bringing the **Offender or Offenders** to Trial and Conviction, will receive the above Reward. **PHILIP HANCOCK.**

FORD, near Wiveliscombe, 16th October 1829.

J. BAKER, PRINTER, WIVELISCOMBE.

Printed Ephemera, 1962. The changing uses of type and letterforms in English and American printing. The two bills on the left, dated 1815 and 1795, might have been printed at any time in the previous two hundred years. Those on the right could not have been printed before the early years of the nineteenth century. The Fat Faces (1803), Shadow Letters and the heavy Egyptians (1815) were a completely new vernacular. It is of some interest that the two auction bills came from the same printer in Dorset, the first printed in 1815, the second in 1827.

and pulled on a shirt, he turned to Françoise and noticed that she had put over her hair a pretty snood of fish-netting intertwined with shells. He made a little 'Tut, tut' noise and, leaning over her, with great delicacy adjusted it to his fancy.

We left the beach, saying goodbye to all but two of the young Spaniards who were lunching with us, and walked up to the Hotel de la Mer, where Henri Laurens and his family were waiting. Laurens was a tall, heavy, grey man, who looked like a retired school master. He had a gentle and courteous manner. His daughter-in-law and her two children completed the party. She was a pretty, vivacious woman, wearing a dress that might have come from Dior or Schiaparelli. Her children, unlike their mother, were completely silent.

Tables were put together on the terrace and the twelve of us sat down to lunch. The meal alone would have made the day memorable. Langoustes and white wine were followed by roast chickens and red wine, to be succeeded by Gorgonzola cheese, a *glace*, Armagnac and wonderful muscatel grapes and other fruits. All the while Picasso talked and kept us in fits of laughter.

As we rose from the table, I handed the *rouleau* to Picasso. He apologised to me for not having done the drawings, but he said he had done no work since 'the English visitors' because he had been to Breslau for a conference of intellectuals. He made a grimace and said, 'Aimez-vous les intellectuels? Je les déteste!'

Françoise interrupted saying, 'Will you both and M. Laurens come with us in our car, the rest can follow in their Citroen.'

With Henri Laurens, we climbed into the back of Picasso's new car, an immense Oldsmobile tourer, which an American admirer had given him. Picasso was apologetic about the opulence of the car, but he demonstrated, with childish pleasure, the press-button electrics for raising the windows or hood or sliding the seats about.

'I much prefer my old Renault,' he said, 'but Marcel likes to drive this.'

Picasso and Françoise sat in the front with Marcel, the chauffer-cum-body guard. He was a large and intimidating individual with close-cropped grey hair. He was dressed in a white singlet and pin-striped trousers.

The Musée Grimaldi at Antibes is built on a rock that juts out into the sea. As we stood in the courtyard looking up at the building, Picasso said, 'It was for sale in 1926 for Fr 20,000. Imagine! But it was too dear for me, even at that price. I hadn't got Fr 20,000 or anything like that. The town bought it the next year and set it up as a museum.'

Françoise took up the story of how it had been a typical, stuffy provincial museum, filled with Napoleonic relics. 'Then it was suggested', she said, 'that some of Picasso's work should be shown here. First one room was filled up with his pictures, and then another and another. Now there are only two rooms left to Napoleon – little rooms down in the basement.'

Picasso cut in with: 'Another perhaps final defeat for Buonaparte – and about time too!'

We entered the museum and Picasso ran across to a small, glass-fronted show case and pressed a button. Immediately it was flooded with light revealing the books he had illustrated for Vollard and other publishers, with the Buffon *Bestiary* in the centre. He chuckled with delight and moved across to another larger case.

'Some of my pottery!' he cried as the light came on. Then he led us off on a promenade through room after room of his pictures. These, mostly large panels were painted on unprepared *cement fibré* in flat colours. They were a paean of praise for the previous eighteen months of happiness. Françoise appeared in picture after picture. The culmination of these paintings was a large panel called '*Pastorale*', with satyrs and fauns and the naked figure of Françoise dancing in the centre.

The climax to this conducted tour was in a relatively small grey-walled room lined with glass cases. In these, two rows of magnificent great dishes were set out, glowing with the brilliance of their glazes. The impact was overwhelming. Dear old Laurens kept muttering, 'He is a genius, he is a genius!'

Griselda remarked on the owl that appeared on a number of the dishes. Picasso explained that the model was a tame Little Owl they had kept in their Paris flat. 'We found it as a fledgling with a broken wing. We had it a couple of years, then, while we were away the servants had not bothered to feed it properly and it died.'

'It was a dear little creature,' Françoise said. 'We were both very sad.'

We climbed into the Oldsmobile, for a moment blinded by the sun.

'Now we will show you where the pots are made,' Picasso said. 'We will take you up to Vallauris to see the factory itself.'

We drove through the narrow streets of this little pottery town and came to the Fabrique de Céramiques Madoura. Picasso led the way into a shed where a number of potters were at work. He said something to the foreman, who turned to one of the men who was throwing a pot. The workman completed a tall vase with a long slender neck and made way for Picasso to take his place. He ran his hands over the damp clay, then started squeezing it one way and another. In a few moments the vase had been transformed into a kneeling pregnant woman. Getting up from his seat, he made some joke to the potter and said: 'Don't throw it away!' Then he led us into the room with the kilns. Griselda asked the foreman about the colours.

'They are limited to the oxide colours – those that will stand up to the temperature of the glaze that will cover them. But this man, M. Picasso has taken our limited colour range and somehow or other has increased it greatly.' He paused for a moment and then said: 'I don't know anything about modern art – they tell me he is a great artist – I don't know about that, but I do know he is a fine craftsman.'

Evening was coming on before we made our farewells to Picasso and

Françoise and the by now dumbfounded Henri Laurens. We walked down the hill to the railway station. Griselda took my arm and said, 'What a wonderful day! He wasn't a bit like I expected. His photographs completely mislead one. He was so sensitive, he reminded me of John Nash.'

It was a day to remember, and so in a different way was the next one. We took a bus from Menton over the first range of the Alpes Maritimes to Sospel. I had last been there with Ralph Cusack in 1936. The road is a series of perilous hairpin bends which the bus driver took at speed, all the while turning his head to talk over his shoulder to his friends in the back of the bus. The bridge at Sospel that had a house in the middle of it and which I, like so many others had painted, had been rather ineffectually blown up by Mussolini's troops. We left the bus and turned up a road which was bordered by a stream on one side, running through lush meadows. At one point there was a thick carpet of wild autumn crocuses. We left the road and climbed up a cart track through an olive grove until we came to a clump of fig trees. We flopped down in their shade and ate our paté and bread, drank Lorenzi's red wine which came from his brother's vineyard in the Var, then stuffed ourselves with ripe figs from the trees above our heads. They were juicy, sweet and utterly refreshing. Butterflies were fluttering round us and a huge dragonfly with an iridescent body, hovered stationary above us for an appreciable time, then darted away. The only sound was the intermittent clatter of cicadas. We lay back on the warm ground and drowsed away the afternoon at peace with one another and happy in our lot.

Two weeks later we were back home. At Cowells I was greeted by Geoffrey's 'Haven't you brought the lithograph from Picasso?'

I explained that he was definitely going to do it. He looked doubtful. However, within a month Peter Kapp had delivered it to us. When the set was published, the prints caused quite a stir.

Sometime in February or March 1948, I had a telephone call from John Piper asking whether Cowells could print the programmes and posters and so on for a new festival that was to be held at Aldeburgh in the summer. I told him I was sure they could.

'In that case,' he said, 'if it is all right for you, Benjamin Britten, Peter Pears and the rest of us will come over at about 11 o'clock tomorrow.'

I had first met John Piper when he did the two illustrations for *Grongar Hill* for my type book. Later I got to know him well, once Griselda and I stayed with him and his wife Myfanwy at their farmhouse near Henley-on-Thames. His austere appearance was no reflection of the kind man he actually was.

I went across the office to tell Geoffrey Smith about the Aldeburgh project. With his usual enthusiasm for anything new he said: 'Good work! Tell them we will do anything we can to help them.'

The party that arrived the next morning consisted of Benjamin Britten, Peter Pears, Eric Crozier, John Piper and Elizabeth Sweeting (she was to become the first festival manager). We discussed all the bits of printing that would be needed. They ranged from stick-on labels to a quite elaborate programme book.

'Do you think we can ask five shillings for it?' Benjamin Britten asked.

'I'm sure you will produce something worth that,' John Piper said, 'particularly with these.' He handed me a bundle of striking photographs of Aldeburgh by Bill Brandt.

That was the first of many meetings. After they had gone, I set to work on the design of the first leaflet. Under Harling's influence, I had become excited by Victorian playbills and other bits of Victorian ephemera, so something of that feeling crept into the designs.

At the end of one of our meetings at Crag House we were sitting having drinks. Ben and Peter had just returned from Holland and that evening they introduced us to Dutch gin. It was then that Ben discovered I was Welsh.

'You know, John, I think you belong to the most unmusical nation in the world,' he said. I was outraged and rose like a trout to the bait.

'How can you say such a thing! With all those Welsh choirs, all the Welsh tenors and the miners returning from work singing in harmony.'

'Oh, yes! I admit they can sing in tune and I know that the Covent Garden chorus breaks into Welsh when they get floored by the Russian of *Boris Goudonov*, but they've got such ghastly musical taste – all this "Bread of Heaven" and "Sospen bach".'

'What about the Irish tenors?' I replied.

'Oh, they are infinitely worse! By the way, do either of you know anything about birds?'

I said Griselda did.

'Can you recognize different bird songs?'

Griselda thought she could.

'Let's go for a drive one afternoon and see what we can hear. This is to do with a little piece I am writing for children – I hope for the next festival, if there is a next festival.'

The following week Ben and Peter picked us up at Melton station. A young friend, George Behrens, who helped out during the festival was driving Ben's car which was a 1925 Rolls 20 Tourer. It was a quiet and graceful old motor. It was a sunny warm afternoon and the hood was down. We stopped in the woods near Butley to listen for a nightingale, but without success. Griselda identified various warblers and song birds. 'The little piece' that Ben had referred to was a children's opera that he had just started work on.

'Have either of you ever done any stage sets?' he asked.

'Only when I was a student,' I answered.

'Would you like to do the sets and costumes for this little opera? I say sets – in fact there is only one set – a children's nursery – in the early 1800s.'

'Of course, we'd love to.'

'What's that?' Peter interrupted. 'Listen! There it is again.'

'It's a nightingale,' Griselda answered, 'but he's only tuning up.' As she stopped talking, a raucous 'Kaark' sounded above our heads.

'I know what that is, that's a heron,' Ben said and as he spoke a huge bird flew over the trees, its leisurely wing beats giving the impression that time was on its side.

'I can certainly fit him into the bird song.'

'What are you calling the opera?' Griselda asked.

'Eric and I are having an argument about it at the moment. He's writing the libretto. He wants to call it *The Little Sweep,* but I think *Let's Make an Opera* would be more suitable. The first act is all about just that and takes place on a bare stage with auditions and rehearsals and so on. The second act is the story of a little sweep boy and a brutal master.'

'Like the beginning of Kingsley's *The Water Babies,*' I said.

'Yes, very like that, though Eric is setting it in Suffolk, not in a Yorkshire mill town. In fact it is based on one of Blake's *Songs of Innocence.*'

As the afternoon drew on we heard various other bird songs, including a particularly melodious chaffinch.

'Good Lord! Ben, look at the time,' Peter said. 'They'll miss their train if we don't hurry.'

George started the motor and we were soon bowling quickly along the deserted Suffolk roads.

'The old girl will still get a move on if we give her any encouragement,' Ben remarked. 'I'm awfully glad you like the idea of doing that set. Of course a lot depends on how this festival goes. We have got to get over the first one first.'

The work for the Aldeburgh Festival went ahead. I was roped in to be a part of the selection committee for an exhibition of the work of contemporary East Anglian artists. The other selectors were John Nash, John Piper and Philip James from the Arts Council, who was our Chairman.

The first day of the festival finally arrived. Everything was printed and delivered on time. Eric Crozier wrote to me that evening saying 'Everyone loves the Programme Book and the other things you have done. You can be the Festival Typographic Designer in perpetuity.'

It was during the Aldeburgh Festival that we first met the Cumberleges. Jock was then the Publisher to the Oxford University Press. His generosity was unlimited. They soon invited us to stay with them in Sussex. Year after year they took us to Glyndebourne and in later years, when I was sailing among the Western Isles, they used to take Griselda to Venice. At one stage, when he thought I was worried about my career, Jock offered me a job at the Press.

Geoffrey Smith, in order to help the Aldeburgh Festival, and as a useful public relations exercise laid on a large party at the Old Neptune. This was George Scott's medieval house near the Ipswich

Docks. Geoffrey invited numerous publishers and also had the inspired idea of asking every artist whose work had been printed by Cowells. In addition to the party, the guests were taken over to Aldeburgh to hear an opera or a concert. The whole affair was such a success that Cowells repeated it the following year.

For someone as ignorant of music as I was, the Aldeburgh Festival was a revelation. The only opera I had ever seen was an uninspired performance of *La Traviata*, which Tony Rhodes had taken me to in Washington during the war. *Albert Herring* at the Jubilee Hall, in comparison was a jolly romp. The fact that the Jubilee Hall became overbearingly hot made the intervals all the more enjoyable, because one could walk straight out on to the beach under the shelter of the lifeboat; or if one was thirsty, into the crowded bar of the Cross Keys.

The second Aldeburgh Festival did take place (and it has gone on ever since). The libretto and the music for *Let's Make an Opera* were finished and we started work on the designs. As Ben had said, there was only one set. Eric Crozier and Basil Coleman, the producer, worked out where the various entrances and exits were, and where there had to be a window. I based the completely realistic set on our drawing-room at Cumberland House, but gave it a yellow-striped wallpaper. We painted the flats on the floor of the Jubilee Hall, whilst rehearsals for *Let's Make . . .* and *The Rape of Lucretia* were going on all round us. Ever since then I have had 'Tarquinius's ride to Rome' inextricably mixed up with the coaching song in the children's opera. The costumes largely followed Kate Greenaway's illustrations for the children's dresses and Rowlandson's drawings for the adults. The only difficulties I had were with the hair styles of the grown-up ladies, who were most reluctant to have their hair dressed in an Empire style and were equally reluctant to have their bosoms hoisted up into the high-breasted line fashionable at that time.

The first performance of *Let's Make an Opera* was a great success and much of this must have been due to Norman del Mar who led the audience into singing the Overture, songs that at first sight seemed so difficult, but in the end proved so simple to sing.

There were breathtaking moments, such as in the first act when a young tenor called Max Worthley, who had a very lovely voice, started to sing 'Early one morning' during his audition for the role of one of the sweeps; and another, when the audience, duly rehearsed by a polo-neck jerseyed Norman del Mar, was, a split second later, as the curtain went up on Act 2, faced by the same conductor in white tie and tails, launching us off into the hauntingly beautiful 'Bird Song', which had its origins in that drive with Ben and Peter past Staverton Thicks and the Butley woods a year before.

There was an operatic feast that year, for as well as the first ever performance of *Let's Make an Opera*, we had *The Rape of Lucretia* and *Albert Herring*.

Ben and Peter were very friendly and quite unspoilt by their growing fame. The Festival in those days had a delightful air of amateurism, yet the quality of the music was anything but amateur.

1948 ended sadly. Denton Welch died on 30 December, though we did not hear until the following week. He had been ill for so long and had fought off crisis after crisis with such indomitable courage that one felt he was immortal. His books in fact have already contributed to his immortality. The first and perhaps the best, was *Maiden Voyage*, which came out in 1943. He decorated it himself, with a self portrait for a frontispiece. This drawing was taken from a photograph by Gerald Leet, a painter who had been at Goldsmiths' with us. *Maiden Voyage* was followed by an autobiographical novel, *In Youth is Pleasure. A Voice through a Cloud* on which he was working when he died, was uncompleted, but even so was a very fine novel. This had been preceded in 1948 by a book of short stories called *Brave and Cruel*.

The Christmas before he died Denton sent us a Christmas card which he had drawn himself. It was printed on a pink card. It was a drawing showing him lying asleep under a tree while above a cock crows 'Nowell, Nowell'. He had written on the back, 'Do you think this puce is pretty? Love D.'

The second Aldeburgh Festival poster.

4. Divided Loyalties

IT WAS NOT long after our return from Rocquebrune that Robert Harling asked us over to their house at Wissington. In those days he might have been mistaken for a racehorse trainer. He had a look of Fred Winter about him. He had a craggy, hatchet-like profile with penetrating blue eyes. He always dressed in drain pipe trousers, as narrow as jodhpurs. He was a brilliant display typographer and a devoted, if irreverent disciple of Stanley Morison and Beatrice Warde. Though actually not much older than me, he was a generation older in experience. Even before the war he had run his own typographic magazine. This was succeeded first by *Alphabet and Image* and then, losing interest in typography, in another magazine called *Image*.

Robert was a superb catalyst. Wherever he was, things happened. More than anybody he helped to launch us on our careers. He also introduced us to most of the people in the Stour valley with similar tastes. His kindness to many others like us has never been adequately acknowledged.

One Saturday evening at Wissington whilst Griselda and Phoebe Harling were sitting chatting by the fire, Robert set about me and my future. He analysed Cowells and the capabilities of the directors.

'Why, if you play your cards right, you could be managing director of that firm in five years.'

It was useless for me to explain that I was no business man and had not the slightest desire for power. He swept aside such arguments, implying that power was the only worthwhile objective. I went home next day feeling somewhat dissatisfied with myself, yet, in another way, re-charged. I was more than ever determined to become my own master.

A step in this direction began when, about ten days later, I found myself lunching with two young men at the Connaught Hotel. Robert had telephoned me.

'John, something that might interest you. Two chaps – Geoffrey Neame and Harry Newman – want to start up a print production publishing outfit and they need a designer to go in with them. I thought it might interest you. They will be getting in touch.' They had, and here I was.

Geoffrey Neame, an ex-fighter pilot, was an elegant, young man with a strong look of a film actor then famous called Tyrone Power. Geoffrey's outstanding good looks were hardly marred by a puckered

scar over his right eye, the remnants of some brilliant facial surgery after he had crashed his Beaufighter and practically burnt his
face off. Harry Newman looked like Tweedledum or Tweedledee. He
was a pear-shaped young American, with shining spectacles. He had
graduated from the Harvard School of Business Management before
going on to Cambridge where he had met Geoffrey. The one significant
fact that Harry had picked up at Harvard was, that if he was going to
own a Cadillac, he would need a staff of not less than twenty-five to
generate sufficient turn-over.

Their proposition was for me to join their firm which they had
already named and registered as Newman Neame. Their plan was to
produce and publish books for industry. In other words, non-risk
publishing and the kind of thing I was already designing for Cowell's
customers. Before lunch was over I had agreed to become a director
and to design for them whilst Cowells still employed me on a part-time
basis. I had already reduced my hours of working at Ipswich.

What my connection with Cowells meant was that I could embark on
a freelance career, with just adequate under-pinning. Soon Griselda
and I were working together. This pattern began by my having a bad
attack of influenza. I lay in bed with a roaring temperature, worrying
about my pile-up of work.

'Can't I help?' Griselda said.

'I don't see how. It's far too complicated to explain. Anyhow, what do
you know about typography?' I answered pettishly.

'Nothing – but I can learn. Come on, show me what has to be done.'
This I did, with a rather ill grace. She mastered the techniques in no
time. At the end of six weeks she was a very capable typographer, as
Robert Harling confirmed when she went up to an advertising agency
called Everett's to help him when they were short-handed. From then
on we worked together, apart from a short spell when she worked for
Henri Henrion at Erwin Wasey, the advertising firm in Park Lane. This
was the same Henri Henrion, who, much to my chagrin had taken
Billie off my hands.

If we had had children, I have no doubt our pattern of life would
have been very different. As it was, we could afford to take risks. By
making sure that the work we undertook was within our limitations, we
never had the worry that some of our designer friends had, of employ-
ing staff. Also, unlike most of them, we never really thought of
ourselves as graphic designers. Our interests were in typography, book
production and book illustration. Over the years these interests expanded into writing and editing. If our work was to dry up, we had a
fail-safe plan of going to America and seeking work as a cook and a
chauffeur or butler. I am rather sorry it never happened.

I thought that when I first became a typographer, I would be a
Sunday painter. I soon discovered that painting was no part-time job for
a designer. All one's visual creative energy is exhausted in day-to-day

141

design work. Far from being a Sunday painter, I soon found I was a Sunday typographer.

The Newman Neame concept of publishing, that the publisher found someone, usually an industrialist, to pay for everything, seemed a sound one.

Among many Newman Neame productions we designed were some books for André Simon, including one called *What about Wine?* for which David Gentleman engraved an attractive set of illustrations.

Following Harry's ideas about the size of the staff needed to generate sufficient turnover, various talented people were taken on. Christopher Bradshaw was the first of these. He was prematurely grey, with the rounded shoulders of the painstaking scholar. The appearance belied the man. He reminded me of Mr Carker the Junior in *Dombey and Son*. In fact Christopher was most athletic and a great enthusiast for a variety of things. When I first knew him, it was sailing. On one wintry day he took me for a sail on Hickling Broad in an International 14, the original Rolls-Royce of sailing dinghies. This beautiful little boat had an appropriately literary title. She was called *Preface*. I have never travelled so fast on water since. After sailing Christopher's interests turned to the restoration of archaic musical instruments and from that to the technology of computer typesetting, and finally to becoming Chairman of the Wine Society.

The fact that I was still working part-time at Cowells as well as doing innumerable jobs for Newman Neame made for divided loyalties which presented some problems, and I was soon faced by a third.

Dick Guyatt, whom I had not seen since we were at Charterhouse, asked me to lunch. We met at a restaurant in Soho. He was little changed except that his hair had receded. He was a good-looking, heavily built man with an air of quiet calm about him, a calm that concealed ambitions, shyness and strength of character. After exchanging commonplaces about what I had been doing, he said, 'I've been appointed head of the new Graphic Design Department at the College.'

'Congratulations.'

'Yes, but the trouble is, I don't know anything about the subject. I can paint a bit, I have a feeling for decoration, but that's about it. I want some help.'

'Well, what can I do?'

'Can you help me to find somebody who really knows the job – that is what we used to call "Commercial Art"? The kind of chap who can supply all the things I don't know.'

I did not have to think very hard.

'Yes, I think I can. His name is John Brinkley, he has been working with me at Cowells since the end of the war. He's a super chap, but he's getting restless. He has grown out of the Cowells job.'

A week later John Brinkley accepted a contract with the Royal College of Art. The typographer at the college who had only just been appointed was Ruari McLean, the same Ruari McLean whose layouts for Penguins John and I had admired a year or so before. During his first term, Ruari invited me to lecture to his students about the work I had been doing for the Aldeburgh Festival. As I talked to the students, I thought 'this is my thing, this is what I ought to be doing,' but I did not say anything to anyone. There was clearly no vacancy at the College with Ruari firmly established there. However, within a couple of years, the pressure of Ruari's outside work had built up to such a degree that he resigned from the College and Dick Guyatt asked me to take his place. I was delighted. It was the year of the Festival of Britain. I felt it was time to resign from Cowells. Teaching two days a week, a lot of free-lance work and Newman Neame were going to keep me busy.

It was at the end of 1950 that Robert Harling asked me to write about John Minton for his new magazine *Image*. Robert took me along to see Minton. I found him rather quiet, even nervous. A few days later I went up to his flat in Hamilton Terrace and he was in a quite different mood, bubbling over with gaiety, laughing and joking as he showed me his work, including his illustrations for Alain Fournier's romantic novel *Le Grand Meaulnes*. He had a complete understanding of this haunting story, which meant a lot to him.

After I had joined the staff of the College I saw quite a lot of Johnny, we used to meet over lunch in the Common Room. Gradually the moments of gaiety became fewer and a brooding sadness settled over his face. Lucien Freud and Robert Buhler both painted very good portraits of him, each were melancholy little paintings, but the most revealing picture of Minton was in Rodrigo Moynihan's large picture of the Painting School staff, with Johnny sitting apart, hunched up, haunted by fears of which the rest of that group seemed to be quite oblivious.

John Minton was a very professional artist; as an illustrator he was quite sure of himself. He illustrated a book about the gold-beating firm of W. H. Whiley for me when I was with Newman Neame. He went down to Whiley's factory and did a series of vivid drawings of the different processes of gold beating. I am not sure whether the workers were more impressed by his dedication to his work or by his total lack of inhibitions.

The Festival of Britain had marked the end of an era. In the years immediately following the war, we had still been living in a pre-war world, even if we did have rationing. The years following the Festival were, as far as English artists were concerned, full of questions and doubts. They were beginning to lose confidence. John Minton had been one of the first to question the whole purpose of what they had to say, or even if they had anything to say at all. With people of Minton's generation, particularly the Romantic painters, this loss of confidence, with rare exceptions continued over the next twenty years or so and it seemed it was not until the late sixties that artists in England began to come out of this period of chronic uncertainty. Graphic designers did not know what they were doing either.

As I was now spending quite a lot of time in London, I needed somewhere to sleep. Freddy Gore, who had been in Camouflage with me, came to my rescue and offered me a bedroom in his flat in Charlotte Street. It was next door to a Chinese laundry and above an antique shop belonging to an elderly spinster called Miss Edith Lee. Freddy soon introduced me to the pubs, the Black Horse in Rathbone Place and the Fitzroy Tavern in Charlotte Street, both haunted by Dylan Thomas and Nina Hamnett. Freddy was living with an intriguing little Armenian girl called Lily. There was still a feeling of the Fitzroy Street Group about the area, though it was soon to change with post-war rebuilding. Occasionally we would be wakened in the small hours by the sounds of a street fight or of tarts screaming at each other.

When Freddy and Lily's menage began to come apart, Griselda found me lodgings with a fascinating Austrian lady of aristocratic birth, who was the mistress of Robin Darwin, the newly appointed Principal of the Royal College of Art. From there I went on to stay first with David Gentleman in Camden Town and then with the Bradshaws in Hampstead.

I had left Cowells in the spring following the Festival of Britain on the friendliest of terms. After much deliberation they appointed an attractive and high-powered young advertising lady and launched her in a blaze of publicity.

Meanwhile, there were financial difficulties at Newman Neame. They were just not getting off the ground. Geoffrey was one of the most urbanely charming people I have ever met, Harry was full of fun and enthusiasm. I had worked for them for over two years without any kind of salary, in order to get things going, but even so we were getting into deep water. I discovered they had an overdraft of £50,000. I began to have sleepless nights. Then one morning I had a private telephone call from their bank manager asking me to go and see him. During this interview he told me Geoffrey's wealthy fruit-growing father might at any moment withdraw his support. As Geoffrey's holdings were limited to £100 and Harry had no funds in this country, I, as the third director, would be held responsible for their debts.

'What on earth am I to do?' I gasped. 'My only assets are my house, my boat and my other paltry possessions.'

The bank manager sensibly and kindly said, 'What I suggest (and this is off the record) is disentangle yourself right away.'

I did. Newman Neame did not go bust but in due time they were taken over. It was a narrow escape. Harry retired into his father's real estate business in California and Geoffrey, still living dangerously, was killed driving his sports car through the New Forest, going from one party to another. His pretty wife, June, had for the first time in her life, refused to drive with him. The girl who had taken her place was killed.

Meanwhile at Cowells things had not gone well. Their new art director, used to the methods of the advertising world, found a provincial printing firm too confining for her talents and had resigned. Geoffrey Smith approached me to see if I could help. After a prolonged discussion we came to an agreement that I would act as design consultant, without any strings attached. Things seemed to have slotted into place.

As soon as our agreement was signed, Geoffrey Smith suggested I might do another type book for them.

'Before you start on that,' Geoffrey said, 'here is something for you to get your teeth into. It is an anthology of Suffolk verse, put together by Lord Cranbrook. He has suggested that John Nash might be willing to illustrate it. If he will, we'll publish it – as a limited edition.'

It was a happy beginning to our new arrangement. There was plenty to rejoice about in this collection of Suffolk verse, which was given the title *Parnassian Molehill*. Even if the anthologist did not unearth any new Wordsworths, at least he found some local McGonagalls.

Jock Cranbrook was a close friend of John Nash. They were both keen fishermen and it was on the lawns of Great Glemham House during the first Aldeburgh Festival that Jock taught John Nash how to cast a dry fly. Apart from his abilities as a fisherman and anthologist, Lord Cranbrook was also a skilled zoologist and an authority on bats. When they lived at Great Glemham House his normal practice was to introduce his bats into the drawing room after dinner. He would persuade his less squeamish guests (Griselda was one of them) to feed these creatures with meal worms. One evening when we were there Jock was very excited. Hugh Barrett, a farmer-broadcasting friend of his had been taken ill with what the pathologists thought was some rare disease transmitted by bats.

'If he dies,' Jock remarked, with a gleam in his eye, 'it will be most frightfully interesting.'

Hugh did not die and though Jock was pleased to see him about again he seemed to have a lingering regret that it had not been possible for the pathologists to delve into Hugh's insides, to see just what the bats had done to him.

Parnassian Molehill came out in the Autumn of 1953. The anonymous reviewer in *The Times Literary Supplement* said of it: 'The binding (a repeat pattern of roses) of the book is exquisite, the paper bland, the typography dignified, while the pictorial comments by John Nash are sometimes Arcadian and sometimes comic. It is a Molehill worthy of Parnassus.'

This was the beginning of a long friendship with the Cranbrooks, who showered many kindnesses on us, not least by inviting us to stay with them on many occasions in their little farm near Ravenstonedale in Westmoreland. It was very primitive but provided the base for wonderful long walks over the fells.

145

There was plenty of variety in our work. At one time we were producing an enormous catalogue for Crittalls, the metal window frame firm. The brief for this was given me by 'Pink' Crittall, the younger brother of Lord Braintree, who was Chairman of the firm. All 'Pink' said to me was, 'Make it big enough so that for years to come architects can use it to prop open their office doors.' The catalogue ended up as quite a handsome book with a reproduction of a painting by Robert Buhler of a view of the Chelsea embankment from an open window on the cover. 'Pink' liked this so much he asked me to organize a series of press advertisements based on the theme 'Seen through a window', by as many painters as I could muster.

'Cottages at Landermere', 1950, drawing by Robert Buhler for Crittalls.

As soon as *Parnassian Molehill* was completed, I started work on the successor to *A Handbook of Printing Types*. Using the same format, I planned a book that would cover both notes on text setting and graphic methods of reproduction. Robert Harling, in reviewing the original little type book had said it would have been better if I had leavened the illustrations of Moore, Sutherland etc, with that of promising un-knowns. I had plenty of those at the College. Apart from some drawings by Bawden, Gross, Minton and Ardizzone, all the remaining illustrations were by contemporary third-year College students including David Gentleman, John Sewell and Len Deighton, who posed in braces and a bowler hat for a photograph to illustrate half-tone methods.

Of the students, the one we remained closest to was David Gentleman. He was a quiet and charming person and a very good draughtsman. He was also a fine wood engraver. From time to time I was able to make some use of his talents.

The only typographic innovations in *A Handbook of Type and Illustration* were two fine titling alphabets, which were specially drawn for the book by David Kindersley, where he indicated for perhaps the first time his ideas on automatic letter spacing.

I did not realize then how lucky I was to be allowed to indulge myself with the production of these typebooks. They led to all kinds of opportunities including the publishing of *Printed Ephemera*.

Meanwhile a stream of work came our way, mainly through our connection with Cowells. One of the more interesting jobs was to design a magazine called *Land* for the Shell Chemical Company. The editor was David Wolfers, a youngish man of some sensibility who was later to start the New Grafton Gallery. For the first number he had chosen a painting by Paul Nash for the cover. Soon we were producing another magazine for him called *Catalyst*. *Land*, as its name implied was about agriculture, *Catalyst* was about the chemical industry. The magazines were illustrated by our numerous East Anglian artist friends.

Edward Bawden, who though he taught at Goldsmiths' when I was a student there, we only got to know well after we had come to live in East Anglia. His austere exterior and apparent shyness, hid a warm personality. His brilliance as an illustrator and print maker was recognized by a few, particularly artists and designers. We made many visits to Brick House, Great Bardfield, where his wife Charlotte, who was as extrovert as Edward was introvert, entertained with great good humour. Edward had a somewhat macabre sense of humour. In the posthumous exhibition, 'A Tribute to Edward Bawden', at the Fine Arts Society in 1992, a drawing he had done of his father on his deathbed was partnered by his son Richard's drawing of Edward in turn on his deathbed. I think he would have appreciated that.

5. The Royal College of Art

COMING TO THE College in 1951 was very like joining a club where one knew most of the members. My first encounter with Robin Darwin was whilst I was lodging in Maida Vale with the lovely and wayward Austrian lady. Robin's appointment as Principal of the Royal College of Art caused quite a furore. Within a few weeks of his arrival he had sacked every member of the staff. One or two of the luckier ones, such as John Nash, were sent a covering note saying 'Of course this does not apply to you'. Gilbert Spencer, the Head of the Painting School, was thrown out without a word of consolation. Christine Nash, an old friend of Gilbert's, was very bitter about it. John Nash, with a certain amount of in-built preservation, said nothing, which was not true of William Johnstone, the pugnacious Head of Camberwell (and later the Central) School of Arts and Crafts. He was vitriolic in his condemnation of Darwin's appointment, largely because he had pinched most of his staff.

The dust had begun to settle by the time I started to work in the School of Graphic Design. As I knew little about teaching, but had spent most of the war lecturing, Dick Guyatt suggested I should do a series of lectures to the first-year students. These were an attempt to give them something of the cultural background to printing. For the next thirteen years, generations of students had to sit through a dozen or so lectures that I gave during their first term. I at least learned a lot from this, for I was educating myself. Every year I re-wrote these talks and nearly twenty years later the results of all this appeared in *Anatomy of Printing*, which Fabers published in 1970.

In the Painting School Rodrigo Moynihan had replaced Gilbert Spencer as Professor. Within a year of his appointment he began his large picture of his teaching staff. Moynihan, one time an abstract artist, had by 1949 become a successful portrait painter, painting in the manner of the Euston Road Group. His students were a little in awe of him, thinking him to be scholarly and sophisticated, though they admitted he was very fair in his dealings with them. His staff were mostly followers of Sickert and the Camden Town painters.

The two members of the Painting School that I knew best were Carel Weight and Robert Buhler. Carel, I had known since Goldsmiths' days. Robert, I only got to know after I had joined the College. He was a pleasant, good-looking fellow with a fairly sharp tongue. He was born in London of Swiss parents. His mother ran a restaurant in Soho where

148

many artists used to foregather. His art training began in Switzerland, but was continued in London at St Martin's School of Art. From there he won a scholarship to the Royal College of Art and remained there for precisely six weeks. That was typical of the man. He developed into the most painterly of painters, usually painting in low tones both portraits and East Anglian landscapes. For a while he had a cottage at Landermere, where Basil Spence, John Hutton and Edouardo Paolozzi also lived at various times.

The painterly qualities of the work of Robert Buhler, Ruskin Spear and Carel Weight had little appeal for their more progressive students. The general opinion was that Robert Buhler was somewhat cynical, Ruskin Spear was clever and worldly and Carel Weight a comforting and kind teacher.

Robert Buhler and Ruskin Spear were an odd couple. They were both good painters. All Ruskin's work had something of his earthy sense of humour. They both painted portraits and both preferred sitters from among their friends rather than commissioned portraits. Buhler painted Ruskin Spear, Barnett Freedman and Madge Garland, but his most telling portrait was his 7 ft high painting of the literary critic John Davenport, who with a cigar in his hand and semi-intoxicated, looks as if he was about to topple out of the frame.

The one tutor that all the students had any real sympathy for was John Minton, who in the College Magazine *ARK 13* wrote a witty piece about the three most successful painters who had left the college in recent years. These were Derrick Greaves, Jack Smith and Ed Middleditch. Minton commented 'Doom being in and Hope being out the search amongst the cosmic dustbins is on . . .'

On the evening of 21 January 1957, I picked up a copy of the *Evening Standard*. Bold headlines across an inside page said: 'Artist John Minton is found dying in his Chelsea studio.' The implications of the report were that he had committed suicide. It was a horrible shock. Most of his friends disagreed with the report and thought that his death was a tragic accident.

The 'cosmic dustbin' searchers that Minton referred to were soon succeeded by the kitchen sink school most powerfully represented by John Bratby. Darwin arranged for Bratby to have a special allowance of paint which he used in a prodigal manner, painting his wife-to-be in varying stages of undress sitting among cornflake packets and unwashed dishes.

A couple of years later the kitchen sink school was succeeded by the Pop artists, led at the College by Peter Blake, whose images of popular culture had absolutely nothing to do with either cosmic dustbins or the kind of painting his tutors practised.

It is surprising that the Pop artists did not have more influence on the Graphic Design School. The cross-fertilization of Fine Art with the various design disciplines so talked about by the art educationalists rarely happened. What the designers needed most of all was drawing, yet most of them had forgotten how to draw if indeed they had ever known. I am not referring to the illustrators and print makers.

Even so the College in 1951 was brimming over with confidence. The staff had played a large part in the success of the Festival of Britain and Robin Darwin seemed to have the world at his feet. He had such charisma that he had only to turn to you and say, 'My dear So-and-So, would you mind doing this or that', and the So-and-So was falling over himself to do it. If there was nothing he particularly wanted of you he would ignore you. I never felt at ease with him. It was as well that I was never one of his favourites, for when they fell from favour, he behaved just as Henry VIII did to his wives and friends. They hardly knew what had hit them and if they did not lose their heads they certainly lost their jobs. Three Heads of Departments, Jimmy de Holdenstone, John Skeaping and Wyndham Goodden suffered this fate, yet at least two of these had been his close friends. In spite of this, he obtained almost total loyalty from his staff.

Johnny Skeaping had been sacked for seducing one of his students, not that she objected. He was the most endearing person. He had been a student at Goldsmiths' many years before I was there. One evening I was seated next to him at a College Dinner. He started talking about his great hobby, greyhound racing.

'Recently,' he said, 'I was at some dinner at Harringay. Next to me at table was a little East End Jewish bookmaker called Ikey Moses. I must have had a bit to drink, because I said to him, "How is it, Ikey, that you are such a rich man, yet you have had no education, whereas I, who am well educated am as poor as a church mouse?"

' "I'll tell you what it is, Mr Skeaping," he replied. "It's nothing to do with education. All you've got to have is a bit of courage. Why, last week there was a lovely greyhound on whom the odds were getting shorter and shorter. Before they got too short, I put £1000 on him. Then I began to lengthen the odds and rumour got round that he had been nobbled. Soon he was 50:1. At that stage, I laid off another £1000 on him."

' "What happened?" I asked.'

' "Cor, 'e just romped home. I cleared over £50,000 that night."

'What do you think of that for a story?' Johnny concluded.

'Marvellous,' I answered. 'Was it true?'

'Oh yes, it was true all right. The trouble is I bet like hell, but like Beerbohm Tree, I must have spent a fortune trying to get back the first half crown I lost.'

Robin had his Achilles' heel and that was his own form of snobbery. One night after some dinner for various VIPs, including Lord Eccles, who was then Minister of Education (and always referred to by Robin as 'Smarty-Boots') we were gathered round the fire in the old Senior Common Room in Cromwell Road. The VIPs had departed. I was sitting on a sofa with Robin. Across the room was a group of the Painting School tutors, including Ruskin Spear, Robert Buhler, Carel Weight and Rodney Burn. We had all had plenty to drink. Robin looked up from his glass of brandy and beamed at the painters in a patriarchal manner, then leaned over towards me and said, 'I do love the Arty Boys.' He paused, smiling to himself then added, 'But I *adore* the Smarty Boys.'

Something of this attitude rubbed off on to the College. It was something the students resented, yet it was through Robin's connections with 'the Smarty Boys' that he achieved so much. Even so, his aims were a trifle confused. The terms Senior Common Room, Rector and Pro-Rector and so on that were introduced with the Degree status that he achieved for the College and his weakness for the paraphernalia of academic ceremony all hinted at a longing for the cloistered world of scholarship and university life, a background that he himself lacked. He must have felt this all the more because his family were so deeply rooted in Cambridge University life. The fact that his students were learning to work with their hands he quite ignored, even though he was himself a skilful painter.

Once over lunch at the Garrick (in fact the only time I ever saw him at the club) he said to me, 'My ideal for the College would be to turn it into a college like All Souls – a civilized place with no students!'

In spite of these moments of self-revelation, even sometimes of weakness, he was a formidable man with a lot of animal power. On one occasion he was faced with a mass demonstration of students. He met them head on, silenced their jeers and cat-calls, talked to them for an hour and a half, and at the end of it received a standing ovation.

Not long after I had arrived at the College, Herbert Read, on behalf of the publishers Routledge and Kegan Paul, approached Robin Darwin about a series of books on design which might be written by the heads of each department at the College. Dick Guyatt, like most of his colleagues felt little inclination to do anything of the sort, but he suggested that John Brinkley and I should do a book on Graphic Design. This we did with enthusiasm, John writing the chapters on lettering and on the technical stuff and I doing the rest.

In the Easter holidays of my first year at the College, I was asked to take a party of students to Amsterdam. The object of this outing was to introduce them not only to the art of the Netherlands but also to see printing and typefounding.

The night before our departure, Griselda and I were going out to dinner in Chelsea with Anthony Gross. We were on a No. 14 bus and I had placed my case with all the students' passports, their currency allowance and the tickets, in the space under the stairs. I was able to keep an eye on it until a little man in a white overall also put his carpenters' tool bag in the luggage space, and then took a seat between me and the bag. He seemed in an agitated state. Just after the bus came

151

to a halt at some traffic lights, he fidgeted until the lights began to change, then jumped up, muttering something about 'going the wrong way', grabbed his bag and leaped off the bus. As soon as he had gone, I saw that he had also taken my bag. I leaped to my feet and, in peril of my life, jumped off the bus, which was beginning to get up speed.

'Stop thief!' I yelled, as I pounded after the little man. As he was carrying my quite heavy case, as well as his tool bag, he was under some handicap and within a short while I caught him up.

'You've got my bag!' I stupidly gasped.

'Have I?' said the little man. 'Oh, sorry Guv!' And with that he put it down and was off, darting down a side street. I was so relieved, I said no more.

Later in the evening, I telephoned the Chelsea Police Station. A bored station officer said, 'What did he look like? And what bus were you on?'

I told him.

'Oh, that's Charlie, he always does the No. 14 route. Only came out of prison last week. Do you want to make a charge? If you do you will have to stay and give evidence.'

I told him I was off to Holland in the morning.

'In that case, you'd better forget all about it. After all, you've got your suitcase back!'

So that was that.

It was an enjoyable couple of weeks and a time for making friends with the students (and life-long friends in the case of one or two of them) and those who entertained us. At Haarlem, we visited Enschedé, one of the great printing houses of Europe and there I once again met Jan van Krimpen and Sem Hartz. Jan was imposing, at first sight rather intimidating. He was probably the best type designer in the world at that time. He was also a great *bon viveur*. Sem was slim, handsome and spoke impeccable English. He had his clothes made in Saville Row and his shoes by Trickers. He was (and is) an engraver of sensibility and has been responsible for the design of many of the Dutch postage stamps. One of our party was David Gentleman, who since then has designed as many, if not more English stamps than Sem has done Dutch ones.

On the last day of our tour, after visiting the Musée Plantin at Antwerp, we went across to *Le Chapeau Rouge* for lunch. The students were bent on ordering fillet steaks and other expensive dishes, when the Madame came to my rescue. She hissed in my ear, 'What about some *moules?*'

I agreed and told the students we would start on mussels. By the end of the meal (it was four o'clock) we had consumed a wheelbarrow full of *moules marinière,* and could not possibly have eaten anything else. As our train was drawing into Amsterdam, a pretty girl called Margot Hamilton-Hill let out a terrible wail. She had left her handbag at *Le Chapeau Rouge.* Her young man, a likeable and very clever illustrator called John Sewell, demonstrated his affection for her by going all the way back to Antwerp to retrieve it.

The next day David Gentleman and I met Griselda at the Hook of Holland. She had brought over our car. Together the three of us drove down to the Camargue, where we found the Mistral blowing and David and I were overcome by the beauty of a fifteen-year-old waitress in a sleazy café in Aigues Morte. It was the sight of her mother who looked like an awful old tart – she would have made a good model for Lautrec – that decided us we had better tear ourselves away, for there was a startling likeness between that lovely young girl and her dreadful old mother. Driving through the flat lands of the Rhône delta, the Mistral, which was practically blowing us off the road, soon cooled down our ardours. It was not until we had reached Rocquebrune, that we were sheltered from that cruel wind. After a couple of nights at *Le Mirasol*, we drove on down to Florence, where David left us. We had grown very fond of him. Within a few years he and his wife Rosalind had taken the ground floor flat at Cumberland House at Manningtree and were in turn providing us with a *pied-à-terre* in Gloucester Crescent.

It was after that visit to Holland that I really began to know Van Krimpen. John Brinkley and I had started work on the book which we called *Graphic Design*. We decided to include a section on Van Krimpen's work in the book. Jan came to lunch at the Garrick and left me a set of proofs of the book that John Dreyfus had just written about him.

'Dreyfus has done your homework for you,' he said, 'but I don't doubt you will be able to add something to it.'

From that time onwards – and for some years – every time Jan and his wife, Toos, came to England on the Harwich boat, they would spend a night with us at Manningtree. Jan loved his food and his drink. At some time or other he had mentioned that he had never eaten grouse. So, when the season was right, Griselda bought a brace, at what seemed an exorbitant price. She cooked them with loving care and the Van Krimpens arrived just in time for lunch.

'I'm afraid Jan is not too well,' his wife said. 'We had a very bad crossing.'

After downing two large whiskies, Jan came to the table and proceeded to dispose of a liberal helping of our home-potted Harwich shrimps. As we have always done, we ate in the kitchen. As Griselda turned to the oven, Jan said, 'I don't think I can eat any more.'

At that moment, the smell of the cooked grouse drifted across the room. He sniffed, then said, 'Perhaps I can just eat half a bird!' If he had been feeling well, we should have gone hungry.

Jan van Krimpen had the most beautiful handwriting. It was his own personal, supremely legible version of a chancery script, written at speed without affectation. Jan was in many ways an inspiration. His situation at Enschedé put into proportion my connection with Cowells. He was at much the same age when he joined Enschedé as I had been when I started work in Ipswich. When we visited the Van Krimpens at their villa at Heemstede, he talked about some of the difficulties of a designer working in a print shop. It was during the winter and there was ice on the canals. He stoked up a good fire and while Griselda talked to his wife, I sat and listened to Jan.

'I had already designed a typeface for Enschedé, when in 1925 they asked me to join the firm. It seemed a great opportunity.'

'What was the firm like then?' I asked.

'Much as it is now, in one of the prettiest buildings in Haarlem.' Then as if in gentle reproof for being interrupted, he continued, 'As I was saying, it seemed a great opportunity, but soon there were difficulties. First, I had opposition from the composing room. They were not used to working with a typographer – but I had even more opposition from the clerical staff, the order clerks who dealt with each job, and so on. They were frightened at the intrusion of an "expert". They feared that my presence would put their jobs in jeopardy. None of them knew much about printing and even less about design. However, this opposition was nothing to what I had to put up with from the directors who were not responsible for my appointment. They were jealous of what they saw as my power and my freedom.' He paused and gave the fire a poke.

'How did that affect you?' I asked.

'They made quite certain I never got a seat on their Board!' he said. 'I resented that for a time, but now I do not think it matters.' He paused again, then said, 'I think there are three qualities that an artist working in commerce must have. Toughness, integrity and resilience. Without these I doubt he can survive.'

We told Jan we were thinking of visiting Italy in the following spring, whereupon he started planning our itinerary.

'First you will go and see Hans Mardersteig in Verona at his Officina Bodoni. Hans is the finest printer in Europe. In Verona you must have a meal at the *Dodici Apostoli*. From Verona you should go to Florence. My little friend Bianca Cavaglieri will put you up. She has a pretty apartment near the Ponte Vecchio.

'When you have exhausted Florence – you must go to the Laurentiana, not that they look after their books – you can then visit Arezzo to see the Piero della Francescas and Siena to see the Palio. If you want to go to Venice, Bianca's cousin takes in paying guests. She lives by the other bridge – the Rialto.'

'What about Leonardo's?' Toos interrupted.

'Of course! Leonardo Walsh! He is one of the best cooks in Europe! He has a little hotel at S.Vigilio on Lake Garda. I will give you a letter of introduction, otherwise he probably won't let you in.'

In due course we followed Jan's itinerary, visited Hans Mardersteig and marvelled at the beauty of his printing, which was done on a couple of German hand presses. We stayed with Bianca Cavaglieri in

Florence and with her cousin in Venice and loved Venice as much as we disliked Florence. As for S.Vigilio, I do not suppose we shall ever stay in such another inn. The sight of Jan's handwriting was enough for Leonardo. His food was perfection, the Italian waitresses charming. Now alas, Leonardo is dead.

We continued on terms of close friendship with Jan until his marriage showed signs of breaking up. Toos came to stay with us and Jan, who was a touchy man, assumed we were taking sides with his wife. It was not until a year before his death that we met again. It was at a Double Crown Club dinner that things were put right. Up until that time we had only one other disagreement. He strongly disapproved of the fact that I had a boat and spent so much time on it.

'Sem Hartz, he has a boat too. Everyone in Holland has boats. They must be the most time-wasting of things. Life is too short – how can you expect to become a good typographer if you waste half the year sailing about the Noord Zee?' I had no answer to that.

By the end of 1953 we had finished *Graphic Design*. It was an unsophisticated mixture of a potted history of lettering and printing, a technical treatise on printing processes and brief monographs on the artists we considered worthy of the term 'graphic designers'. We chose them, because, like Paul Nash, Eric Gill, Reynolds Stone, Van Krimpen, Eric Ravilious and Edward Bawden they had worked mainly in the fields of fine art or fine printing and so were uncontaminated with the coarser aspects of the advertising, publishing and printing trades.

The book was well produced and well printed by Cowells and Robin Darwin, on receiving one of the first copies, said: 'Ah! Now this is a work of real scholarship. This will do much for the College!' I caught John Brinkley's eye. He knew and I knew. Neither of us had any pretentions to scholarship. What we both had was what might be called a 'seeing eye'. Apart from that we had good and helpful advice from friends more learned than ourselves. We were also fascinated by the subject's historical background. We ingenuously hoped our enthusiasm made up for our other deficiencies.

Part-time teaching can have a very salutary effect on any practising artist or designer. After my first feelings of euphoria had worn off, I found working at the College a chastening experience that involved me in a loss of confidence and in an undermining of my beliefs.

I was comforted when Ted Ardizzone, who joined the College staff not long after I did, said to me one morning in the coffee break that the students made him feel that he was nothing but a bumbling, old, commercial hack, and he had never felt so unhappy in all his life! I found that even after years of arguing some point with students, that one would suddenly begin to question whether one was right or wrong. It was all rather painful. Henry Moore made it clear to me that the time to teach for a practising artist or designer is when he is searching for his own means of expression, so that he can take the students with him on his questing. Moore thought he had been a good teacher while he was trying to find his way, for he could take his students with him on his voyages of discovery, but from the moment he discovered what he wanted to do, he was of no more use to them. He just wanted to go away and get on with his own work.

Coming to teaching after a spell as a practising designer, I had already developed a pragmatic outlook. This implied that I had a sufficient know-how of my job so that I could solve my problems quickly along known lines of approach. Students do not *think* like this. They have no experience to help them or to limit them. They have to draw on their imaginations as they have little else to call to their aid. The good student often approaches things in the most impractical way, creating monstrous difficulties over a problem that a professional designer would ride over with barely a glance. Yet in spite of, or because of this approach, the student often arrives at a fresher solution than the professional. Sometimes something of this freshness of approach would rub off on to the teacher, in the nature of 'feed-back'.

I do not think I was a good teacher. For one thing I had not the technical dexterity of someone like John Brinkley to hand on to them. The lectures I gave had but one objective, that was to communicate something of my enthusiasm for the subject. That was quite a different thing from day-to-day teaching. The fact that I could stand up and talk was incidental, maybe something to do with my Welsh blood. In spite of everything, I found some rewarding things about being at the College, and most of all the stimulus of constant contact with the young, no matter how much they cut one down to size. There were moments of surprise and pleasure when on rare occasions some highly successful ex-student would come up and say, 'I shall never forget what you said about so-and-so!' It was by the way that the remembered remark was usually something quite banal.

One of my jobs was to keep an eye on the students' publication, the journal *ARK*, which was always tottering on the edge of some crisis or other. One number had to be destroyed after it was printed because of some references to Princess Margaret that were thought to be scandalous.

The most interesting work that I did at the College was helping to start and run a private press. This all began with one of my book production exercises. I took a translation of Giambattista Bodoni's Preface to his *Manuale Tipografico*, as a test run for what our printing and binding departments could do, and what benefit students could get from such an exercise. In fact it was a satisfactory little book. Dick Guyatt approved of it. Robin Darwin not only liked it but soon had visions of an endless supply of slim volumes to give to his friends. This thought was immediately succeeded by the idea of producing a succession of slim volumes to SELL to his friends. So in 1956 the Lion and Unicorn Press was born.

The plan was that there were to be three books each year, in editions of 200, for a subscription of five guineas. I think our subscribers had good value for their money.

The programme of supplying them with three books a year went tolerably well until Robin Darwin began to take an active interest in what we were doing. Few things are more appealing to the layman than the operation of a private press. Because of such interest and so interference, our speed of production, in spite of more equipment, began to slow up alarmingly. Darwin infiltrated various books by his friends and relations.

The Lion and Unicorn struggled on for several years, with an increased circulation, but the demands on our limited resources caused further difficulties and delays. In 1963 the idea of the College entering the commercial publishing field was also raised again. Robin Darwin proposed that the Press might publish various successors to *Graphic Design*. He also suggested that I should look after their production. Working in the context of the College with so many people liable to interfere, apart from the inevitable inertia of reluctant authors, I could see nothing but frustration, blood and tears ahead.

It was at this stage that Eddie Penning-Rowsell, who was directing Studio Vista for Odhams, put a proposition to me that I might edit a series of paper-back books on design for them. I could not do this as well as the Lion and Unicorn project so I decided in favour of Studio Vista and resigned from the College. I had been there thirteen years and my third five-year contract had two years to run. I was sad to go, yet my feelings were mixed. I liked belonging to the College, yet I disliked not having a free hand. Once again it was my problem of wanting to be my own master.

As soon as John Brinkley heard I was leaving, he said, 'I think I have had enough too. Can you find me a job?'

Before I could leave College, I had to attend Convocation. Robin Darwin, with all his talents, was no orator. His speeches at Convocation, punctuated with attempts at humour, were something to be endured. Over the years the only two events that were in any way memorable were firstly, the occasion when all graduating students, gowned, mortarboarded and ranged in ranks behind the speaker, suddenly lowered their faces into their laps. A moment later and again in perfect unison, they lifted their heads to reveal the fact that they were all caricaturing Darwin with heavy, black-rimmed glasses and black moustaches. The audience roared its approval. Darwin, quite unaware of what was happening behind him, thought that one of his feeble sallies had provoked this response and beamed contentedly as he continued his peroration. The second event – and I am not sure it was not on the same day – was the appearance of the graduating David Hockney who, spurning mortar-board and gown, had peroxided blond hair and was wearing a sparkling gold lamé jacket. He looked like a shining star in that soberly clad company, which was not so inappropriate, in view of what lay ahead of him.

NEARLY THE END OF AN ERA

Ever since our marriage, Griselda had been fighting against ill health. Holidays abroad became an ever increasing anxiety. In the mid-fifties a holiday in Venice ended up for her a nightmare journey back to England. She was losing weight rapidly, but her doctor (he is dead now) told her she was just a silly, neurotic woman. It was not until she paid her annual visit to John Cambrook, our dentist in Queen Anne Street, that any positive action was taken. Cambrook was the chief dental surgeon at Bart's and over the years he had become a good friend. He took one look at my wife and said quietly, 'Good gracious girl, you are very ill. You shouldn't be walking about like this.' He turned to his receptionist and said, 'Cancel my appointments for the rest of the morning.' He then started telephoning various people. After about half an hour he turned to Griselda and said, 'I have arranged for you to see Dr Cullinan at the Gordon Hospital, and what is more, I am taking you there.'

It looked as if she was dying. For some weeks it was touch and go, and then by a process of elimination the doctors discovered that she was a coeliac, a condition that up to that time the medical profession thought only affected children. They were just in time. Once she was on a gluten free diet, she went within a few days from being at death's door to looking almost well. In fact it took her a couple of years to regain her strength.

Later that year, it was 1956, my mother died very suddenly, leaving my father overcome with grief. As a memorial to her passing he had the kitchen done up.

My parent's house had the most apalling kitchen, open raftered and with a stone sink with taps set 3 ft above it and a dreadful old boiler that my father used to rake most unmercifully. For thirty years my mother had begged my father to do something about her kitchen. Now, ironically, he set about having it modernized, regardless of expense. When it was completed, he proudly showed it to me.

'She would have liked it, don't you think?'

I was tempted to say that she would have liked it even more at any time during the previous quarter of a century.

My mother's younger sister Katharine came to keep him company. She was a fey little creature who had once been on the stage. She had run through quite a lot of money and had become adept at moonlight flits, a hangover from her days of touring with bankrupt theatrical companies. She had also spent a small fortune on storing her almost valueless furniture. On two occasions my father had reluctantly paid off massive bills to Harrods and some other furniture repository in the west country. While my mother was alive he would not have her in the house. But now, perhaps because she had a faint look of her elder sister, he seemed to take pleasure in her company, though she exasperated him beyond belief. At least she was someone he could shout at.

Pen drawing by Auguste Renoir from *Graphic Design*, 1954.

6. Trans-Atlantic Ephemera

MY HABIT OF collecting pieces of ephemeral printing began as a result of finding the Palgrave Album. Soon I was adding to the collection from many sources, including waste-paper baskets and garbage bins. I found one beautiful hardware label in a muddy Ipswich gutter. My main source, however, was Andrew Block's dusty little shop in Barter Street, a few hundred yards from Holborn Underground Station. Andrew Block was a remarkable man, without a grey hair, even when he was in his late seventies. He spent most of his time shouting at his very deaf wife who sat hunched up in a corner of the shop oblivious to his thundering tirades. Every time Mr Block struggled past her, his arms full of dusty files, he would fall over her. Then there would be another volley of abuse, which passed unnoticed over her silent world.

Nothing in his shop was catalogued or arranged chronologically. The files were headed Food, Politics, Sanitation, Police etc. To find a seventeenth-century Royal Proclamation, I had to look through mountains of dusty pieces of paper, to discover it sandwiched between a copy of the *Daily Worker* and a 1910 Report on the Suffragettes.

All the while the idea of a book was growing in my mind, but there were obvious gaps in my collection which I could not fill, except by getting photographic copies of material in museums and public collections. I started with the collections at the British Museum and moved on to the Pepysian Library at Magdalene College, Cambridge, and then to Dr John Johnson's vast collection at Oxford. 'The Sanctuary of Printing', as the learned doctor named it, was housed at the Oxford University Press. Soon after I had bought the album, I had written to Dr Johnson asking him if I might see his collection. I received a curt letter from this eccentric printer explaining just why I (or anyone else) could not see his collection.

Dr Johnson was married to a first cousin of my mother-in-law, possibly a good enough reason for refusing me access to his 'Sanctuary'. In fact the nub of his argument was that all through the war he had never left the press buildings, literally sleeping with his treasures, and he would need at least 'five uninterrupted years before he could consider ANYONE looking at his "Sanctuary"'. He concluded his letter to me with, 'Am I to be allowed to have those uninterrupted years?'

Even after the learned doctor had retired, he still kept his hands on the archives and objections to my looking through all this ephemera were not brushed aside until Vivian Ridler had become Printer. By this time Dr Johnson had been separated from his beloved collection and I was at last able to get to work in the 'Sanctuary'. Harry Carter, a good, wise and learned man had been appointed Archivist. With his and Vivian's help I found a mass of material for my book. Harry had said to me, 'If you want to find anything, Lil Thrussell is the only person who will know where it is. She has been cataloguing the collection for about thirty years.'

Dr Johnson had spotted Mrs Thrussell when she was still a girl, helping on her father's vegetable stall in the Oxford market. He must have been taken with her pretty colouring, for he persuaded her to come and work for him. He trained her in how to sort and file and mount this ever growing pile of material. In spite of marrying and bringing up a family, she had been hard at it ever since. When the collection moved to the Bodleian, Lil Thrussell went with it. The collection is a monument not only to Dr Johnson's foresight, but to Mrs Thrussell's industry. She had an encyclopaedic knowledge of its contents.

The scope of my studies was widening. From Oxford and elsewhere I had already gathered a number of American pieces. Phil Hofer, the Librarian of the Houghton Library whom we had met at the Cumberleges, suggested we came over to the United States to visit various collections there, including the Bella C. Landauer Collection at the New-York Historical Society. He also generously invited us to stay with him and his wife at Cambridge in Massachusetts. I told Geoffrey Smith about all this and the projected book. He immediately became most excited.

'If you can find an American publisher for it,' he said, 'we will underwrite an English edition and get Fabers to publish it.'

*   *   *

We left Liverpool on a Friday evening in April, bound for Boston in the *SS Newfoundland*. The Furness Warren Line ran two small passenger-cargo ships on this route, the *Newfoundland* and the *Nova Scotia*. It was a shuttle service that ran throughout the year. They called at St John's, Newfoundland and Halifax, Nova Scotia and took thirteen days for the voyage. These 7000 ton ships not much bigger than the Channel packets, carried 4000 tons of cargo. They were fine sea boats, as they needed to be on their North Atlantic run. The cost of a first class ticket was not much more than tourist on one of the Queens. It was a thoroughly enjoyable trip.

As a prelude to our search for an American publisher for *Printed Ephemera*[1] as the book came to be called, we stayed for the promised weekend in Cambridge with the Hofers at their handsome old house on Appleton Street.

Bunny Hofer greeted us warmly and took us up to our guest suite, the first time in our lives we had had such special treatment. Bunny was a bright-eyed, bustling little woman. 'I was born in a brownstone house in New York, but I'm not entirely American. My mother was Lord Esher's sister,' she told us as she showed us into our apartments. She was certainly a high powered lady and moved in a rarified stratum of society, both social and intellectual, that was quite outside our experience.

Some weeks later after we had returned to England, I ran into John Carter at the Garrick. He was the scholarly old Etonian brother of Will Carter and a director of Sotheby's. He was a superior person if ever there was one. 'I followed you as house guest at the Hofers,' he said. 'What a house! What a cook! And what people – there is no one they don't know. They made me feel a complete provincial!'

I found that rather reassuring.

That first evening, at dinner, Phil Hofer gave us our first insight into Boston life. 'A couple of years ago,' he said, 'I was asked to go and see an old lady who lived on Beacon Hill. She had been a recluse for over thirty years. She is dead now. Let us say her name was Miss Adeline Vanderbank – she might have been one of Henry James's Bostonians! I was ushered into her presence and a very severe old dame she was. "Mr Hofer," she said, "I understand you know about pictures. I would be grateful if you would look at my ancestral portraits and tell me whether they are in good shape – whether they need cleaning or anything." She conducted me through room after room filled with Reynolds', Copleys' and Gainsboroughs' until we came to face to face with a portrait of George Washington. Somewhat surprised I said, "I didn't know that George Washington was one of your ancestors Miss Vanderbank."

' "Well, Mr Hofer, as a matter of fact he wasn't, but he was courting my great-great-Grandmother Rebecca Vanderbank. Whilst he was court-ing her the family had the portrait painted. Then she turned him down, but they kept the painting. After all they had paid for it. He was a tall, good-looking young man."

' "Oh, what a pity Miss Vanderbank that your great-great-grand-mother Rebecca turned down George Washington."

' "I'll say it was a pity! As you know, he went off and married that Martha Dandridge, who might have been anyone's housemaid. Why, if Rebecca Vanderbank had married George Washington, she'd have seen he was loyal to his Queen!" '

The next morning we went to the Houghton Library with Phil Hofer, to look at his incomparable collection of illustrated books. I was able to beg for my book, a pile of trivia, consisting of book lists, prospectuses and the like to do with the Private Presses.

'If you have seen enough here,' Phil said, 'I think we ought to go and have a look at Boston. There are some nice old houses and squares there. Then we might call in at the Athenaeum, which is more like the London Library than the club of that name.'

Later as we walked into the Athenaeum, a white-haired, heavily built, very upright old man passed us on the stairs.

'I'm glad you saw him,' Phil Hofer said. 'He's old —. Quite a character. Shot his wife on their honeymoon. It was in Paris and he found her in bed with the room service waiter. Shot him as well. Good thing it was in Paris. He was very well connected, so they hushed it all up and he was hurried home. Never married again and to this day he wears on his hip the same pearl-handled revolver with which he did the deed.'

'How very aristocratic!' Bunny said.

'Oh, he's aristocratic all right, and no one has ever dared to remark on his pistol until the other day. He was in the wash-room. He had taken off his jacket. A new member, a rather brash young man suddenly noticed the revolver in its holster on his hip and said, "My! Sir, that's a cute little gun. Ever shot anyone with it, Sir?" The old boy stopped towelling his face and replied in a very gravelly voice, "Matter of fact, I have!" '

On Saturday (we were organized down to the nearest minute) Bunny drove us over to Salem to visit the Peabody Museum. The speedometer on her Jaguar was not working and we were gonged by a traffic policeman. She pulled up sharply and was out of the car like a shot. She had her licence in her hand as a large, fresh-faced young cop got off his motor cycle.

'Do you realize you were doing 87 mph?' He said.

'Oh, no Officer, surely not? If I was it must be the spring! My speedometer is not working.'

What was working was her charm. The overbearing manner of the policeman evaporated. He glanced at her licence and read out: 'Frances Hofer, 88 Appleton Street'. Then he handed it back to her with a grin, saying, 'O.K. Fran! Just watch it, that's all.' And he waved us on.

'What a dear young man,' she said as we drove off, 'so democratic!' Bunny, with the organizational powers of a Presidential Aide, had warned Mr Brewington, the Curator of the Peabody Museum, of our impending visit and the kind man devoted a couple of hours of his time to showing us his collection of scrimshaw work, Liverpool transfer jugs, ship models and literally hundreds of primitive ship paintings.

We were back in Cambridge just, but precisely just, in time to bath and change for a large dinner party the Hofers had arranged for us. It was intellectually rather an intimidating gathering. One of the guests, who looked as bemused as I felt, was Gyorgy Kepes, the Hungarian Professor of Visual Arts at the Massachusetts Institute of Technology. The conversation was on a very elevated level. We did not feel we had been a great success.

To help finance my trip, Phil Hofer had arranged for me to do a series of lectures. The first of these was at the Museum of Fine Art in Boston, which went off without any untoward reactions.

The second of my lectures was to the Alumni Association of Harvard. This was done on a substratum of rice and prawns and sherry served in paper cups. As *l'après-ski* can be more exhausting than actually hurtling down the *piste*, so is *l'après-conference* to the delivering of a lecture. On that particular evening, after I had completed my talk, I was jammed into a corner of a small ante-room being bombarded with questions and observations for upwards of two hours, when, whether it was from lack of air, or just sheer exhaustion, the room began spinning and I gently slid to the floor in a dead faint.

Before our visit to Boston was over, we met Martin Simmons, who was known as 'Cowell's Man in New York'. Martin had been a good friend to us and had pushed various interesting jobs our way, including the designing of a number of books for the Limited Editions Club of New York. He arranged to drive us down to New York on the Sunday. He looked like a well-bred gangster.

To begin with the day was overcast with a promise of rain. The long Merritt Parkway ran through woods of sugar maples, birches, prunus and dogwood which was in full flower. We stopped at a Howard Johnston for hamburgers and then drove on. By the time we reached the outskirts of New York it was pouring with rain.

That evening we dined with Martin and Doreen in their apartment. After dinner, as the night had cleared, they walked back with us to our hotel and Griselda could see for the first time, the skyscrapers towering upwards into the night sky. As we were saying goodnight, Martin said, 'I have arranged for us to see the publisher Alfred Knopf tomorrow morning. He likes the idea of your ephemera book.'

The meeting with Knopf's senior editor went off well. As I was on the point of leaving, the editor said, 'We'll do the book all right, just work out a dummy for us so that we can cost it and you shall have a contract.'

I was delighted for this was then one of the most distinguished of the American publishers. After that I spent days at the New York Public Library and at the New-York Historical Society, working my way through the Bella C. Landauer Collection, gathering material to fill the gaps in my book and so, I hoped, making the book that much more appealing to the American market.

At the end of another week we travelled up to New Haven. Alvin Eisenmann, the printer to the Yale University Press who had been over in London working at the College a couple of years back, collected us from the station.

'Good to see you, John,' he said. 'Had a good trip?' I said we had.

'Fine! I've got a big audience for your talk tonight. The whole of the Arts Faculty. I told them they would be fired if they didn't turn up.'

We arrived at the University campus just before mid-day and were shown up to our guest suite. It was in one of the oldest of the University buildings, high up and overlooking a quadrangle.

In the evening I gave my lecture to the Faculty. Alvin had set me up on a wide stage with a lectern and a reading light to one side. The audience seemed rather remote, so after I had been talking for a short

Griselda and Bolivar at Meadow Cottage, 1959. *Photograph by Anthea Sieveking.*

The author and Minky on the back cover of *Typography: basic principles*, 1963.

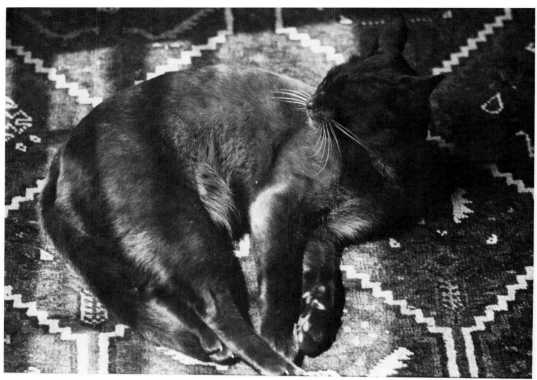

The Burmese cats Minky and Moosie.

Patient Griselda in the Hollandsche Diep, 1962.

'Wal'r, my boy,' replied the Captain, 'in the Proverbs of Solomon you will find the following words, "May we never want a friend in need, nor a bottle to give him!" When found, make a note of it.'

Captain Cuttle – *Dombey & Son* by Charles Dickens.

Harvey's Wine List, 1962. Drawing by Edward Ardizzone of Captain Cuttle and Walter Gay.

Harvey's Wine List, 1961. Wood engraving by David Gentleman.

Shell *Land*, 1967. Illustration by John Nash to an article by the Earl of Cranbrook.

John Nash, 'Snow art is good for Biz', 1972. *Photograph by S. S. Walia.*

William Heath Robinson, self-portrait, with his much loved cat 'Saturday Morning'.

Rowland Hilder at Blackheath, 1977. *Photograph by Rado Klose.*

John Lewis and printed ephemera.
Photograph by Dominic Turner.

The two sides of a typographer's life.

John Lewis at the tiller of *Patient Griselda*.

while I departed from my script with some story that I hoped would loosen them up. As I digressed I walked away from my lectern to the front of the stage. I finished my anecdote, the audience responded, then I realized that I had not only lost the thread of my dissertation, but I could not remember which lecture I was doing. The lectern with my script was 20 ft away. I turned to the audience and saw a very intense lady in the front row gazing hopefully at me. Chancing my arm I said, 'You know, I haven't the faintest idea what I was talking about!'

She came straight back at me, 'Oh, you were saying so-and-so,' and she then repeated verbatim all that I had said before my digression. The audience burst into laughter and all went well from that moment.

The most gruelling experience of the week was a lecture I gave at the Parsons School of Design in New York. On this tour I had four different set pieces. One was called 'English book illustration from Francis Barlow to Aubrey Beardsley', and this was the one they had chosen. When I arrived at the Parsons School of Design, the Dean conducted me into the lecture hall. Of the students assembled, 125 of them, many were negro, Porto Rican or Chinese. I had a feeling they would not make much of my English illustrators. The curtains were drawn over the windows, the slide projector was switched on and I started my lecture. Perhaps, not surprisingly, I could not feel any response from my audience. However, after about a quarter of an hour there was a diversion.

There was a sound of voices and furniture being moved about. Then there was a tap-tap-tap and a full symphony orchestra started off into Stravinsky's *Rites of Spring*. I was screaming at the top of my voice, when the music stopped in the middle of a bar and stopped too quickly for me to lower my voice. I must have been audible right across the East River. A member of the staff had gone to remonstrate with the music class, apparently effectively, for with sounds of muttered grumbling, they withdrew.

That was not the end of it, because as I came into the last lap of my performance, two workmen outside the windows started beating the daylights out of a 40-gallon oil drum. I kept going to the end. The students looked utterly bewildered. However, I was politely thanked by the calligrapher, Paul Standard, with whom I had exchanged letters over the years.

'I'm afraid you were working under difficulties,' he said as he shook me warmly by the hand. 'This used to be a boxing gymnasium. The sound-proofing is not quite one hundred per cent.'

The last evening in New York, we had dinner with Alan Fletcher who had been a student at the College and his pretty Italian wife Paula in their one-and-a-half room apartment in Greenwich Village. Alan had left the College a couple of years previously. He already had an aura of success about him. Pentagram lay ahead.

A week later we boarded the SS. *Manchester Mariner* at Montreal.

165

Apart from steaming through pack ice for nearly thirty hours and cutting across the bows of another of the same company's ships in the river Mersey, forcing her on to a mudbank, it was an uneventful voyage.

The night we arrived back in London, my father died. The same night, the boiler in the kitchen at 9 Castle Street also expired, weeping rusty tears across the floor. Every night for over thirty years, my father had beaten it into submission.Clearly it could not face a future without such violent attention.

*   *   *

When I had returned from the States, our work was going well. I told Geoffrey Smith about the arrangement with Alfred Knopf for *Printed Ephemera*. 'Splendid,' he said, 'let's reproduce the pictures and then you can do a really good mock-up.'

This was done and early in the following January I flew out to New York to show them the result of my labours. I felt there was a slight constraint in the air when Martin Simmons and I were ushered into the publisher's office. I handed the editor the *Printed Ephemera* dummy. He slowly turned over the pages.

'I don't quite see the point of all this,' he said, 'not that it isn't an interesting collection of material. However, I'm afraid that is by the way. Since I last saw you, things have changed here. We have new masters and they have laid down that we do no more books on the arts or in related fields. I'm truly very sorry – I hope you find another publisher.'

We staggered out into a blizzard and made for the nearest bar. Martin for once could think of no alternative outlet.

When I returned to Ipswich, I had to face Geoffrey with this problem. The best part of £2,000 (a large sum in the 1960s) had already been spent on reproduction work for the book and it looked as if we would have no American sales. It did not take him, courageous man that he was, more than a moment to say, 'Don't worry, we'll go it alone.' He turned over the pages of the dummy. 'Amazing!' he said. 'Fancy finding all that stuff. Is there anything you can do to make it more interesting to printers and publishers?'

I took the dummy away and looked at it. Then I remembered how the American publisher had said, 'I don't quite see the point of all this.'

'Well,' I asked myself, 'what is the point of it?' After I had been turning over the pages for a while, my eye was caught by two little auction bills from a Dorset printer, one dated 1815 and set in a bookish manner in old style typefaces that had been in use for the previous 200 years; the other, looking quite different, had been printed a dozen years later and was set in the first of the Victorian display letters, a Fat Face and a Shaded Letter, both from Robert Thorne's typefoundry. It was the beginning of a new vernacular. Here was a theme, the changing uses of type and letter-forms in English and American printing; and that proved to be the making of the book.

Ten days later Geoffrey had a letter from Martin, saying that he had sold a large edition to Dover Books in New York. Eight thousand copies were beautifully printed by Cowells and with some inspired promotion the edition soon sold out. In 1969 Fabers published a selection of the illustrations from the original edition as a paperback. It was an offset job and was an unattractive production compared with the original. However, they cleared a large edition of that as well.

In 1990 Diana Steel under the imprint of the Antique Collectors' Club, printed and published a facsimile of the original edition, with a new introduction and many of the subjects that had been in monochrome, now in full colour. It was well printed and sold well. Of the numerous books that I have written, it would seem that this is the only one for which I am remembered!

Diana Steel followed this up with *Railway Printed Ephemera* written by William Fenton, whom I had first met when he was a student at the College. He had followed me to Cowells and for some years had run their London Studio. William was a great railway buff. I wrote an introduction for *Railway Printed Ephemera*, it was most interesting and more than a worthy successor to my book.

7. Meadow Cottage

I PONDERED OVER the problem of parting with No. 9 Castle Street. Much as I loved it, we were too entrenched in East Anglia to think of returning to Farnham. Eventually I put it up for sale and it was knocked down for a miserable price. The agents had persuaded us not to put a reserve on it. Sick at heart we put it out of our minds and went house hunting. We had lived for nearly twelve years in Manningtree. Griselda thought it was time she had a real garden – and she found it – 7 acres of marginal land surrounding a primitive and isolated cottage about three miles outside Woodbridge. It was a quarter of a mile from the nearest road. The garden was non-existent, but there was a wood, meadows and a stream called the Lark running along the boundary. Over the next eighteen years, Griselda created her garden, or rather her controlled wilderness. It was really a spring garden with drifts of daffodils and narcissi and thousands of snowdrops all along the edge of the stream.

We bought Meadow Cottage, as it was appropriately called, when it had no electric light and we had to pump the water from our well by hand. During the first winter we lived a restful existence with evenings spent sitting in soft lamplight, just staring at the great wood fire. The following year, we enlarged the house, with an upstairs room that would serve as a studio. Electric light was installed and an electric pump for water. We soon grew to love the place.

We had moved to Meadow Cottage with our two elderly cats. First one and then the other came to the end of their lives. It was then that we saw an advertisement in the local paper for Burmese kittens. We drove over to a village called Finningham and came to a house full of beautiful cats. They were either brown or grey. Mrs Swan, the owner of these lovely creatures, produced a large open basket with six kittens in it, three of each colour.

'This is the mother,' Mrs Swan said, pointing to the most aristocratic of all the cats. 'She would not look at a brown tom, so we mated her with a grey one.'

'Can we have one of each?' I asked.

'Of course!' she answered. And that was how Minky (who was brown) and Moosie (who was grey) came into our lives. Their real names were Limberlost Meadow Brown and Limberlost Chalkhill Blue.

The breeder did not believe in inoculating her kittens against cat 'flu or any of the other complaints that they were liable to catch, so we did nothing about it. However, when the kittens were about four months old they both caught feline enteritis. If it had not been for Dick Shorter, a Stowmarket vet, who was also an old friend, they would certainly have died. However, he kept them alive with saline injections. Moosie the grey one, recovered first. From the moment we had started nursing them, we had to have them in bed with us at night to keep them warm. Every day for twenty eight days we drove 20 miles to Stowmarket and 20 miles back, and though Moosie was almost well by then, Minky was too weak to walk. After a dozen or so visits, as soon as he was put on the vet's table, he started a faint purr, then actually held out one or other of his front paws to have his injection.

We began to despair, for the little cat would eat nothing. Whilst Moosie daily grew stronger and was soon joining us on our walks round the wood, all Minky could do was to lie feebly but contentedly in my arms. It was actually on the evening of the twenty-eighth day that Moosie caught a baby rabbit and brought it into the house, plonking it down in front of his brother. Minky looked at it with an expression that clearly implied, 'What am I meant to do with this?'

Griselda picked it up, took it outside and gutted it, then, cutting out the liver, which was still warm, she brought it in and offered it to the little cat. He looked at it, sniffed it; a gleam came into his eyes and he grabbed hold of it. That was the turning point. The battle was won but another battle had been lost. We were clearly their chattels and their servants and our bed was no longer just ours, it was theirs as well. We used to sleep, four in a row, the cats stretched out alongside each of us with their heads on our shoulders. They were the cleanest animals imaginable and smelled like warm biscuits.

*   *   *

In 1960 Ben and Peter asked us if once again we would do the programme book for their Thirteenth Aldeburgh Festival. We had designed and produced the Programme books for the first seven years of the Aldeburgh Festival's existence, then Benhams, the Colchester printers had taken it over. Ben thought that over the years the Programme Books had grown rather stodgy. We redesigned the whole thing, giving it an asymmetric layout and using a tinted paper for the actual programmes. This was not liked at the time. However, a year or so later they adopted the same scheme.

8. The Book Factory

THROUGHOUT THE SIXTIES our work continued, but was beginning to be limited to the production of our own books, or to producing and editing the series of paperbacks for Studio Vista. However, Griselda and I were still designing the two magazines for Shell Chemicals.

They were attractive magazines with a lively sprinkling of good illustrations and covers by artists as varied as Stanley Spencer and Ivon Hitchins.

I was at the same time acting as typographic consultant to S.H. Benson Ltd, the advertising firm at the top of Kingsway. This one day a week job was through the kindness of Bobby Bevan, who was the chairman. It was my one and only experience of advertising. I would not have found it very rewarding if Bobby had not asked me to occupy part of my time by setting up a permanent exhibition of the history of printing. This was hung on the walls of the third floor corridors.

Bensons had always been a literary agency. Dorothy Sayers was once a copy-writer there. The setting for her novel *Murder Must Advertise* was based on Bensons. Bobby Bevan had an encyclopaedic knowledge of English literature. Anyone less like the popular concept of an advertising tycoon it would be hard to imagine. His office at Bensons might well have been the room of a Fellow of an Oxford College – and a rather unusual Fellow at that, with an esoteric taste for ocean racing and fine painting. Photographs of his yacht *Phryna* were flanked by paintings by Gilman, Gore and Robert Bevan. As the last named was his father, preference for the Camden Town Group was not surprising.

Bobby was a formidable figure but he was a very kind man. His real and tangible kindnesses to innumerable people were done very privately. John Nash was one of those on whom he lavished his support.

It was in 1948 that we first met Bobby. He had only recently married Natalie, who had been previously married to Lance Sieveking. We met them at a Regatta Party at Wivenhoe, given by Dicky Chopping and Denis Wirth-Miller. Natalie, on that day, looked as beautiful as anyone I had ever seen.

The regatta party was notable for some dignitary who was being constantly summoned on the loud hailer by the somewhat unfortunate name of 'Mr Anus'.

It was towards the end of 1960, while I was still at Bensons that I had a telephone call from David Wolfers, asking me if I would be interested in designing a wine list for Harveys of Bristol. I replied that of course I would be. 'They have seen a copy of *Land* and like the look of it. A chap called Robin Don will be getting in touch with you.'

Robin Don called to see me at Bensons. He was an elegant, slightly pompous young man with dark hair and a pale complexion. We discussed the project of the wine catalogue and its illustrations. I showed him David Gentleman's engravings for the book we had done for André Simon and he liked them.

David did a brilliant set of engravings for the first of the many wine lists that we put together for Harveys. Cyril Ray, writing in *The Sunday Times* described this catalogue as 'the prettiest wine list ever produced'.

Edward Ardizzone, John O'Connor, Asgeir Scott and Leonard Rosoman were some of the artists who illustrated these wine lists. The last one that we did had a fine set of drawings of ships and boats by John Gardner. It was then that Showerings of 'Baby Cham' fame bought up Harveys and that was the end of our wine lists.

Robin left Harveys and returned to his Norfolk farm at North Elmham. The next I heard of him he was working for Brown and Pank, the wholesale wine department of Watneys the brewers. This company was run by an ex-Guards Officer, a youngish man called Simon Heneage. For him we produced a book called *Off the Shelf*, once again with David's engravings. This looked to be as promising a connection as Harveys, but history repeated itself. Watneys sold the business to Distillers and Simon Heneage was out of a job, as of course was Robin Don, who decided to start his own vineyard in Norfolk. Heneage left the wine trade with no regrets and spent the next few years studying the English illustrated book, before in due course launching into the book trade, publishing and the art market.

From that time onwards, apart from my periodic visits to art schools and consultancy work with Dunlops and the University of Essex, where I helped to build up a printing centre, it was books. We had indeed become compulsive book-makers. From the time I put together *A Handbook of Printing Types*, this book-making slowly replaced any desire I had to paint.

As soon as I left the College, I became heavily involved in the editing and production of the Studio Paperback series on art, design and architecture. Eddie Penning-Rowsell had originally commissioned me to produce three titles. By the time these were completed, Odhams had sold Studio Vista to the Rev. Timothy Beaumont. Penning-Rowsell left to devote his life to writing about wine and was replaced by David Herbert, who had learnt his job at Penguins. Working with David, my three titles quickly grew to twelve and eventually to over forty, until they came to an end in the early 1970s, when Studio Vista had once again been taken over, this time by an American firm.

Of the forty odd titles, we must have designed all but half a dozen. They were economically produced in a square format, which gave scope for illustrations. Each book was printed on only two sheets of paper by a firm called Koch and Knuttel at Gouda in Holland. On one occasion we actually corrected a set of proofs in the cabin of my boat, moored behind the gasworks at Gouda. These books were published simultaneously in Britain and America.

From the time *Printed Ephemera* was published in 1962, hardly a year passed without a new book appearing from either Griselda or me. What made possible such a spate of authorship was that practically all our books were picture books. We approached them as book designers who were lucky enough to have the opportunity to write their texts as well. The element of chance always came into it. The discovery of an unlikely picture would be the cause for further research and more text or some unexpected facts would set off a search for additional illustrations. It was a bit like a juggling act. The writing and designing were completely interlocked.

My most ambitious book was *Anatomy of Printing* (over-ambitious was how one reviewer described it). In this I tried to place the design of printing in the context of its time, relating the printed page to contemporary movements in art and architecture. I had originally planned the book twenty years before, when the story was to have been told almost entirely by illustrations. I might have been wiser if I had followed the original plan, but over the years I had acquired such a mass of information which I used for lectures at the College, that I could not resist the temptation to put it all in. I was supported in this by my two editors at Fabers, first David Bland, who sadly died in 1970 while I was still writing the book and then by Berthold Wolpe, the same Berthold Wolpe who during the war had designed the jacket for Tony Rhodes' book *Sword of Bone*. Berthold was one of the most endearing of men and a famous letter designer. He read the completed manuscript and was full of kind words about it. It would have been better for me if he had subjected the book to some fairly swingeing criticisms.

I sought far and wide for the illustration material and also had the help of Helen Wodzicka from the St Bride Printing Library. Griselda and I made various journeys to Amsterdam, Antwerp and Paris. It was at the Bibliothèque Nationale that we met Mme Jeanne Veyrin-Forrer in the *Rèserve*, the rare book department. (Today she is the head of it.) She was charming and helpful. As we were about to leave, she suggested we went to her apartment for supper. 'I am sure my husband will like to meet you,' she said. 'He is a painter.'

Mme Veyrin-Forrer had told us her flat was opposite Les Invalides, but we had not expected the restrained opulence of the apartment block. A lift took us up to her floor and she greeted us warmly. It was like a Park Avenue setting, with the walls covered with Impressionist paintings, including two by Camille Pissarro. Her husband arrived soon after we did. He was tall, good-looking and beautifully dressed.

'I am sorry I am late,' he said. 'I have just flown in from Tokyo.' I wondered if he was a successful portrait painter. He had brought a huge tin of caviar back with him. It was not until the end of dinner that he told us that he was the publicity director of Air France. He was a direct descendant of Camille Pissarro and on the shelves of the sitting room was a complete set of all the books his grandfather, Lucien Pissarro had published at the Eragny Press in London.

The colour transparencies of pages from the *Sacramentary of Gellone* that Jeanne Veyrin-Forrer found for us were the most handsome things in *Anatomy of Printing*. The book was beautifully printed by Cowells. It was the last piece of fine bookwork that they printed by letterpress.

Griselda and I passed every sheet both in the composing room and again as they came off the machines, going into Cowells' letterpress department at any hour of the day or night. Ernie Mills, a big placid man was the night shift overseer of the letterpress machine room. He said to us, 'You know, it makes such a difference, printing a book like this. All the good jobs seem to go to litho nowadays. This is something you can get your teeth into. It's quite interesting to read too.'

When I finally parted company from Cowells, I particularly regretted leaving behind all those on the shop floor. Over the years my relationship with the firm had become more and more tenuous. With the retirement of Geoffrey Smith and Eric Hanson, it soon came to an end. Under their guidance Cowells had prospered. Geoffrey in his heyday was a brilliant salesman and Eric a very shrewd handler of the firm's finances. In later years, he most generously sorted out Griselda's and my muddled financial affairs in an attempt to save us from having to end our days in the workhouse.

9. Art Schools

ONE DAY OVER pre-lunch drinks in the Senior Common Room (it must have been about six months after I had left the College), I was talking to Bernard Meadows, who had succeeded John Skeaping as head of the sculpture school. He and I were both Governors of the Norwich School of Art. The Norwich principal was due to retire and we were discussing whom we could find to run the school, when John Brinkley broke into our conversation.

'Would you consider me?'

'Consider you!' we both repeated.

'Do you mean to say you would leave these fleshpots', Bernard said, 'to go and live out in the sticks, not that Norwich isn't a jolly fine place; I was born there!'

'I have already told John that I wanted another job, and there is nothing in the world I'd like more,' he answered.

'In that case, the job is yours. We will have to do a bit of lobbying, but we'll get you in.'

A month later John Brinkley was appointed principal of the Norwich School of Art. He was faced with a very run-down school and there were problems ahead. As a result of the Coldstream Report, a new kind of art and design diploma was being introduced, to replace the old National Diploma in Art and Design. The idea behind this, was to produce not only better trained, but better *educated* art and design students. It was thought that they should have a diploma course of a standard comparable to a degree course at a University. These new courses were intended to provide a liberal education as well as a training in art. With the same students and the same teachers, it was a matter of their pulling themselves up by their own bootstraps. Sometimes the educational pendulum swung too far and they had so much philosophy, sociology and art history that they came out into the world as very inadequately equipped craftsmen, even if they were marginally better educated.

As soon as this scheme was announced, all the art schools in the kingdom clamoured for diploma status. Apart from anything else, it meant that the staff would get better pay. It was decided that the schools should be inspected, not by Her Majesty's Inspectors but by panels of practising designers and artists. I, amongst a lot of my friends, was co-opted onto the Summerson Committee Graphic Design Panel and soon found myself heading for the outback.

It was a revelation. There were marvellous schools in unlikely places and in places where there should have been marvellous schools, there were dreadful ones. We found good painting, sculpture and print-making in far off places, for good young painters and sculptors were quite willing to go far afield to teach, because it provided them with a livelihood and still left them time for their own work.

The picture for graphic design, the portmanteau title under which all of our trade was taught, was very different. Good, young graphic designers had no need of teaching as a full-time occupation; they were only too often fully occupied and well rewarded. In Britain, London was their place. A principal of an art school remote from London, with aspirations towards running a graphic design course, had to be very persuasive to lure bright (which I suppose is synonymous with young) graphic designers to his school.

This was one of the problems that faced John Brinkley when he arrived at Norwich. Applications had already gone in for recognition for the new diploma courses in painting and graphic design and agreement had been reached for a new establishment of teaching posts. Brinkley appointed Edward Middleditch, a distinguished and very lively ex-College painter as head of the painting school. After a lot of talking he persuaded Frank Ariss, a young former student of his to run the graphic design school. Middleditch soon established a good staff around him and in no time had an excellent fine art diploma course under way. Frank Ariss had other problems, apart from the fact that he commuted from Croydon to Norwich. He had to show that he was running a viable course and he had only six not very promising students in their final year. Frank thought for a while. It was obvious their individual talents were not up to much, so he set them a group project. This was to design a package for a Rolls-Royce Turbo-bypass Jet engine. The students were flabbergasted.

'Don't worry,' he said to them. 'It's a nice little problem. I'll work on it with you.' The students looked doubtful. 'First of all,' he said, 'we'll build a simple mock-up of the engine in aluminium. Can anyone read engineering drawings?' There were dull shakes of the heads. 'Never mind, I'll soon show you. Now, has anyone had any welding experience?' None of them had. 'Well, I'll show you that too.'

They set to work and in six weeks had produced a most beautiful, 17 ft long, gleaming, aluminium artifact and those six, apparently dull students, had been metamorphosed into different people. The problem of packaging they took in their stride, dealing with all the stresses and strains needed for a box of that size to carry that weight. When this lovely aluminium object was nestling in its crate, Frank said, 'What about the graphics?'

One of the students walked forward with a stencil and slapped on to the outside of the box the words 'Made in Britain'.

It was on the dazzling mock-up of the Rolls-Royce engine that the visiting panel, without hesitation, awarded Norwich the right to run a graphic design diploma course.

Service on one of the Summerson Committee validating panels led in due course to most of the members becoming external examiners. When we started on this it was not considered necessary to interview the students, unless it was for some very special reason. I caused some alarm both at the schools and with my fellow assessors by insisting on having a lengthy talk with each student.

'In graphics,' I rather pompously insisted, 'you cannot separate the man from his work.' This became accepted practice and a meeting with the students earlier in the year served to break the ice. I found the work very stimulating. It had all the feed-back of successful teaching, but none of the day-to-day responsibility.

From the validating visits (something like thirty-six in the first three years) a few memories stick. One was of visiting three Welsh schools in succession. Ranging from very good to very bad. The most interesting of them was Newport and that was where I first met John Wright. He was clearly an inspiring teacher. With the help of Bob Falla, who had been one of our students at the College, John ran a lively graphic design course with a higher standard of drawing than any of us had so far seen.

Not long after our visit to Newport, John Wright, at the age of thirty-two was appointed principal. He made a brilliant success of the school. He was a very good painter, an excellent designer, a political animal and an afficionado of the bull fight. He covered the walls of his lavatory with bull-fighting ephemera. I visited Newport many times. The last time I was there the whole place was in mourning. The All Blacks had just beaten Wales at Cardiff Arms Park by precisely one point, with the last penalty kick of the game.

Liverpool was another school I had been to many times over the years. On one visit, I had completed my examining, except for a student who had failed to turn up. A message had come that she had domestic problems but would be in early next morning, so at some inconvenience I had to stay another night.

I was waiting for this reluctant young woman at 9 o'clock the following morning. She finally turned up at a quarter to one, by which time I was getting very angry. She was a poor little waif, with bedraggled fair hair.

'Where on earth have you been?' I asked.

She answered in a rich Scouse accent: 'I've been up all night with the baby.'

'Couldn't your husband have looked after it?'

'Husband? I haven't got a husband, he's a little bastard!'

I was completely deflated and in a wave of sentiment, I passed her. As a result of this, she got a job with a window-dressing firm the very next day.

As a Governor of Brinkley's school, I was having to make weekly visits to Norwich. These visits were enjoyable. John had made an unqualified success of the school, but he was having problems with the local education authorities. They were bombarding him with paper work and every day he seemed to be beset with needless bureaucratic pin-pricks. This began to tell on his health. He had always been asthmatic. Finally things got to such a pitch that his doctor ordered him to go away for a couple of weeks and to forget all about the school and its problems.

It was only a few days later that I had a call from the Chairman of the Governors, telling me that John Brinkley had died of a heart attack while on holiday in Wensleydale. He was fifty-seven.

In due course we had a Governors' Meeting to appoint a new principal. From a not very strong field, there was one possible candidate who was a sculptor. Bernard Meadows, Christopher Cornford and myself, the first two from the College and Peter Laslo from the University of East Anglia, all voted for him. The result was a dead heat with another candidate. The Chairman, ignoring the way his so-called experts had voted, cast his vote for the other candidate. As a result we resigned.

I had only one other experience of sitting on a Governing Body and this was for one of the technical colleges. I had been asked to sit on this body by the local art school, whose affairs were governed by it. At the first meeting I attended, I got the impression that the chief interest in the art school affairs of the Governors was how the various building contracts were going to be shared out. The only matter with any relevance to students was on the point of being brushed aside, when I leaped to my feet and made some contentious remarks about how I appeared to be the only person in the room who had any interest in student affairs. In spite of some grumbling from the Chair, I achieved some action on the matter.

At the end of the meeting, the Chairman said: 'This is an occasion when three Governors are due to retire and three new Governors will be elected. I will now draw lots.'

The first name that came out of the hat was mine. I have never sat on a Governing Body since.

*   *   *

For a spell of five successive years I visited the National College of Art and Design in Dublin. At meetings, and the Irish are great ones for meetings, we would soon get bogged down over some controversial point, tempers would begin to flare, then someone would say, 'We are not getting anywhere. Let's just go across the road to Buswells (that was the nearest bar). Maybe we'd do better over a jar.'

An hour later and after several pints of Guinness, we could not remember what we had been arguing about.

On one of my visits, I expressed concern about a particular student. He was a simple inarticulate country lad who was producing no work at all. I could see no way that he could gain his degree. After his tutor Iseult McCarthy had come all the way from Dublin to Suffolk to plead the boy's case, I said, 'You will have to do something pretty desperate to get him through.'

'I'll think of something,' Iseult said.

The shock treatment that they applied to this student was to take him, in company with one or two others, to Paris for a fortnight. It worked. The log jam was broken. Work flooded out of him and when some months later I examined him he proudly exhibited an impressive array of drawings. He also talked like a seasoned boulevardier and sailed through his examination.

10. An Irish Story

RALPH CUSACK HAD been my closest friend at Charterhouse, yet apart from a letter in 1947 and a catalogue or two from the nursery garden that he had established at Annamoe in County Wicklow, catalogues which were remarkable more for the quality of the prose than for the quality of the bulbs he was advertising, we had heard little from or about Ralph. We had been told by Louis Le Brocquy, the Irish painter who for a while taught at the College, that Ralph and Kira had parted and that he had taken up with a girl called Nancy, who was a cellist and as unconventional as Ralph. It was not until sometime later that we heard more. I was lunching at the Senior Common Room with the Guyatts and a friend of theirs, an Irish painter called Norah McGuinness. I asked Miss McGuinness if she knew Ralph.

'Knew him! Of course I knew him. Everybody knew Ralph. I suppose you heard how he had to leave the country?'

I shook my head.

'Bless the lad! Such an event hadn't happened since the Troubles. It must have been in the summer of 1948, Lady Cork and Orrery threw a garden party. A real, old-fashioned Edwardian do, with marquees and waiters and champagne and cucumber sandwiches and croquet. Everybody was there, and of course Ralph and Nancy were asked. They had not got quite the right kind of clothes for that sort of an affair, so to dull their senses a bit they finished off a bottle of paddy before they started out. At least they had the right sort of motorcar. It was a huge Renault of great age that Ralph had inherited from his father. The champagne on top of the whiskey was all that was needed to put Ralph into a fighting mood. He was in the big marquee and in no time he was having an argument with Mr Erskine Childers. Being unable to express himself fully enough, he knocked poor Mr Childers to the ground. Nancy hurried him away and into the car. He got the great old thing started up and slowly drove away.

' "Nancy, I'm afraid you don't love me any more!" he said.

' "That I don't," she replied. "Not if you go on behaving like you have today."

' "I was afeared of that," he said and put his foot down on the accelerator. When he had urged the Renault up to its maximum speed of about 50 mph, he swung it off the drive, on to the grass and headed back towards the centre of activity.

' "Where are you going?" Nancy cried.

' "Back into the tent!" he shouted. "I want another drink!" '

'By this time he was scattering people right, left and centre as he roared up to the marquee. In fact he did not get into the marquee, but he brought it down about his ears.'

'Wasn't anyone hurt?' I gasped.

'No, it was a miracle. Oh, I think some old waiter fell over and broke his leg, but no one seemed to worry about that.'

'What on earth happened then?' Dick Guyatt asked.

'I'm not too sure,' Norah McGuinness answered, 'but the next I heard he had sold up his nursery and departed with Nancy for the south of France. Ireland was the poorer for his departure.'

The next I heard from Ralph was one Christmas at the beginning of the 'sixties. He sent us a Christmas card with a few lines scribbled on it. I replied in kind. Early in January I heard from him again. He was living in a Provençal village called Spéracèdes.

After some contentious references to our old school he said:

> We live in a fantastically old troglodytic overcrowded house, which is gradually falling down (and not so gradually either in bad weather) but which, pace nuclear interference or the children setting fire to it, should stand for another couple of millenia. The place is like an Irish cabin (indeed it is one) transplanted to the south, but we have no pigs; only hens, wine, olives, fruit, vegetables, and eau-de-vie. I am the same age as yourself (fifty this autumn) but have been most fearfully ill for the past four years and have just recently pulled out of it so I am suffering from the dangerous delusion that I am getting younger every week: it is a matter of comparison. Formerly I could neither see nor walk: now I can do both in moderation . . . Your job seems to me ideal and I am so very glad you have been able to follow your bent with profit too. Louis Le Brocquy (an old friend of ours) lives 35 km away. He is very wealthy now and has a most beautiful wife. In spite of all his terrible nonsense I like him well. Sad to hear of your parents' death: I remember them, voices and all, very vividly, in Castle Street . . . Now DO come here. I think it would be fun and maybe somehow reassuring: I do not know how.
>
> Best wishes meanwhile,
> (Sgd) Ralph

After that we exchanged many letters. I wrote that we hoped we would be able to come over in the autumn. In one letter he told us:

> Over four years ago, I had a frightful operation called 'Smithwick's Sympathectomy' – invented by some bloody American surgeon. It has been given up now – it was so infrequently successful – in spite of which I survived. My back was slit open from top to bottom. They said it was meant to relieve hypertension and high blood pressure!

I fixed up our visit to Spéracèdes for the last week in September. Just before we left I had a note from Ralph saying he had arranged for us to stay very near their house at a little inn, *La Soleillade*, which was run by a youngish couple named Forest, who had worked in a circus. He ended this letter with:

> . . . Forest's grandfather, so he says, was the first man to put an internal combustion engine into a boat! . . . I wonder if we will know each other. If my old – 15 years old – car holds together, we'll be at the airport to meet you.

Our Comet landed at Nice on time and there at the barrier unmistakably was Ralph, with Nancy. They looked like a couple of peasants, just off the land, as in fact they were, for they had been picking jasmine since dawn. Nancy had a sweet gentle face, marked by a terrible scar that ran in a half-moon from her cheek-bone to her jaw. It was not until some days later that she told me that Ralph in a moment of madness, had smashed a broken tumbler into her face.

'Poor darling, he didn't know what he was doing,' was all she said.

In our respectable clothes, I felt they must have thought us very bourgeois. A couple of miles from the airport, we pulled up at a little café overlooking the sea. As we ate our meal, we were still shy of one another, still taking stock. When the bill came, I reached for my wallet.

'Oh! You oughtn't to do that!' Ralph said, but made no attempt to stop me. It was not until later that I found out how short of money they were and that he could not possibly have paid even that modest sum.

We dropped our bags at *La Soleillade* – the Forests were not in – and drove the few yards to the Cusack's troglodytic home. It was a tiny old cottage, hewn out of the rock. Behind it were steep little fields of jasmine, vines and olive trees. In front, the ground fell sharply away to a well-treed valley far below. It was all very primitive, with the bare rock serving for the walls at the back of the house, with geckos scuttling about everywhere. Ralph's and Nancy's ground floor bedroom looked like a second-hand bookshop with piles of books scattered over the floor. It had open rafters and just above the head of the bed was a wild bees' nest.

It was not long before all the barriers were down and we were talking each other's heads off. The years fell away and we might have been still at Charterhouse, whiling away long summer afternoons ostensibly watching cricket, reading and talking.

'Did I ever tell you why I had to leave Ireland?' he asked me.

'Was it anything to do with Lady Cork's party? I heard about that from Norah McGuinness.'

'What did she tell you?'

'Only that you had punched Mr Erskine Childers on the jaw and had run over an old waiter.'

'The trouble had nothing to do with Childers – after all he is a politician and should be used to that kind of thing. The old waiter was the rub.'

'As far as I remember, you only broke his leg!'

'Devil a bit of that! He was not hurt at all, but he had an acute heart condition and I was told by my solicitor that if I did not settle for a tidy sum right away, I would be up before the courts and if he died, I'd be on a manslaughter charge. The final advice my lawyer gave me was to get to hell out of the country.' He paused and smiled rather ruefully. 'I had to sell up everything in Ireland. My only other asset was my mother's villa at Menton.' He stopped and looked at me. 'Of course, you stayed there, when we went to the Monaco Grand Prix in the pouring rain. Well, I had let it over the years to some old girl who was always wanting to buy it. So I sent her a telegram saying she could have it if she could find me a small-holding, where I and my concubine (that's what they call them in France) and our numerous children could earn enough to exist on. Within forty-eight hours, she wired me back to say she had found this little place.'

'Can you make a living off it?' I asked.

'Just about, there's a hectare of jasmine. We sell the crop, which goes on for about four months, to the scent factory at Grasse. We have another hectare of olive trees – the olives go to the co-operative in the village – and our vineyard. That produces an average of about 1800 litres, which, since I stopped drinking, just about keeps Nancy going until the next harvest.'

'Did the waiter die?'

'Good heavens! No! He's now a prosperous hotelier on Achill Island.'

A few days later, Ralph's eldest son, Roy, who earned his living as a house painter, came over to help with the *vendange*. He was a dear gentle fellow with considerable organizing ability. We started picking the grapes at dawn. As soon as our baskets were filled, the grapes were tipped into a huge stone vat at the back of the house. Meanwhile, as Nancy after a certain amount to drink had retired to bed, Griselda after sweeping about a ton of rubbish out of the kitchen was cooking half-a-dozen chickens and about fifty kilos of potatoes to feed the helpers and the family.

The most memorable sight of the day was Susannah, Ralph's and Nancy's lovely sixteen-year-old daughter, practically naked, trampling the grapes and covered with grape juice up to her thighs. It was like a pagan rite. The lasting impression of that household, with all its Irish squalor and its primitive vagaries, was a feeling of love. The fact that there were old bones and crusts and other unmentionable things scattered over the kitchen floor, and that the bedroom had not been dusted in living memory counted for little in the balance against that.

Over the years, we have stayed in a fair variety of pubs, including Leonardo Walsh's *Locanda* at S. Vigilio, but none has matched the idiosyncratic *La Soleillade*. Michel Forest and his pretty little wife Josette had for twelve years earned their living as circus performers. They called themselves 'Les Deux Crags' after some English woman who had had quintuplets. Their act, so they told us, consisted of Michel holding a long stainless steel pole with a vertical ring at the top into which a bicycle was fixed. Josette would climb up the pole and mount the bicycle. Then like a squirrel in a cage, she would pedal frantically looping the loop inside the ring. Meanwhile Michel, as if he was a Salvation Army lass holding a banner, would be doing a tap dance.

'You must be very strong,' Griselda said.

'Pas du tout,' he answered, 'c'est seulement l'équilibre!'

We asked Josette if she had ever fallen and hurt herself. Apparently she had broken four ribs in Madrid, both arms in Stockholm, her collar bone in Warsaw; and as for her head, she had fallen on it more times than she could remember.

'C'est pourquoi elle n'est pas très intellectuelle!' Michel said.

I had a letter from Ralph a couple of days after we had returned home. He wrote:

> I cannot really believe that it is only a week since the *vendange*, when you both came to our aid so magnificently. More like six months I'd say. And we both, *all*, miss you sorely ever since . . . it was a great joy meeting you and Griselda too. A kind of very special life encouragement. Nancy and the children never stop singing your praises . . .

This was followed three days later with another letter:

> Nancy quite well again – whilst I am a bit off colour. We seem to be a bit like those dreadful Swiss barometers with either the man or the woman coming out of the doors, but never both.
>
> Somewhat shaken yesterday by a telegram from Brendan Behan announcing his imminent arrival; we had just read he is being chased by solicitors on account of a libel action on account of his new book – so he is taking refuge here: I have put him on to the Forests, hoping that their experience in the circus will have made them the people to deal with him . . .

We waited with some apprehension to hear what effect one explosive Irishman would have on another, even if most of the fireworks had been knocked out of Ralph. In due course we had a report:

> Brendan's visit was a nightmare. The Forests behaved marvellously, managing to deal with him with a mixture of cajolery and toughness. He was at last got off with the help of the BBC and the *Daily Mail* and the Forests and the male nurse, to appear in some crapulous T.V. programme called *This is your life* to whose lustre I can hardly imagine he added. But it was all tragic, worse than Dylan: his wife treated him *dreadfully* . . . We were horrified at his decline in the last eight years both physically and mentally: a veritable dollar pimp. Oh, America ruins everything and everybody it touches . . .
> P.S. Brendan says he was at the Borstal at Woodbridge!

As Ralph for the previous ten years had not drunk a drop of alcohol, his great need was for tea. This we dispatched to him, and Griselda found a mohair blanket which we sent them as a thank-you present for all their love and kindness. The blanket took a couple of months to reach him. By mid-December, we had decided it was lost, when we heard it had at last reached Spéracèdes.

> Vasty thanks for that utterly magnificent blanket which arrived perfectly (and freely) last Monday. Nancy was ill in bed. I was just well enough to go to Grasse to pick it up at the railway office, and the next day joined her under it, where I stayed grievously afflicted for 48 hours. Since then it had been very hard for us to drag ourselves out of the marvellous warm cocoon into which it has turned the bed. We have slept better and fantastically late under its magic nonsensically named (O Sole Mio) down, the first new bed covering we have ever had! Repeat, ever!

The following summer, Ralph was in hospital at Grasse for nearly three months, with supposed threatened T.B. At the beginning of 1965 he wrote to me:

> It would be lovely to see you again and talk to you both. I fear I have run a little further down the hill since last we met – but I hope to be in good form by March and be able to enjoy your visit and not be a wet rag.

I had almost left it too late. We had a sad little visit. Ralph never left his bed, though his conversation was still pointed and witty. We laughed a lot, but when I left him, we both had tears in our eyes. We knew we would never meet again, at least in this life.

At the end of July, we had a letter from Michel Forest telling us that Ralph had just died in the hospital at Grasse. After that, we had one or two quite cheerful letters from Nancy, but in the following January we heard from her boy Colin, telling us that she had committed suicide by taking a huge quantity of sleeping pills.

'She never really got over Daddy's death,' Colin wrote, 'though she had often been happy since.'

Poor Nancy! I can see her now as I first saw her at the airport, looking like a gypsy, with a shawl round her shoulders, her feet in old gardening shoes and that great scar in some way not disfiguring her kind, smiling, sunburnt face.

11. Boats and Books

IN SPITE OF Jan van Krimpen's strictures, I had continued to sail. In 1960 I had a new boat built. I called her *Patient Griselda*. Soon after her launch, I nearly ended my days whilst laying out an anchor in the Orford River. After that she served us well. She was a pretty boat and heavily built. Her solidity was a comfort to us on our journeys through Dutch canals. On the first of many cruises across the North Sea, I ended up in Friesland with shingles. The old Zuider Zee ports were still uncrowded, though, with the shutting out of the North Sea, Zeeland was changing. The fishing fleet had departed from Veere. Van Loon would have been sad, for his beloved Veere had become fossilized into a museum town and the once deserted Zaandkreek was alive with sailing dinghies.

In 1967 Griselda and I were invited by John Dixon, a casual acquaintance at the Garrick, to join him for a cruise on the west coast of Scotland. It was an uneventful couple of weeks but it gave us a taste for those incomparable waters. A year later we sailed *Patient Griselda* up there, for the first of many seasons among the Western Isles. In the same year Adlard Coles published *A Taste for Sailing*. This was an account of Griselda's and my fumbling attempts to learn how to sail. The book sold only 1800 copies and was then pulped. Yet of all the books I have written, this is the one about which I have had by far the biggest fan mail. A kind review in *Blackwood's Magazine*, led to the publication of accounts in *Maga* of our cruises in *Patient Griselda* to the west coast of Scotland and the Outer Hebrides.[1]

On one of these cruises, Tom Nunn, my old compositor friend from Cowells joined me at Mallaig. We had an easy sail southwards and after passing through the Crinan Canal, we anchored for the last night in the Kyles of Bute just off the entrance to Loch Ridden in Glen Caladh. Two other boats were at anchor, both of them venerable craft. They added to the charm of the place.

We sat on deck, watching the reflection in the water of the lights on the other boats. We talked until late about this and that. One of the subjects we touched on was industrial relations and Tom's experiences at Cowells.

'You take Mr Geoffrey,' he said. 'You know, he never came on the works without asking me how my wife was, or how the boy was getting on. Somehow you felt he cared – not like most of them nowadays. If only they would realize that sometimes a kind word means more than another quid in your pay packet. It's all much more impersonal now; that's what's wrong with industry.'

The happiest cruises that I had on the west coast of Scotland were with Tom Nash. He was a young architect and a second cousin of John Nash, but a couple of generations younger. The pleasures of sailing depend largely on the company. Griselda had had to give it up because as a side effect of her coeliac condition, she could not bear the cold. She was no spoil-sport and cheerfully sent me off for weeks at a time while she looked after the cats, the house and the garden. Tom was not only a good crew but a good companion and a fine cook.

Though we have sailed to the Outer Hebrides and up the west coast many times, my favourite place is Canna. Rhum, Muck, Eigg and Canna make up the Small Isles that lie between the islands of Skye and Mull.

On one occasion, returning from further north, we sailed out of the fishing port of Mallaig. We had Roger Finch[2] with us. The morning forecast offered us cyclonic winds backing into the north west. We had a quiet sail round the Point of Sleat then the wind eased away to nothing. The sea had a silken, somewhat ominous look about it, and as we approached Rhum the gentle underlying swell began to increase. The wind came up out of the north-west and was soon blowing hard.

The Sound between Rhum and Canna is only a couple of miles wide. With a northerly wind funnelling through that narrow stretch of water against the tide, an ugly sea soon gets up. As we came into the Sound, the wind increased. *Patient Griselda*'s side decks were awash and she began to wallow. We managed to drop and stow the main sail, then under storm jib and the diesel we battled our way across the Sound. By this time, a big hollow sea was running and I began to wonder if we would reach the harbour. The alternative was to make for Tobermory. The thought of running thirty or forty miles through the night, before what looked like the beginnings of quite a gale was not pleasant to contemplate.

Slowly we inched our way across the Sound, sometimes being stopped dead as our little boat butted her full bows into the wall of a hollow sea. The Lister diesel, bless its heart, never faltered and at last we came into the harbour and were soon under the shelter of the cliffs. Canna has the most secure of harbours and is quite landlocked.

'I think we have earned a wee dram,' Tom remarked as we struggled out of our oilskins. *Patient Griselda*'s cabin was in some contrast to the scene outside, where it was now blowing a full gale. The soft lamplight lit up the unpainted woodwork as well as our flushed faces. Tom was a master cook and we dined off Dublin Bay prawns and fillet steaks with fried potatoes and a ratatouille and drank a bottle of Moroccan wine.

'I think this is the great joy of sailing,' Tom said. 'You have all that awful buffeting about and yet within half an hour of dropping the anchor with the lamps alight and the coal stove going, there is nowhere in the world I would rather be.'

186

'That must be the malt whisky talking,' Roger Finch, the third member of our crew said. Roger who had once been the mate of a Thames barge and had had more experience of sailing than Tom and I put together, was never one to see the romantic side of the sport.

'Thank God we are in here and not outside,' I interjected.

'I should say so,' Roger said. 'This harbour is well sheltered, but I reckon these seas are no place for a small boat like this in bad weather. I'd prefer to be among the soft mudbanks of the East Coast to banging into all these rocks.'

That night it blew a full gale. A dozen or so fishing trawlers joined us, Moored close together in tiers, they made an eerie sight in this normally deserted bay. Their decks were flooded with light, and on every boat, in spite of the wind and the driving rain, yellow oilskinned figures were working on deck repairing their nets and going over their gear.

The next morning the sun was shining. I went on deck to take down the riding light. A curlew was calling from the rocks and a couple of oyster catchers were chattering away on the nearby tide line, poking about in the seaweed looking for shell fish.

Canna that morning looked like paradise. Its fresh greenness was in some contrast to the tundra bleakness of the Outer Isles. Later when we went ashore and climbed up Compass Hill, we found a carpet of wild flowers under our feet including the rare Hebridean orchis. Canna always seemed to be a sunny island, in some contrast to the great rocky, cloud-shrouded pile of Rhum.

The following day, it was still blowing quite hard but the sun shone and it was a fair wind. We rolled our way southwards over a brilliant cobalt sea, a big rolling sea, sparkling and white crested. And so we came to Tobermory.

Like most typographers who write, I wrote mainly about design and printing or about illustration, and only incidentally about boats and sailing. At the same time Griselda was writing about English pottery. The articles I wrote for the yachting press and later for *Blackwood's Magazine* and the books about sailing began as a means of financing my boats, but developed into a pleasant hobby. Writing about experiences of sailing through the waterways of the Netherlands and along the coasts of the North Sea or through the Western Isles was a way of repeating the enjoyment of those often blissful, sometimes frightening times. I am not sure that the writing was not more enjoyable than the actual sailing.

My writing about boats, which began with the lifeboat book and continued with a much larger book called *Small Craft Conversion*, was followed in turn by *Vintage Boats*, the reverse side of the coin. This book described how old, often converted craft were restored to something like their original form. My most helpful editor at David and Charles was James Moore, himself a keen sailor. I met some wonderfully dedicated characters including a Colchester dental surgeon who spent eight years rebuilding the oldest Colchester oyster boat that was still afloat, and a retired Wing Commander from the Australian Air Force who devoted nearly twenty years to re-rigging, re-engining and bringing up to a state of perfection the schooner, *Heartsease*, making her the most beautiful sailing boat that was still afloat. Sadly in 1993 she was sold to a new owner, who within a few months had her broken up.

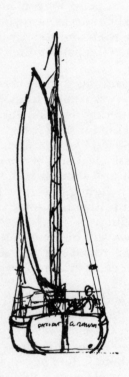

12. Casting Off

IT WAS TOWARDS the end of 1975 that we bought a little house in the centre of Woodbridge, in a backwater called Doric Place. It was in a terrible condition though its nonagenarian owner was proud of the fact that her scullery was separate from the kitchen. Both rooms were Dickensian in their primitiveness. The stone sink was a replica of the dreadful old one at 9 Castle Street with the taps a good 3 ft up from it. However, the house had character and a garden of nearly half an acre with an old stable building that we thought might serve as a work room.

We missed the space of our surrounding wilderness at Meadow Cottage, but soon found compensation in living in the town close to the shops, the post office and the railway station. The river and my boat were a mere 300 yards away. It was remarkably quiet, except for the cries of the gulls and the occasional redshank and during the day the hum of the machinery in the mill on the quayside.

Eighteen months before we left Meadow Cottage, Minky, our beloved Burmese cat died, and within a year his brother Moosie followed him. They had given us unalloyed pleasure and happiness for fourteen years, the span of their all too short lives. We felt we could never have cats again.

Within a week of Moosie's death, a little brown and white tortoise-shell cat came into the garden. She was quite wild and clearly very hungry. Griselda put out some milk for her and the next day she arrived with a kitten. The following day she arrived with two kittens, the day after with three and finally four. Each time we put something out for them. After that we saw no more of her, but she left us with three of the kittens – two girls and a very plain black and white tom. They were as wild as their mother. We discovered later that they had been born in a hollow tree stump and had been badly frightened by a couple of village lads who had tried to winkle them out of their lair. They remained very wild, and within six months one of them had produced a litter of four. We found homes for three kittens and had to keep the plainest who we called Emma. She turned out to be a boy, but Emma he remained. The other female who had remained untouchable, then in her turn had a litter of four. Even though she was so wild, she sought Griselda's help with her accouchement.

We moved to Doric Place with seven semi-feral cats and very plain they all were. We left the black and white tom with the new owners of

Meadow Cottage and found homes for the four kittens. That reduced the score to three. The intrusion of these country cats into Doric Place did not please the local cats at all. Night after night there were fearful punch-ups. Among the prowling town cats was a stray, a large pathetic looking, obviously starving ginger tom. One afternoon in order to chase him off, I bent down to pick up a stone. He saw what I was doing and let out so miserable a wail that I dropped it, whereupon he rushed up to me and rubbed his mangy old pelt against my legs. I was so moved by this that I fetched him some food. He was ravenous, but his mouth was so ulcerated he could barely eat. In spite of his shabby appearance, there was something nice about him. We were not going to have him in the house, so I made him a kennel out of an old tea chest and placed it near the tool shed. We took him to the vet, who cured his ulcers and his other sores, and neutered the poor old thing at the same time. After that he began to put on weight and grew into the most handsome cat, but he still lived in his kennel. It must have been at least two months before anything else happened, then one night I was awakened by a noise like an outboard motor battering my ears and a great weight on my chest. It was the stray – he had found his way into the house. Things moved quickly after that. The other cats accepted him, but when they were fed, he would sit back as if to say, 'I know my place, I'm much too 'umble to put myself forward.'

To the end of his life he was head cat, though he still let the others eat his food if they wanted to. They were still rather wild and quite different creatures from the Burmese, or even from the stray who finally answered, when he felt like it, to the name of Marmalade. But they all had their individual charms.

*   *   *

Just after we had bought the Doric Place house, Griselda was working in the garden when one of our geriatric neighbours leant over the garden gate and said in a tremulous voice, 'Are you the people who have bought No. 6?' Griselda said we were. In reply she quavered: 'Oh! I'm so glad an elderly couple have come here!' With which she tottered off. That made us feel rather depressed.

The Spences were almost our first visitors after we had moved. Basil approved of what we had done to the house. In his praise of others he was always the most generous of men. We had seen very little of them from the time Basil and Joan left Landermere, which coincided with the completion of Coventry Cathedral. After that came the years of his great successes, culminating in the British Embassy building in Rome. Each Christmas we had a card from them, but it was not until 1974 that they came back into our lives. They had wearied of the Beaulieu River where they had built a house. Until such time as they could find a house in East Anglia, they had rented a small farmhouse near Bures. From that time on we saw a lot of them and in the autumn of that year they invited us to stay with them in Malta. We were their first – and indeed last guests, apart from their family, to stay at Dar-Tal-Ghar, their house which was built on the side of a hill. It was on the south coast, overlooking the island of Filfla. It was built of honey-coloured stone in the local idiom. It was a very pretty house with cool marble floors and a garden with orange, lemon and pomegranate trees.

One afternoon Basil took us down to visit Victor Pasmore. He lived in a house with a rectangular courtyard, just like a Roman villa. He told us they kept well clear of the sociable comings and goings of the local people. 'I have to tell them I have come here to paint, not to attend coffee mornings,' he said. 'It is a painter's island.'

Viewed from the heights of the old city of Medina, it certainly was. The landscape looked like a patchwork quilt worked in shades of dusty green and old gold. The natives were an unsmiling lot. At weekends the peace of Dar-Tal-Ghar was shattered by the local lads blazing off at anything that flew, and particularly at the migrating birds that used Malta as a staging post in their flight across the Mediterranean to North Africa.

A mile or so from the Spence's house were some high cliffs. These were penetrated by numerous caves which were still inhabited. The sound of transistors coming from the cavernous depths and the shiny Volkswagens parked at the entrances struck a somewhat incongruous note. One afternoon we climbed up the cliffs to a tableland where there was a pre-historic Clapham Junction, a marshalling yard of railway lines cut out of the surface of the rock. Beyond were some standing stones. These were the remains of megalithic temples that had marked similarities to Stonehenge. There seemed to be little interest in the English community about such things. Their thoughts were mostly about their bridge, or golf or the iniquities of Dom Mintoff.

It was during this holiday that Basil began to feel the first symptoms of the cancer that was so soon to kill him. In spite of that, he was as full of life as ever, even though there were times when his resentment against the critics would come bubbling up. He had clearly been deeply hurt by some of the things that lesser men had written about his buildings. Hugh Casson later said, 'Basil was born with a skin too few, if he was going to have the success he so rightly deserved.'

It was soon after our visit to Malta that the Spences bought Yaxley Hall, near the Suffolk–Norfolk borders. It was an intriguing house – in fact it looked more like a street of houses with one part Tudor, one part seventeenth century Dutch and one part Regency. In six weeks Basil had had the house stripped and completely redecorated. His genius was manifold. He was a perfectionist craftsman, and he had a capacity to inspire people to work for him. These two facets were combined in the exquisite little Chinoiserie pavilion that he designed and had built to decorate the courtyard below his bedroom window.

The fact that his cancer was developing fast in no way seemed to

191

lessen his delight in living, his enjoyment of good wine and food and his pleasure in his friends' company; even though he was undergoing the most painful deep-ray treatment, he would not give in. Three weeks before he died, he drove Joan down to Woodbridge to have lunch with us. It was his last outing. He knew he was dying, but he lived his life to the full to the very end. Each day he woke up saying to Joan, 'Well, I've got another day.' The pavilion – the last thing he ever designed – was completed the day before he died.

Basil was buried in the church yard at Thornham Parva. The little church was filled with family and one or two friends. As the young priest began to take the service, a shaft of sunlight suddenly illuminated the coffin. It looked as if Basil had arranged with the Almighty to fix the lighting.

It was in many ways a sad decade, for although they were very productive years for us, a number of our friends had died. Anna Hadfield was the first. In December 1975 we saw the first of three obituaries in *The Times* to Valerie White (the Billie of Goldsmiths' days). Every Christmas we had exchanged cards. She had always written, 'Let us meet this year.' We never had. Then in succession Freddy Mayor, Bobby Bevan, Nick Bentley and Brian Robb died. Last and most tragically, John Sewell, who had been on that student trip to Amsterdam in the early 'fifties, threw himself in front of a train at Holland Park station. Six weeks before I had talked and laughed with him at a gallery in Cambridge where he was having a one-man show of his work. It was well received, but he did not sell a single picture. Margot Hamilton-Hill, the girl whose handbag he had travelled half across the Netherlands to retrieve, broken-heartedly told me the news.

It was in 1974 that Larry Lamb had had a stroke. Within a week or so I had quite a cheerful letter from him. Though he could no longer work, he continued to write amusing letters to his friends. It was not until nearly three years later that Griselda and I, after a visit to the Cumberleges, called in to see the Lambs. We were horrified to find how crippling the stroke had been, yet we marvelled at his fortitude. His eyes sparkled even through his tears of pleasure. The spirit had conquered the flesh. Two weeks later, he was dead. Lamb's funeral was in a curious way a joyous occasion; we all felt, and most of all his wife Biddy felt, that he had been released from intolerable bonds.

Jock Cumberlege and Larry were devoted to each other. Jock wrote to me just after our last visit to Lamb. 'The day following your visit to him which brought him intense pleasure, he battled against his handicap and wrote us a long letter, full of twinkle – I wonder if in the end he could still emit that squirting chuckle! Fortunately he is to me clearly seen, full of life, vigour and enthusiasm and the L L of perhaps 1950. I know of none who can fill his place as an illustrator of the Victorian age.'

John Nash, ever since we moved to Manningtree in 1946, had been one of our closest friends. When I was working with Studio Vista I tried to persuade them to publish a monograph on his work, but they said there was no market for such books. It was not until Simon Heneage suggested that I wrote a book on John Nash's works as an illustrator that any publication seemed possible. John seemed pleased, though no doubt he would have preferred a book about what he used to call his more serious work.

I discussed the project with him. He was as helpful as could be and dredged up a surprising amount of information from the depths of his memory; yet he was not really interested. It had come too late. It was while I was working on the book that Christine died quite suddenly. I went over to see John the next day. He was quite shattered.

After a while he started to talk. 'The old girl hadn't been in very good shape over the last week. She was sitting down a lot, which wasn't like her. Then yesterday morning, she brought up my early morning tea as usual; she had given the postman his usual cup . . .' He stopped talking for a moment, wiped his nose and then continued, 'that'll be the last cup of tea he will ever get . . . then she collapsed. By the time the ambulance arrived I was only half dressed and never even said goodbye to her. I ran after the ambulance with my trousers half on and half off, but they didn't stop . . .'

Over the next few months, he must have had a series of small heart attacks. Ronald Blythe moved in to look after John, almost abandoning his own work. Before long the strain began to tell on Ronnie and he rang me up. 'I'd no idea what Christine had to put up with!' he said. 'The old man's so demanding. He's an absolute monster!'

I drove straight over to Bottengoms to see if I could help. Ronnie was in his bedroom trying to finish an introduction to a new edition of *War and Peace*. I walked into the sitting-room to talk to John. After a few minutes he began to fidget. 'Where is Ronnie?' he asked querulously. 'What is he doing?'

'He is finishing his introduction to *War and Peace*.'

'Bloody old Tolstoy!' was all he said. Then after a moment or two he looked up and said, 'It's no fun, old boy, this business of slowly falling off a twig!'

A few days later I telephoned Ronnie to see how John was, only to hear that a specialist had been to see him. He had said that John must have had another stroke during the night, and was quite unfit to be at home.

'The poor old dear was eating nothing and trembling badly,' Ronnie said. 'Yesterday he insisted on changing his clothes no less than five times. Last night we watched the Covent Garden Gala on television and John suddenly became convinced we were sitting in the stalls and were improperly dressed. "What will they say, seeing us dressed like this?" he kept repeating."'

The last time I spoke to the old man he was in a geriatric ward in one of the Colchester hospitals. He looked very ill and very old. However, he cheered up when he saw Griselda.

'We have just come from seeing Natalie,' I said, referring to Bobby Bevan's beautiful widow.

A gleam came into his faded eyes. 'Oh! To be seventy again!' he said.

We called once more at the hospital. We found him asleep. For a moment I did not recognize him. I gave his shoulder a gentle nudge and then a firm shake, but he did not stir. His face was twitching like that of an old dog, dreaming of the chase. We stood by his bedside for a little while and then crept away. That night he died. In his will he left me his water colour drawing of the Gower that used to hang in the kitchen at Bottengoms, with a note saying that Christine wanted me to have it. He also left me the task of being his literary executor.

It would be an understatement to say that I missed him and his old fashioned ways, his courtesy, his earthiness and his sense of values. I hoped that he had gone to join his friend Clarence Elliott and that they were beating the reaches of Elysian rivers in search of such trout as they never caught on earth. In many ways John Nash had been *in loco parentis* to me. He taught me so much – and there was no one to fill the gap.

The book came out in 1979, eighteen months after he had died. I am sorry he did not live to see it. An aspect of his work that surprised many people was the chapter devoted to his funny drawings. If he had never done anything else, he could have made a career as a comic draughtsman.

John had been a marvellous correspondent. Every year when he was on a painting holiday and it was too wet to paint he would sit and write to those he called his 'dear ones' or even his 'inner ring dear ones'. Just after his golden wedding celebrations, when the Cranbrooks had given him a splendid garden party, we heard from him. After thanking us for some little present we had given them he wrote: 'I forgot that we had been the cause of your knowing Jock and Fidelity (Cranbrook) – well, that was a happy chance and I should be grateful, as I am, to old Lance (Sieveking) for bringing us together with them and that camouflage course for the pleasures of our friendship with *you*. Old Wolfers has borrowed something of mine from Agnew's for his new gallery – there's something rather endearing about him, though he always sounds so low. No chance now of us beating the bloody Aussies owing to this beastly weather. . . .'

In a letter written from Ironbridge in 1956, he wrote: 'Here we are with acid Edward (Bawden) and jovial Carel (Weight), jolly Charlotte (Bawden) and the old trout Muriel Rose, and talking of trouts, I caught two beauties with Clarence on the way here . . . I've done three paintings and a bit – but Carel has done an oil painting every day it seems while Edward keeps his work secretly in his room and does not divulge progress. Carel and I play bar billiards every night, but Bawden will not join in these simple diversions.' John Nash's relationship with Edward Bawden was given some piquancy by Edward's acerbic, if teasing, remarks about John's sketches. He would lean over John's shoulder and say, 'That's a very unpromising viewpoint,' or, 'Do you think you will be able to make anything of that?'

Before I had finished the John Nash book, Barrie and Jenkins, through James Moore, who had moved on from David and Charles, said they would like to publish a book about Rowland Hilder that I was already working on. From the time when we moved to Manningtree we had seen little of the Hilders. At one stage they had joined some communal living scheme down in Kent. It was not exactly our scene and we seemed to have grown apart. Also Rowland viewed my connection with the College with grave distrust. He associated the College with the art establishment he so feared and disliked.

When *A Taste for Sailing* was published, I sent Rowland a copy and had a most appreciative letter in response. It was not until five or six years later that he wrote to me, asking me if I would be willing for him to illustrate it. We met and picked up the threads where we had left off thirty years before as if there had been no lapse of time. We discussed *A Taste for Sailing* and within a few days he had knocked off twenty or so sketches. It was then that we decided to modify the book and to call it *From Limehouse Reach*. It soon became obvious to me that my book would be swamped by Rowland's drawings, but for a while we persevered with the idea. Then one day, when I was down at Blackheath, he rather nervously asked me if I would be willing to do a book on his work. Perhaps I hesitated for a moment, for he immediately said with an embarrassed laugh, 'Of course, it is probably the last thing you would want to do!' I put his mind at rest and said I would be proud to do it. From that moment *From Limehouse Reach* was put in limbo.

A day or so later, Rowland wrote to me: 'Regarding the book on my work – it suddenly struck me that although I knew about your later work, your books and so on – you can't know mine for the last fifteen to twenty years, and it was presumptuous of me to suggest you "write me up" – you may well think my developments in art are quite horrid!'

On my next visit to Blackheath, I once again settled that, but not before, over a bottle of whisky, I had had to sit through a passionate diatribe against the art establishment and the critics.

When he next wrote to me he said: 'I know I had a good bind over far too much whisky – but I felt fine after that – quite cured but had a feeling that you took what I said to heart. What I would not like to see happening is for you to get involved in defending me against all those bastards. All that is past now. Things like advertising and illustration, once dirty words, are now becoming an interesting facet of history.'

He may well have thought that such worries were things of the past, but every so often these complaints would erupt as if they were some festering sore.

I spent many hours at Blackheath talking to Rowland and going through his sketches, paintings and illustrations. The book began to take shape. The early drawings of shipping must have been a revelation to those who only knew his much reproduced paintings of Kentish oast houses.

We had various signing sessions; one at Blackwell's bookshop in Oxford, when we cleared sixty-one books in one hour. The book sold well but was practically ignored by the critics, though there was a short notice in the Robert Harling-edited *House and Garden* which said, 'Everyone, apart from a blinkered aesthetic minority, understands and appreciates his drawings and paintings, and likes the subjects he chooses to draw; ships, barns, waterside houses, estuaries, windmills. The artist's multitudinous admirers will find this a highly covetable volume.' In a talk on the BBC, Jane Gibb said, 'This really is a lovely book and it gave me a lot of happiness over Christmas.' Maybe that sums it up. Rowland Hilder had become a people's artist. When we were having our signing sessions, person after person came up to say how much pleasure his work had given them over the years. The artist himself positively glowed at these spontaneous tributes.

Before the Rowland Hilder book was published, Griselda and I started work on the production of a book about Edward Bawden for Simon Heneage. This was to be a follow-up to my book about John Nash. Heneage had persuaded Douglas Percy Bliss to write the text. Bliss, who for many years was the Director of the Glasgow School of Art, had known Bawden since they were at College together. He was also a close friend of Rowland Hilder's and I had met him more than once when I was living at Blackheath.

On a warm September day Griselda and I drove over to Saffron Walden to Bawden's house, into which he had moved from Great Bardfield, not long before his wife died. It was a small terrace house just off the main street behind the Co-op. It was chock-a-block with pretty things; it might have been the home of a tasteful maiden lady instead of such an apparently austere person as Bawden. The austerity was not even skin deep. Over the years he had mellowed. He had also become a very good cook and seemed to delight in entertaining his friends.

Bliss was in some awe of Bawden and was clearly overwhelmed at the prospect of going through literally hundreds of drawings and boxes of printed reproductions. He did not seem to know where to start, so Edward said rather firmly: 'I think you had better leave it to John and Griselda to choose the pictures. They are designing the book. They will make a better job of it than you will!'

Douglas Bliss, far from being affronted by such a blunt statement, was delighted to be relieved of this chore. When we discovered how much work Bawden had done during his long career, we also were somewhat daunted.

I had written about Bawden's work in *Graphic Design*, the book on which I collaborated with John Brinkley in the 'fifties. Brinkley admired his work as much as I did. At the time *Graphic Design* came out, Bawden was very much a designer's artist. Robert Harling collected and used his work extensively; Ruari McLean did the same. The Curwen Press, that patron of the arts, used his work more than that of any other artist.

The book slowly grew. Bliss's text was sympathetic and the Scolar Press printed it well. It was the first book that had Griselda's and my name as co-designers and it was the nicest book we had done. For the jacket we used a wallpaper design that Bawden had done for Coles. It was the same one that lined the walls of the College Senior Common Room in Cromwell Road.

*　　*　　*

'You must have very catholic tastes,' John Hadfield remarked on the day my book on Rowland Hilder's work appeared. 'First Heath Robinson, then John Nash and now Hilder, let alone the Bawden book you are working on. Unlikely bedfellows, I would have thought.'

They were unlikely bedfellows. The Heath Robinson book had happened in a roundabout way. I had known Heath Robinson's eldest son Oliver since we had been in Camouflage together and I had often talked to him about his father's work. Oliver's younger brother Quentin had been planning to write a life of his father, but hearing I was interested in Heath Robinson, suggested we collaborated. Soon after that, pressure of work caused him to withdraw and I was left to do the book alone.

Ever since my father had sent me a copy of *The Water Babies* during the First World War, I had loved his work. Not so much for his funny drawings and strange inventions but his illustrations to such books as *Bill the Minder* or *A Midsummer Night's Dream.* At Goldsmiths', Hilder had tried to steer me away from my attempts to draw in a Heath Robinson manner.

William Heath Robinson had died in 1944. By 1972, when I started work on the book, his widow Josephine was ninety-four. She was living with her daughter Joan at Hornchurch in Essex. After an exchange of correspondence we visited her in April and found her to be a sprightly, bright-eyed little woman with the mind and charms of a girl. She talked at length about her husband. The first revelation was when she said, 'Will hated doing all those funny drawings. If I looked out of the kitchen window and saw him pacing up and down his studio, we knew things were not going well. At the end of the day he would bring his drawing in for me to see. If, as sometimes happened, I didn't see the joke, he would get awfully cross.' She stopped and sat silent for a moment, twisting her shawl in her hands, then said, 'What he wanted to be remembered for was what he called his "serious work", his illustrations for books like *A Midsummer Night's Dream*. He thought the pen drawings in that were the best things he had ever done.'

Those remarks confirmed my own feelings. I decided there and then that I would try and make sure that Heath Robinson's 'serious work' really would be remembered.

Griselda and I spent many hours at Hornchurch with Josephine (as she soon asked us to call her) and her daughter Joan. Our visits, which took place in the afternoons, were always punctuated with large nursery teas. Josephine had a great weakness for potted meats. I soon fell in love with that delightful old lady, who in many ways seemed anything but old.

In answer to some question that I put to her, Josephine said, 'You know, John, we were very ordinary people. We lived a happy life and Will earned enough to educate the family well. Of course he had no idea of money and never saved any.'

In fact, Josephine had been left quite badly off. One day at the Garrick I happened to mention this to Nick Bentley. 'I am sitting on the Civil List Pensions Committee,' he said. 'I'll see what I can do.' In due course Josephine was awarded a pension which gave her particular pleasure, because she regarded it as a tribute to Will.

When the book had been set, I sent the proofs to Josephine; she not only read them carefully, but picked out several literals, marking them with the proper proof-correction marks. I marvelled on this but all she said was, 'I was brought up surrounded by galley proofs, we were always being pulled in to help correct proofs.'[1] Nick Bentley wrote a perceptive introduction to the book.

In December 1974 Josephine Heath Robinson died, just thirty years after Will's death. I felt I knew Will almost as well as I had known Josephine. Larry Lamb was the only person, outside his family, that I knew who had actually met Heath Robinson. Larry had been taken up to Highgate to have tea with him by his son, Alan, who was a fellow student of Lamb's at the Central.

'He was a lovely man,' Larry said, 'not at all melancholic as most humorists are. He had a great sense of fun, but he knew full well that to make his comic drawings work, all the little people in them had to be immensely serious. The idea, current at the time, that he was mad, pleased him no end!'

*   *   *

Every time I had been to the Reading Room at the British Museum, I had passed Weinreb and Douwma's print shop on the corner of Bloomsbury Street and Great Russell Street. In the 1930s it had been the premises of Dryad Handicrafts, where Griselda once bought a loom. By the time I first met Ben Weinreb at the Garrick he had separated his part of the business from Rob Douwma's, and was occupying the top two floors. Here he ran what must have been the largest and most important antiquarian architectural bookshop in the world. Yet Ben had the cosiest little outfit imaginable. His staff appeared devoted to him.

Ben was a perfectionist and took great trouble over all his catalogues. We designed many of these. The details of the design were discussed in Ben's office, over glasses of Madeira, in the company of Julia Elton, or other members of his staff if they were involved. It was a civilized way to work, even if there were periodic traumas as Ben flew into a towering rage over some mistake that he attributed to their or our shortcomings. 'Calm down, Ben,' Julia would say and slowly the clouds would clear and the sun would come out again.

When Barrie and Jenkins proposed remaindering a book on typography that I had written for them, even though it had sold over 5000 copies, Ben promptly bought up the rest of the stock. After the publication by the Antique Collectors' Club of the second edition of *Printed Ephemera*, I decided to try to get rid of my quite large collection. Ben Weinreb bought the lot with the intention of selling it to a Japanese University.

In 1980, after a short and enjoyable cruise to Holland with Roger Finch, I put *Patient Griselda* up for sale. I had had a very happy twenty years with the old boat and I wanted to end on a high note. I still enjoyed sailing but I wanted to spend more time with my dear wife.

On the day I sold the boat, Griselda said, 'Now you have got that out of your system, what about us doing a book together on pottery, perhaps on Pratt ware?'

We had bought our first Pratt jug in 1944, at about the same time we found in a second-hand book shop a copy of Woolliscroft Rhead's *The Earthenware Collector*. In this delightful and useful book, Rhead was the first person to write about this ware. When we started collecting this type of pottery it was thought to be of little value, but it was not very common. When we began to write the book we thought we knew quite a lot about the subject. We soon discovered we had much to learn. It was about this time that Arnold Mountford, the Director of the City Museum at Stoke-on-Trent and an old friend of Griselda's, suggested we should join the Northern Ceramic Society. It was one of the most sensible things we have ever done. Members of the Society, some of whom had spent half a lifetime on a particular area of study, with great generosity threw their researches open to our scrutiny. They conducted us to sites of old potteries in which we were interested; they introduced us to other collectors and they directed us to relevant archives in local libraries and record offices.

Griselda was both surprised and pleased how many members had got one or another edition of her *A Collector's History of English Pottery*. More than one person came up to her and said, 'You know, it was your book that started me collecting.'

We spent days and weeks visiting museums all over the country and hours in their dusty cellars photographing pieces of Pratt ware and always returning to Stoke-on-Trent or to the Wedgwood archives at Keele.

Finally we found a publishing house on our doorstep. It was called the Antique Collectors' Club and was run by John and Diana Steel and later by Diana alone. They willingly undertook to publish *Pratt Ware*, but were somewhat surprised when we said that we would like to design it ourselves. Rather reluctantly they agreed. Since then we have designed a number of books for them. We followed up *Pratt Ware* with a new and much enlarged edition of Griselda's *A Collector's History of English Pottery*. Diana Steel has her own printing works. Talking to her pressmen and camera operators made me feel I was once again part of the print production, it was a bit like being back with Cowells.

Lynton Lamb's words, 'Being a typographer means occupying a shadowy post, always playing second fiddle to authors and illustrators etc.,' were very apposite. Yet it has been an agreeable business, bringing one into contact with many talented people. Book design is a fascinating trade and with each new book one is faced with a new set of problems. It never seems to pall.

NOTES

Part 2: *The Printer's devil*

1.1. The foreman of a companionship of compositors, who distributed the copy etc. A term that dates from 1808.

1.2. The other gaps in my knowledge were the actual processes by which Cowells printed – letterpress and offset lithography. The preparation work for letterpress was of course done in the composing room. The text matter, set on Monotype composing machines and casters was made up into imposed formes by Harry Hogger or one of the other stonehands and then locked up in iron chases with line or half-tone blocks for the illustrations. The blank spaces were taken up with 'furniture', which consisted of metal leads and blocks of either metal or wood, locked into position with wedges called quoins. The type was finally levelled with a planer and mallet. It was just the same when Caxton was printing. In fact the only real advances since Caxton's time were the typesetting machines and type casters and the speed of the printing machines.

Once the forme had reached the printing machine, the laborious business of make-ready had to be undertaken. This consisted of pasting in overlays so that there was an even pressure of ink on the type and illustration surfaces. On a large machine this make-ready used to take about four and a half hours for each forme. During this time proofs were taken until the result was perfect.

For letterpress printing the reproduction of the illustrations was done by process houses, who were known as block makers. For offset lithography, at Cowells all the reproduction work was done in the house. This department was run by Fred Fenner, a Suffolk man of great knowledge and experience. For offset the typesetting was still done in the composing room and reproduction proofs of the text matter were sent over to the photo-litho department for imposing and photographing onto the offset plate.

When I first joined Cowells, most of Fenner's staff had been trained as chromo-lithographers. They could take an oil painting and reproduce it faithfully by literally drawing each colour. Anything up to twelve or fifteen separate plates were drawn either as flat colours or with delicate chalking onto a key outline. The ability of Fred Fenner to assess what extra colours were needed for photolithography was quite remarkable. It was all a matter of a trained eye.

By 1946, as in most printing houses, chromolithography had been superseded at Cowells by photolithography. The artwork would be photographed by huge Hunter Penrose cameras using filters to separate the colours. Cowells rarely printed colour work with less than six separations, much more often it was nine or ten. In the case of the King George V stamp collection, that they printed soon after I had joined the firm, as many as thirty-seven printings were used on some of the stamps and some of the sheets went through the presses fifty-three times.

Accurate registrations could only be achieved in a press room that had complete humidity control.

In photolithography the job was only begun by the camera. After the negatives were developed, they were handed to the re-touchers (the former chromolithographers who were always referred to as 'the photo artists'). They would do hours of work on these negatives, painting out irrelevant areas or strengthening or reducing the size of the dots on the halftone screen. These re-touched negatives were converted to transparent positives and after further re-touching were assembled in correct imposition on a plastic sheet placed on a light table. This was the offset equivalent of the letterpress forme and the work of the stonehand.

This assembled plastic sheet was put up in front of a sensitized zinc plate and exposed to light. After developing it was ready for proofing. In those days all colour jobs were proofed in full colour, and as often as not, more than once. Finally the job was ready to print on big 2- and 4-colour German machines, running at 5000–6000 impressions an hour. Runs of 100,000 could be made off nickel-faced plates.

1.3. Stuart Rose CBE, who was born in 1911, was a most successful free-lance graphic designer. He was the typographical adviser to the Post Office for some years. He also worked for the Federation of British Industries, was editor of *Design* Magazine and was an associate of Milner Gray and Misha Black in their Design Research Unit. From 1965 to 1974 Stuart Rose was a Governor of the Central School of Art and Design and for some years he was associated with the printing firm of Benhams in Colchester.

1.4. Ruari McLean CBE, DSC was one of the most successful of the scholar-typographers of our generation. He was born in 1917 and after leaving school he worked with B.H. Newdigate, then spent some time gaining industrial printing experience in Germany. This was followed by jobs with *The Studio* and with the printers Percy Lund Humphries. In the war he was commissioned into the RNVR and was seconded to the Free French Navy, serving as a liaison officer aboard one of their submarines. For this service he was awarded the DSC and Croix de Guerre.

After the war McLean free-lanced, then in 1948 became the Tutor in Typography at the Royal College of Art, where he remained until 1951. From that time onward he had various jobs including co-founding the book-packaging firm of Rainbird, McLean Ltd. He was the founder and editor of the journal *Motif*, which ran from 1958 to 1967. From 1966 to 1980 he was the typographic adviser to H.M. Stationery Office. He has written a number of books on the history, the design and the typography of books and magazines, including *Modern Book Design, Victorian Book Bindings* (2 Vols), *Magazine Design* and monographs on the Victorian printers Edmund Evans, Joseph Cundall and Benjamin Fawcett. He also produced studies of the Swiss typographer Jan Tschichold and the artists Edward Bawden and Nicolas Bentley. For some years Ruari McLean has lived in idyllic surroundings on the south coast of the island of Mull.

1.5. This was Sem Hartz.

1.6. In this process, grained transparent plastic sheets provided the artist with an easier and more flexible medium than the grained zinc litho plate. It was originally intended that the artist would do his drawing in chalk as if he was doing an ordinary lithograph. However someone (it may have been Henry Moore) discovered that by using dilute photopaque, it was possible to achieve gradated washes. The photopaque, which was jeweller's rouge in suspension, lodged in minute particles on the grained sheet.

The completed drawing on the plastic sheet was then exposed to a sensitized zinc lithoplate, as if it was an ordinary positive. As the drawing was not used on a printing surface it had an unlimited life.

2.1. Will Carter was not only a letter cutter but was also a superb printer. From his Rampant Lions Press at Cambridge, run later in collaboration with his son Sebastian, Will produced books that would more than rank with the best of the Private Press productions.

2.2. Edward Young, DSO, a very good looking young man, had like Ruari McLean, always been involved in design and typography. It was he who designed the early Penguin Books for Allen Lane and actually drew their Penguin trademark. He had a most distinguished war career. He was the first RNVR officer to join the submarine service and the first to get an operational command, operating in the North Sea, North Russia, the Bay of Biscay and the Mediterranean and the Far East. The story of his adventures is vividly told in his book *One of our Submarines* which Penguin's published in 1952. This incidentally was the 1000th Penguin book. Edward Young finished his publishing career as managing director of George Rainbird Ltd. After his retirement he lived for some years in France.

2.3. *A Taste for Sailing* Adlard Coles 1969. Second Ed. Terence Dalton 1989.

2.4. One of the first books on single-handed cruising by R.T. McMullen published in 1869.

6.1. Alan Clinton in his *Printed Ephemera Collection, Organization and Access* in 1981 wrote, 'It does seem that the term "Printed Ephemera" must be attributed to John Lewis, and particularly to his excellent illustrated book on the subject, published in 1962.' This was something of which I was quite unaware!

11.1. *A Taste for Sailing* was republished in an enlarged edition by Terence Dalton in 1989. The *Maga* articles appeared in March and May 1972 and May 1973.

11.2. Roger Finch, who was a retired school master, crewed for me several times. He was not only a fine seaman but he was also a considerable naval historian. He wrote a number of books about the sea and ships. He and I worked together on a book called *Pierhead Painters*. It was published by Barrie & Jenkins in 1983. While Roger was writing it, I had to go over to America to see the publisher of some of my nautical books. This meant visits to Maine and Massachussetts, where I was able to find a number of relevant photographs for Roger's book.

12.1. Her father, John Latey Jr, was for many years the editor of *The Illustrated London News*.

202

Appendix 1 Books by John Lewis

Such Things Happen Unicorn Press 1994

Pratt Ware: An Introduction (with Griselda Lewis) Shire Publications 1993

Pratt Ware 1780–1840 (with Griselda Lewis) Antique Collectors' Club 1984, 2nd Ed. 1993

John Nash: The Painter as Illustrator Pendomer Press 1978

Rowland Hilder: painter and illustrator Barrie & Jenkins 1978, Antique Collectors' Club 1987

Typography: design and practice Barrie & Jenkins 1977

The Repair of Wooden Boats David and Charles 1977, 1979

Collecting Printed Ephemera Studio Vista 1976

Vintage Boats David & Charles 1975

Restoring Vintage Boats International Marine (USA) 1975

Restauratie Klassieke Schepen De Boer Maritiem (Netherlands) 1978

Heath Robinson: Artist and Comic Genius Constable 1973, 1982

Small Craft Conversion Adlard Coles 1972, 1977

Anatomy of Printing Faber and Watson Guptill (USA), 1970

Printed Ephemera Faber (paperback) 1969

A Taste for Sailing Adlard Coles 1969, 2nd Ed. Terence Dalton 1989

Reproducing Art (with Edwin Smith) Praeger (USA) and Faber/Cowell 1967

The Twentieth Century Book Studio Vista and Reinhold (USA) 1964, Herbert Press and Van Nostrand, Reinhold 1984

Illustration: Aspects and Directions (with Bob Gill) Studio Vista and Reinhold (USA) 1964

Small Boat Conversion Adlard Coles (paperback) 1963

Typography: basic principles Studio Vista and Reinhold (USA) 1963, 2nd Ed. 1966

Typografi-grundprinciper Bonniers (Sweden) 1966

Typografie: Grundlagen und Experimente Otto Meier Verlag (Germany) 1969

Principios basicos de tipografial Editorial Trillas (Mexico) 1974

Printed Ephemera Cowell/Faber and Dover (USA) 1962, 2nd Ed. Antique Collectors' Club 1990

A Handbook of Type and Illustration Cowell/Faber 1956

Graphic Design (with John Brinkley) Routledge and Kegan Paul 1954

Small Boat Conversion Rupert Hart-Davis 1951

A Ship Modeller's Logbook Percival Marshall 1950

The Three Spaniards by J.G. Venner (*nom de plum* of J. and G. Lewis) Chambers 1949

A Handbook of Printing Types W.S. Cowell 1947, 2nd Ed. 1948

Commercial Art and Industrial Design Robert Ross 1945

Appendix 2 Lion and Unicorn Press Books
1953–1970

Marrot, H.V. Bodoni's *Preface to the Manuale Tipografico*, London, 1953. Paper covered boards.

Vallans, W. *A Tale of Two Swannes*, Ill. David Gentleman, London, Lion and Unicorn Press 1953. Paper covered boards.

Hughes, E.H. *The Gates of London*, Ill. by author, Lion and Unicorn Press 1953. Paper covered boards.

Ward, James. *In Defence of the Beard*, Ill. Roy Morgan, London, Lion & Unicorn Press 1954. Paper covers.

Anthology. *Births, Marriages and Deaths*, Ill. David Gentleman and other students, London, Lion and Unicorn Press 1954. Cloth in dust jacket.

Fugger, Wolffgang. *Handwriting Manual*, Facsimile of 1553 edn., London, Lion and Unicorn Press 1955. Paper covered boards blocked in gold and black.

Wilkes, John. *The Life of John Wilkes, Patriot*, Ill. Donald Higgins, London, Lion and Unicorn Press 1955. Paper covered boards blocked in gold and black.

Greenwood, Ormerod. *Sir Gawain and the Green Knight*, Ill. Roy Morgan, London, Lion and Unicorn Press 1956. Portfolio covered in a printed pattern paper.

Lee, Laurie. *Imaginary Journeys*, Ill. John Griffiths, London, Lion and Unicorn Press 1956. Printed paper covered boards.

Casson, Hugh. *Red Lacquer Days*, Ill. by author, London, Lion and Unicorn Press 1956. Shantung covered boards, printed in red.

Ireland, G. *Epstein 1956, A Camera study of the sculptor at work*, Intro. by Laurie Lee. 1956. London, Lion and Unicorn Press. Blue canvas covered boards.

Fiera, Battista. *De Justicia Pingenda*, Trs. James Wardrop, London, Lion and Unicorn Press 1957. ¼-bound black morocco and green paper covered boards blocked in gold and red.

Welch, Denton. *I left my Grandfather's House*, Ill. by Leslie Jones, London, Lion and Unicorn Press 1958. ¼-bound suede and printed paper covered boards.

Yciar, Juan de. *Arte Subtilissima*, Facsimile of 1550 edn., Trs. E. Shuckburgh, London, Lion and Unicorn Press 1958. ¼-bound black morocco and cloth with label.

Anon. *A Newe Book of Copies*, Facsimile of 1574 edn, Edited by Berthold Wolpe, London, Lion and Unicorn Press 1959. Lithoed cloth covered boards blocked in gold.

Chaucer, Geoffrey. *The Merchant's Tale*, Trs. by Neville Coghill, Ill. D. Cousins, London, Lion and Unicorn Press 1960. Cloth and boards.

Carolino, Pedro. *English as she is Spoke*, Intro. by Paul Jennings, Ill. Edward Bawden, London, Lion and Unicorn Press 1960. Lithographed cloth covered boards.

Woodall, Mary. *The Letters of Thomas Gainsborough*, London, Lion and Unicorn Press 1961. ¼-bound black morocco and printed paper covered boards.

Girling, F.A. *English Merchant Marks*, London, Lion and Unicorn Press 1962. Drawn-on embossed paper cover.

Paolozzi, Eduardo. *The Metallization of a Dream*, Commentary by Laurence Alloway. London, Lion and Unicorn Press 1963. ¼-bound in black morocco and blocked paper covered boards.

Momens, Norman. *ZOZ*, Illustrated by the author, London, Lion and Unicorn Press 1964. Printed paper covered boards.

Hayes, Colin. *Scrap book drawings of Stanley Spencer*, London, Lion and Unicorn Press 1964. ¼-bound printed cloth sides.

Stokes, Adrian. *Venice*, Ill. John Piper, London, Lion and Unicorn Press 1965. Black buckram covered boards. blind blocked.

Morison, Stanley. *Splendour of Ornament*, Selected from *Essempio di recammi*, Venice 1524 by G.A. Tagliente, London, Lion and Unicorn Press 1968. Bound in woven silk covered boards. Note: This was in production when John Lewis left the R.C.A. in 1964.

Hockney, David. *A Rake's Progress*, Poems by David Posner, London, Lion and Unicorn Press 1970. Black buckram with plastic gripper spine. Note: this was in production when J.L. left the R.C.A. in 1964.

Appendix 3 Studio-Vista Paperbacks

Titles in this series edited by John Lewis FSIAD 1963–1972

Typography: Basic Principles by John Lewis 1963, 2nd Ed. 1966

Graphic Design: Visual Comparisons by Alan Fletcher, Colin Forbes and Bob Gill 1963

Basic Design: The Dynamics of Visual Form by Maurice de Sausmarez 1964

Illustration: Aspects and Directions by Bob Gill and John Lewis 1964

The Nature of Design by David Pye 1964

Creative Photography by Aaron Scharf 1965

Painting: Some Basic Principles by Frederick Gore 1965

Architecture: City Sense by Theo Crosby 1965

Sculpture: Form and Method by Bernard Myers 1965

Signs in Action by James Sutton 1965

Trademarks: A Handbook of International Designs by Peter Wildbur 1966

Graphics Handbook by Ken Garland 1966

TV Graphics by Roy Laughton 1966

Ships and Boats: The Nature of their Design by Douglas Phillips-Birt 1966

New Movement in Cities by Brian Richards 1966

The Artist as Reporter by Paul Hogarth 1967

Architecture: Action and Plan by Peter Cook 1967

Transport Design by Corin Hughes-Stanton 1967

Corporate Design Programs by Olle Eksell 1967

Urban Structuring: Theories of Alison and Peter Smithson 1967

Stage Design by Kenneth Rowell 1968

Kinetic Art: The Language of Movement by Guy Brett 1968

Colour: Basic Principles and New Directions by Patricia Sloane 1968

Machines and Perception in Industrial Design by W.H. Mayall 1968

Stained Glass by John Piper 1968

The Nature and Art of Workmanship by David Pye 1968

Typographics by Michael Hutchins 1969

What is a designer: education and practice by Norman Potter 1969

Grammar of Drawing by Colin Hayes 1969

Grafilm: an approach to a new medium by Jack Bryne-Daniel 1970

Designing for Visual Aids by Andrew Wright 1970

Good or Bad Design? by Odd Brochmann 1970

Thoughts on Design by Paul Rand 1970

Fashion Design by Joanne Brogden 1971

The Computer in Art by Jasia Reichardt 1971

Mathematics in Art by Michael Holt 1971

Exhibition Design by Arnold Rattenbury 1971

Structure: the essence of architecture by Forrest Wilson 1971

A Basic Course in Graphic Design by Richard Taylor 1971

Art and Science by Dolf Rieser 1972

Drawing Systems by Fred Dubery and John Willats 1972

Published by

UK Studio Vista Publishers London

USA Van Nostrand Reinhold Company New York

206

Index

Numerals set in bold refer to the illustrated sections.

Abergavenny, 2, 3, 8, 28, 37, 48–9
Adaptive Colouration of Animals, 55
Aigues Mortes, 153
Albert Herring, 138–9
Aldeburgh Festival, 135–9, 143, 145, 169
Aldershot, 6, 15, 25, 35
Alexander, Gen., 85
Algiers, 81, 91
Algonquin Hotel, 73–5
Allen, Rev. L. J., 15, 57
Almansora, SS, 46
Alphabet and Image, 98, 126, 130, 140
Amsterdam, 151–2, 172, 192
Anatomy of Printing, 148, 172–3
Anderson, S., 31
Angharrad, vii
Antibes, 132–3
Antique Collectors' Club, 126, 167, 199, 200
Antwerp, 115, 152–3, 172
Archer, T., 26
Ardizzone, E. & C., 44, 56, 83–4, 104, 147, 155, 171, 184, **15, 28**
Ark, 149, 156
Arriss, Frank, 175
Art and Technics, 126
Arts Club, 130
Arts Council, 106, 112, 137
Asturias, SS, 46
Athenaeum, Boston, 162

Baden-Powell family, 18
Bagford, J., 115
Baltimore Museum, 77
Banff, 78–9
Bari, 81, 89
Barletta, 82–3, **11**
Barrie, J. M., 7, 47
Barrie & Jenkins, 195, 199, 202
Barrett, Hugh, 145
Barry, viii, x, 1, 4
Bart's, 25–9, 158
Baskerville, J., 113–4

Baskerville type, 117
Bateman, H. M., 53
Bateman, J., 31
Battersea, 39, 40–1, 48–50
Battle of Britain, The, 104
Bauhaus, 78, 113
Bawden, Edward, C. & R., 31, 34, 106–7, 118, 147, 155, 194–7, 201, **17**
Beaumont, Rev. T., 171
Beddington, Fred, 41, 54–5
Beddington, Jack, 41, 54
Bedford, N. S., 79
Beerbohm, Max, 20
Beggar's Opera, The, 18
Behan, Brendan, 183
Bell, M. F., 55–6
Bella C. Landauer Collection, 161, 164
Benhams, 169, 201
Benson, S. H., 170
Bentley, N., 192, 198, 201
Beresford, L., 97–8
Berté, Jean, 39
Betjeman, J., 41
Bevan, R. A. & N., 170, 192, 194
Bevan, Robert, 170
Berwick, T. & J., 113
Bibliothèque Nationale, 172
Bigshot, 7–10, 12, 18
Bill the Minder, 197
Blackheath, 32, 40–1, 49, 83, 196
Black, Misha, 36, 47, 201
Black Watch, 25
Blackwell's Bookshop, 196–7
Blackwood's Magazine, 185, 187, 202
Blake, Peter, 149
Blake's *Songs of Innocence*, 137
Bland, D., 172, **20**
Bliss, D. P., 196–7
Block, A., 160
Bluenose, 79, 97
Blythe, Ronald, 193
Bodleian Library, 161
Bodley, G. F., 105
Bodley-Scott, G., 105, 138
Bodley-Scott, R., 105
Bodoni, G., 113, 156

Boland, K. & J., 42, 45–6
Book Collector, The, 109
Book of Beauty, A, 121
Bone, Muirhead, 37
Boston, Mass., 161–2, 164
Bottongom's Farm, 127, 193–4
Boudreau, J. V., 78
Boyd Houghton, A., 37
Bradshaw, C., 142, 144
Bragge, Mr, 66–7
Braintree, Lord, 146
Brandt, Bill, 136
Brangwyn, F., 37
Braque, G., 35, 131
Bratby, J., 149
Brave and Cruel, 139
Breton, Capt. G., 27
Brewington, M. V., 163
Brierley, G. G. & M., 7–9, 12
Brinkley, J., 110–2, 126, 142, 151, 153, 155–7, 174–7, 197, **14**
British Medical Journal, 116
British Museum, 115, 160
Britten, Lord, 135–9, 169
Brixham, 33–4
Brunel, I. K., 49
Brotherhood of Man, The, 9
Buchan, J., 42
Buckle, Miss G., 7
Buckley, R. McL., 54–6, 95
Buffon's Bestiary, 134
Buhler, R., 143, 146, 148–9, 151, **19, 23**
Bulmer, W., 113
Burn, Lt Col, 95
Burn, Rodney, 151, **23**
Burton, Mrs & D., 1
Buttery, H., 56, 81–2, 85, 90–1

Camberley, 6, 16, 25, 55
Camberwell School of Art, 148
Cambridge, 8, 25–6, 115, 141, 151, 160, 162, 192
Cambridge, Mass., 161, 163
Cambrook, J., 158

Camden Town Group, 93, 148, 170
Camera, M. & T. da, 45–6
Camouflage, 54–96, 144
Camouflage, Canadian Army School of, 68, 74, **9**
Campbell-Gray, Hon. I., 55, 81
Camperdown, HMS, vii, **2**
Campobasso, 89
Canadian Railways, 40, 71, 73, **9**
Cannan, G., 47
Carriere, J., 70, 79
Carrington, D., 97
Carrington, N., 96–8, 107
Carter, H., 161
Carter, J., 162
Carter, B., S. & W., 162, 202, **15, 20**
Case, Mr & Mrs F., 74
Cassandre, 35
Cassirer, B., 104
Castle of Otranto, The, 113
Castle Street, No. 9, 12, 24, 93, 180, 189
Catalyst, 147
Cavaglieri, B., 154
Central School of Arts and Crafts, 50, 95, 129, 148, 201
Champion, J., 105, 119
Charterhouse, 12–25, 28, 41, 45, 52, 57, 112, 128, 142, 179, 181
Cheek, L., 77
Chester, 47
Childers, Erskine, 179, 181
Chopping, R., 170
Churchill, W., 79
Churchward, 49
City Museum and Art Gallery, Stoke-on-Trent, 199
Clinton, A., 202
Colchester, 122, 127, 169, 188, 194, 201
Coldstream Report, 174
Coleman, B., 138
Coles, Adlard, 97–8, 185, 202
Collectors' History of English Pottery, A, 126, 199, 200
Commercial Art and Industrial Design, 97, 99
Connolly, C., 99
Constant Nymph, The, 39, 40
Cook, T., 113
Cooper, Bob, 103
Cooper, Mary, 103
Cooper, Mr, 105
Cork and Orrery, Lady, 179, 181
Cormorant, 125–6
Cornford, C., 177
Cott, Dr Hugh, 55
Coventry Cathedral, 190

Cowell, S. H., 100, 102
Cowell, W. S. Ltd, 96–7, 102, 104–6, 109–19, 122, 126, 131, 135, 140–2, 144–5, 147, 153, 155, 164, 167, 173, 185, 200–1
Craig, C., 12, 45
Cranbrook, Earl of, 127, 145, 194, **29**
Crawford's Advertising, 84
Crittall, 'Pink', 146
Crittalls, 146
Crowell, T. Y., 75
Crozier, E., 135–8
Crum, Canon, 6, 23–4
Crusader, The, 83
Cullinan, Dr, 158
Cumberland House, 122–3, 153
Cumberlege, Jock, 129, 137, 161, 192
Cundall, J., 201
Curwen Press, 197
Cusack, R., K. & N., 17–20, 22, 24, 40, 42–3, 135, 179–84, **7**

Dalton, M. & N., 14
Dandridge, Martha, 162
Darling, J. R., 20, 52
Darwin, Sir R., 112, 144, 148–9, 150–1, 155–7, **23**
Davenport, J., 149
David & Charles, 187, 195
Davis, Mrs J., 3, 4, 7, **1**
Deanmount, SS, ix
Deighton, Len, 147
Deptford, 26, 29, 33, 39, **4**
Design Research Unit, 201
Dinkle, E. M., 31
Disney Studios, 79
Dixon, J., 185
Don, Robin, 171
Doric Place, 189, 190
Double Crown Club, 129–30, 155, **20**
Dover Books, 167
Dreyfus, J., 130, 153
Drury, A. & P., 31
Dublin, 17, 177–8
Dufy, R., 131
Dunkirk, 68–9
Dunlops, 171
Dunraven Colliery, vii
Durst, A., 63

Earthenware Collector, The, 199
East Anglia, 147, 149, 168, 190
Eccles, Lord, 150
Ede, C., 130
Edgar, Miss E., 22–3

Edmonton, 71
Eisenmann, A., 164
El Alamein, 74, 83
Elliot, C., 194
Elstead, 23
Elton, Julia, 199
England, Major A., 57
Enschedé, 152–4
Eragny Press, 173
Euston Road Group, 148
Evans, E., 201
Evans, Rev. L., 48–9
Evening Standard, The, 141, 149
Eve's Journal, 45
Everett's Advertising, 141
Eye to the Future, An, 17
Eynsford, 47

Faber & Faber, 148, 161, 167, 172
Fairbanks, D., Jnr, 69
Fairbrother, A., 111–2
Falla, B., 176
FANY, 57, 59, 99
Farnham, 6, 7, 18, 22–3, 35–7, 41, 45, 50, 53, 55, 60, 63, 93–4, **12**
Faversham Creek, 36, 42
Fawcett, B., 201
Fenner, F., 104, 109, 200–1
Fenton, W., 167
Festival of Britain, 143–4, 150
Finch, R., 186–7, 202
Fine Arts Society, 147
Fletcher, A., 165
Fletcher, Sir F., 19
Florence, 153–5
Foggia, 83
Folio Society, 130
Forest, M. & J., 180–4
Forsyte Saga, The, 119–21, 131
Fort Belvoir, 77, 79
Fournier, A., 143
Foyle's Bookshop, 42
Fraser, C. L., 18, 20, 23
Freedman, Barnett, 107–8, 149, **19**
Frensham, 94–5
Freud, L., 143
Fulham, 15

Garda, Lake, 154
Gardiner, C., 30, 37
Gardner, James, 94–6, 104
Gardner, John, 171
Garland, Madge, 149
Garnett, R., 125
Garrad, 'Flossie', 122–3, **20**
Garrick Club, 127, 151, 153, 185, 198
Gaskell, 'Goldie', 66

Geelong Grammar School, 20, 52
Genesis, 106, **16**
Gentleman, D., 123, 142, 144, 147, 152–3, 171, **28**
Gerrard, H., 55, 67
Gibb, J., 196
Gibson, C. D., 17
Gill, E., 155
Gillot, F., 131–4, **21**
Gilman, H., 170
Giorgione, 35
Giotto, 35
Glasgow School of Art, 196
Glyndebourne, 137
Godfrey, M. & L., 72, 75
Golden Treasury, The, 113
Goldsmiths', 29–39, 41, 69, 97, 107, 121, 147, 150, 192, 197
Golfe Juan, 131–2
Goodden, W., 150
Gordon, C. & M., 12, 14, 34
Gore, F. & L., 93, 95, 144
Gore, Spencer, 93, 170
Gouda, 172
Gourock, 69
Graphic Design, 153, 155, 157, 159, 197
Grasse, 182, 184
Gray, Milner & G., 36, 47, 97, 201
Grazebrook, D., 7, 27
Great Bear, The, 5
Great Glemham House, 145
Great Missenden, 37
Greaves, Sir G. & Lady, viii
Green, C., Archbishop, vii
Greenaway, Kate, 138
Greenwich, 33, 36
Greenwich Village, 165
Greyfriar, The, 22, 24
Gropius, W., 78
Gross, A., 119–121, 131, 147, 151
Grove-White, Lt Gen., 57, 61
Gstaad, 27
Guyatt, R., 18, 142–3, 148, 151, 156, 179, 180, **22, 23**
Gwynne, H., 3

HMSO, 201
Haarlem, 152
Hadfield, A. & J., 121, 125–6, 192, 197
Hadleigh, 128
Haines, R. Lett, 128
Hale, K., 104
Halifax, N. S., 79, 161
Hall, Mr, 110
Hamford Water, 125
Hamilton-Hill, M., 152, 192
Hamnett, N., 144

Handbook of Printing Types, A, 109, 146, 171, **16, 17, 18**
Handbook of Type and Illustration, A, 147
Hanson, E., 96–7, 109, 111–2, 173
Hardcastle, Kate, i, x, **2**
Harling, R. & P., 98, 105, 126, 130, 140–1, 143, 146, 196–7, **19**
Hart-Davis, R., 125
Hartz, S., 152, 155, 202
Harvard, 141, 164
Harveys of Bristol, 170–1, **28**
Hayes, C., **23**
Hayward, J., 109
Heals, 50
Heartsease, SS, 188
Heemstede, 154
Heinemann, 119
Heneage, S., 171, 193, 196
Henley-on-Thames, 135
Hennessy-Smith, I., 30, 39, **5**
Henrion, H., 32, 47, 141
Herbert, D., 171
Hilder, R. & E., 31–2, 36–7, 40, 44, 51, 195–7, **6, 31**
Histoire Naturelle, L', 104
Hobbs, J., 16
Hockney, D., 157
Hofer, P. & B., 161–3
Hogger, H., 103, 200
Holdenstone, J. de, 150
Holloway, 'Beak', 73
Hope-Wallace, P., 18
Horizon, 65, 99
Horne, C. & J., 73–74, 77, 79
Houghton Library, 161–2
House and Garden, 196
Howe, E., **20**
Hughes-Stanton, B. & A., 93–5, 106, 123–4, 126, **14**
Hulton Press, 126
Hunting with 'The Fox', 104
Huskinson, L., 63, 93
Hussey, Dr 10
Hutton, J., 55–6, 125, 149

Illustrated London News, The, 202
Image, 140, 143
Industrial Design Partnership, 36
Introduction to English Pottery, An, 126
In Youth is Pleasure, 139
Ipswich, 97, 122, 126, 154, 160
Ipswich Art School, 102
Itten, J., 78

James, H., 162
James, P., 137
Jasper National Park, 71
Jenkins, Herbert, 46
Johnson, A. F., 115
Johnson, C. W. R., 17
Johnson, J., 160–1
Johnston, W., 148
Joie de Vivre, La, 121
Joseph, K. & T., vii, viii, **1**
Joseph-Watkin, T., vii, **1**

Kapp, E., 131–2, 135
Kauffer, E. McK., 35
Kelly, R. B. Talbot, 93–4, 104
Kemp, Dixon, viii
Kennedy, M., 39
Kepes, G., 163
Kerr family, 11, 80, 131
King, G., 105–6
Kindersley, D., 147
Kingsley, C., 137
Kipling, R., ix, 5
Knopf, A., 164, 166
Koch & Knuttel, 172
Kostellow, A., 78
Krimpen, J. van, 112, 152–3

LPTB, 37
Lamb, L. & B., 93, 95–6, 99, 111, 126, 129, 130, 192, 198, 200, **13, 20**
Lancaster, O., 17, 20
Land, 147, 171, **29**
Landermere, 125, 146, 149, 190, **22**
Lane, A., 202
Langston, J., 127
Lark Hill, 55, 67, 81
Laslo, P., 177
Latey, J., Jnr, 202
Laurens, H., 132–3, 135
Laurentiana, 154
Lautrec, H. de T., 30, 104, 153
Lear, E., 32
Le Brocquy, L., 179, 180
Leech, J., 20
Leet, G., 139
Leger, F., 131
Legrand, E., 42
Le Grand Meaulnes, 143
Les Diablerets, 27
Let's Make an Opera, 137–9, **13**
Levy, M., 99
Lewis, C. P. & M. M., viii, ix, x, 2, 4, 6–7, 9, 10, 12, 48, 128, 158–9, 166, **2**
Lewis, Dr C., x
Lewis, Rev. F., 7, 8, 12, 26, 34

Lewis, Griselda, 45, 47,
49–53, 57, 61–2, 65–6, 77,
80, 93, 96–9, 110, 112, 119,
124, 126, 131–2, 134–7,
141, 144–5, 153–4, 158,
164, 168–9, 170, 172–3,
182–3, 185, 186, 189, 190,
192, 198–9, **14**, **25**
Lewis, Rev. T., 8
Lewis, W. D. & R., ix, 2, 23,
38, 48–9
Lieven, A., 69
Limehouse, 36–7
Limited Editions Club, 164
Lion and Unicorn Press,
156–7
Lisbon Story, The, 69
Little Sweep, The, 137
Little Tim books, 104
Liverpool, 105, 176
Llangattock, ix, 38
Llewelyn ap Mervyn, vii
Lockites, 14, 15, 18, 19, 21–2
Lodge, Dr, 115
London Daily News, The, 37
London Mercury, The, 131
London School of Printing,
99
London University, 28
Loon, H. W. van, 73, 75–7,
185
Lucera, 83, 85, 89
Lumpkin, T., ix, **2**
Lund Humphries, P., 201
Lunenburg, 79, 97
Lutyens, Sir E., 94

Macao et Cosmage, 42
McCarthy, I., 178
McGuinness, N., 179–80
McLean, R., 111, 143, 197,
201–2, **21**
McMullen, R. T., 125, 202
Madeira, 45–6
Madoura Pottery, 134
Mafeking, 18
Magazine Design, 201
Magdalene College, 115, 160
Mahoney, C., **23**
Maiden Voyage, 39, 139
Mallaig, 185–6
Malta, 191
Manchester, 47, 103
Manchester Mariner, SS, 166
Manner, F., 35
Manningtree, 122–130, 153,
168, 192, 195
Mansbridge, J., 31, 35, 97
Manuale Tipografico, 156
Mar, N. del, 138
March Field, 79
Mardersteig, H., 154
Mahoney, C., **23**

Mark Hopkins Hotel, 99
Marlborough College, 7, 12,
14
Marrakech, 81, 91
Marshall, Lord, 41
Martens, T., 115
Massachusetts Institute of
Technology, 163
Matisse, H., 131
Maufe, Mrs, 50
May, Phil, 17
Mayor, F., 63, 93–5, 105, 192
Meadow Cottage, 166–9, 189,
190, **19**
Meadows, B., 174, 177
Medway, river, 36
Meynell, Sir F., 109
Mellon, A. & P., 125
Meninsky, B., 93, 129
Menton, 18, 41–2, 44, 46, 135,
182
Merriman, S., 20
Messel, O., 59–60, 67–8
Methuen, 45
Middleditch, E., 149, 175
Midsummer Night's Dream, A,
197–8
Milford, Sir H., 129
Mills, E., 173
Minton, J., 126, 143, 147,
149, 175, **15**, **23**
Mistley Thorn Church, 124–5
Modern Book Design, 201
Monaco Grand Prix, 43
Monmouth, 48
Montgomery, Lt Gen. B., 62,
84–5
Montreal, 70, 74, 166
Moore, H., 106, 146, 155–6,
202, **14**, **16**
Moore, J., 187, 195
Moorland Birds, 104
Morison, S., 107–8, 113, 115,
140, **18**
Morley, F., 74
Morning Post, The, 3
Morris, Rev. B. and Mrs, vii,
viii, **1**
Morris, Rev. E., vii, **1**
Morris, K., 158
Morris, L., viii
Morris, M. N., viii
Morris, Rev. R., ix
Morris, Rev. S., vii, **2**
Morris, T., ix
Morris, Sir C., 93, 118, 124,
127–8, **14**
Motif, 201, **22**
Mountain Ash, x
Mountford, A., 199
Moynihan, R., 143, 148, **23**
Mumbles, The, 3, 4, **3**
Munnings, Sir A., 118
Murder Must Advertise, 170

Murray, J., 98
Musée Grimaldi, 133
Musée Plantin, 152
Museum of Fine Art, Boston,
163

NDHQ, 73, 79, 99
Naples, 85–6
Nash, J. & C., 37, 63, 106,
118, 126–7, 129, 135, 137,
145, 148, 170, 192–7, **20**, **29**
Nash, P., 37, 147, 155
Nash, T., 186–7
National Book League, 121
National College of Art and
Design, Dublin, 177
National Diploma in Art and
Design, 174
National Museum of Wales,
128
Neame, G. & J., 140–1, 144
Netherlands, 151–2, 155,
172, 187, 192
New Cross, 29, 35
New Grafton Gallery, 147
New Haven, 164
New York, 70, 73–4, 77, 162,
164–5
New-York Historical Society,
161, 164
New York Public Library, 164
New Yorker, The, 73
Newdigate, B., 201
Newfoundland, SS, 161
Newman, H., 140–1, **15**
Newman Neame, 141–4
Newport, 176
News Chronicle, The, 40
Nicholson, I., 42
Nordlunder, C. W. F., **18**
Normandie, SS, 70
Northern Ceramic Society,
199
Norwich School of Art, 174–6
Nottingham, 57–8, 61, 66
Nunn, T., 104, 185

Oare Creek, 52
O'Connor, J., 171, **20**
Odhams, 46, 157, 171
Off the Shelf, 171
Officina Bodoni, 154
Ohly, Mr, 106–7
Old Bailey, 29
Old Greenwich, 75
One of our Submarines, 202
Orford, river, 185
Orlando books, 104
Orwell, river, 185
Oss, T. van, 55
Ottawa, 68, 70–1, 73–4, 77
Outer Hebrides, 185–6

Owain ap Howell Dda, vii
Oxford, 160–1
Oxford University Press, 95, 104, 129, 137, 160

Page 'Daddy', 15
Pageites, 15, 20
Paignton, 5
Palgrave, F. T., 113, 115, 160
Palin, S. & H., 15, 18, 40, 52
Palin, W. M., 15
Palmer, S., 37
Panacea, 116, 118–9
Paolozzi, Sir E., 125, 149
Paris, 178
Parnassian Molehill, 145–6
Parsons School of Design, 165
Pasmore, V., 191
Patient Griselda, 185–6, 199, **27, 32**
Patrick, Mr, 104, 110
Paul, Mme, 35
Pavitt, D. E. J., 56, 60
Peabody Museum, 163
Peake, M., 98
Pears, Sir P., 135–9, 169
Pegler, H. & S., 2, 3, 8, 38, 49
Pell, Mr, 104
Penguin Books, 111, 143, 171, 202
Penning-Rowsell, E., 157, 171
Pentagram, 166
Pepysian Library, 160
Petawawa, 70
Phipps, Mr, 8, 9
Picasso, P., 35, 131–5, **21**
Pickering, C., **20**
Picture History of English Pottery, A, 126
Pierhead Painters, 202
Piero della Francesca, 154
Pierrepont House, 94–5
Pilgrim's Progress, 20
Pilsberry, Mr, 15
Pinwell, G. J., 37
Piper, J. & M., 106–7, 135–9
Pissarro, C. & L., 172–3
Plastocowell, 131, 202
Playfair, N., 18
Poole, R., 21
Pop artists, 149
Popski's Private Army, 88, 99
Porter, W. & D., 124–5
Powell, R., 115
Powell, W., 73
Pratt Ware, 200
Pratt Institute, 78
Prestwick, 81, 91
Princeton University, 75
Printed Ephemera, 115, 147, 161, 166, 172, 199, 202, **24**
Puffin Books, 96, 104

Q Ships, 23
Quebec Conference, 79
Queen Elizabeth, SS, 69, **8**
Queen Mary, SS, 70, 79

RMA, Woolwich, 68
RNVR, 53–4, 201–2
RORC, 56
Radcliffe-Wilson, H., P. & A., 21–2, 29, 34, 45, 65
Railway Printed Ephemera, 167
Rainbird, G., 202
Rainbird McLean Ltd, 201–2
Rape of Lucretia, The, 138–9
Ravenstonedale, 145
Ravilious, E., 155
Rawnsley, B., 131
Ray, Cyril, 171
Read, H., 39, 151
Redfern Gallery, 93
Renard, J., 104
Renoir, A., 159
Repton, 30, 34
Rhead, G. W., 199
Rhodes, A., 68–70, 74, 77, 79, 122, 172, **9**
Rhoose, x, 1, 4, 5
Rice, 'Cissy', 13
Ridler, V., 160–1, **20**
Riley, E., 75
Robb, B., 82–3, 85–7, 89, 92, 192, **9**
Robb, Rev. D., 26, 34, 39
Roberts, Lord, viii
Robinson, Edward G., 69, 70
Robinson, W. H. & family, 4, 46, 94, 197–8, **3, 30**
Rocquebrune, 11, 131–2, 140, 153
Roeder, H., 30
Rogers, C., 30, 44
Rolls, C., ix, x
Rommel, Gen., 74
Rooke, N., 129
Rose, M., 194
Rose, S., 109, 201, **14, 20**
Rosomon, L., 171
Rothenstein, Sir W., 108
Routledge & Kegan Paul, 39, 151
Rowlandson, T., 27, 59, 74, 138
Rowntree, K., **23**
Royal Academy, 36, 93
Royal College of Art, 18, 36, 42–4, 69, 108, 112, 115, 142–4, 146–159, 164–5, 171–2, 174, 176, 179, 195–7, 201, **23**
Rugby School, 93
Rye, 66–7

SIA, 36, 97
SPG, 35, 39–41, 44
Saanenmoser, 27
St Bride's Printing Library, 172
St John's College, 25
St Paul's Church, 26, 33, **4**
St Paul's House, 26, 34, 36
St Martin's School of Art, 95, 149
San Vigilio, 154–5, 182
Sao Vicente, 46
Saffron Walden, 196
Salem, 163
Salisbury Plain, 56
'Sanctuary of Printing', 160–1
Sangorski & Sutcliffe, 110
Saskatchewan, 71
Saskatoon, 71
Saundersfoot, viii
Saunderites, 18
Sayers, D., 170
Schofield, Mr, 103–4
School Prints, 131
Schneider Trophy, The, 23
Scolar Press, 197
Scott, Asgeir, 171
Seago, E., 55, 67, 118
Sewell, J., 147, 153, 192
Shand, J., 126
Shaw, Dr, 29
Shaw, N., 94
She Stoops to Conquer, ix, 2
Sheffield, 59
Shell Chemicals Ltd, 147, 170
Shell-Mex, 37, 41
Shenval Press, 126
Shelter Sketchbook, 106
Shorncliffe, 55
Showerings, 171
Sickert, W., 65, 99
Sieveking, L. & N., 170, 194
Signature, 108
Simmons, M., 164, 166–7
Simon, A., 142, 171
Simon, O., 108
Sinclair, E., 34, 39
Sitwell, E., 34, 39
Skeaping, J., 150, 174
Sketty, 127
Slade School of Art, 55, 67, 93
Small Boat Conversion, 125
Small Craft Conversion, 187
Smith, R. G., 96–8, 102–3, 105–10, 131, 135, 138, 161, 166–7, 173, 185
Smyth, E., 28, 99
Somerville's *The Chase*, 113
Songs of Innocence, 137
Sospel, 43, 135
Sothebys, 162

Spear, Ruskin, 149, 151, **23**
Speede, J., 107
Spence, Sir B. and Lady,
  94–5, 125, 149, 190–2, **22**
Spencer, G. & S., 148, 170
Spencer, Maxine, 35
Spéracèdes, 180
Squire, J. C. & R., 131
Standard, P., 165
Staunton Harold, 58
Steel, D. & J., 167, 200
Steele, Mr, 110, 115
Stepney, 60–1, 108
Stiebel, V., 67, 80, 91, 94
Stone, R., 18, 155
Stonehenge, 56
Story of Mankind, The, 73, 75
Story of Rolex, The, 129
Stower's Printer's Grammar,
  113
Stretton-Smith, G., 45, 47, 77
Strangeways, Lt Col D., 81–2,
  89–91
Stromboli, 81
Studdert-Kennedy, Rev. H.,
  23
Studio, The, 201
Studio Vista, 121, 126, 157,
  170–1, 193
Such Things Happen, 46, 53
Sullivan, E. J., 37
Summerson Committee, 174,
  176
Sunday Times, The, 171
Sutherland, G., 106–7, 146
Swale, river, 36, 52
Swansea, 3, 4, 127
Swanwick, B., 30, 37
Sweeting, E., 136
Sword of Bone, 69, 172

Talybont-on-Usk, ix, 3
Taste for Sailing, A, 99, 185,
  195, 202
Tate Gallery, 106, 128
Tempest, The, 107
Thackeray, W. M., 20
Thirsk, J., 13
This Year of Grace, 60
Thomas, Dylan, 144, 183
Thompson, J. W., 66
Thorne, Lt Gen. 'Bulgy',
  61–2
Thornfield, 9, 12
Thornham Parva, 192

Thrussell, Lil, 161
Thurber, J., 73
Tilford, 7, 11, 80, 94–5, 99
Times, The, viii, 40, 192
Times Literary Supplement, The,
  145
Tobermory, 186–7
Todd, Miss J., 3, 4, 23
Tonbridge, 39
Toronto, 73–4
Tryon, Admiral, vii
Tschichold, J., 201
Tunbridge Wells, 60–3, 66–8,
  85, 89
Tunis, 81
Turner, J. M. W., 106
Typography: basic principles,
  25

UBC, 72–3, 99
University of East Anglia, 177
University of Essex, 171
Usborne, R., 130
Utrecht, University of, 75

Vallauris, 134
Van Loon's Lives, 76
Vanbrugh, J., 26
Vancouver, 70–2, 78–9
Veere, 75–6
Velvet Glove, The, 20
Venice, 137, 154–5, 158
Verona, 154
Veyrin-Forrer, J., 172–3
Victoria and Albert Museum,
  66
Victoria, BC, 71
Victoria, HMS, vii, **2**
Victorian Book Bindings, 201
Viney, E., **20**
Vintage Boats, 187
Vogue, 46
Voice through a Cloud, A, 139
Voysey, C. F. A., 11

Walberswick, 15
Walbrand-Evans, M., 65
Walpole, H., 113
Walsh, L., 154, 182
Walworth, 111
War and Peace, 193
Warde, B., 140
Warner Brothers, 79

Wasey, Erwin, 141
Washington, DC, 79
Washington, G., 162
Water Babies, The, 4, 107, 137,
  197, **3**
Waters, P., 115
Watneys, 171
Watts, R., 105, 115–7
Wayne, J., 102
Weekites, 14
Weight, C., 30–1, 48–9, 99,
  148–9, 151, 194, **23**
Weinreb, B., 198–9
Welch, D., 30, 33–4, 38–9, 52,
  64–5, 99, 139, **5**
Welch Regiment, x, 1, 25
West Cross, 3
West Mersey, 125
Western Isles, 137
Westminster Hospital, 26
Westminster School of Art,
  93
What about Wine?, 142
White, G. & B., 55–6, 83–4,
  106
White, V., 30, 32–4, 39, 47,
  69, 141, 192
Whitstable, 36
Whistler, J. McN., 37
Wilkinson, N., 54
Wilson, F. R. L. & P., 16, 20–1
Wind in the Willows, The, 8
Wine Society, The, 142
Winnipeg, 71
Wirth-Miller, D., 170, **14**
Wissington, 140
Witt, J. Le, **14**
Wivenhoe, 170
Wodehouse, P. G., 20
Wodzicka, H., 172
Wolfers, D., 147, 170, 194
Wolpe, B., 69, 172
Woodbridge, 74, 168, 183,
  189, 192
Worthley, Max, 138
Wreford, J., 111
Wright, J., 176

Yachtsman, The, 97
Yale University Press, 164
Yorke, F. R. S., 65
Young, E., 125, 202

Zwemmers, 42